Saul Bellow's Enigmatic Laughter

Sarah Blacher Cohen

Saul Bellow's Enigmatic Laughter

UNIVERSITY OF ILLINOIS PRESS
Urbana   Chicago   London

The University of Illinois Press wishes to express its gratitude to the Andrew W. Mellon Foundation for a grant which has made possible the publication of this book.

The author wishes to thank the following publishers for permission to reprint the designated selections. Rights in all cases are reserved by the owner of the copyright:

From *Dangling Man* by Saul Bellow, © 1944 by the Vanguard Press, Inc., and from *The Victim* by Saul Bellow, © 1947 by Saul Bellow, both reprinted by permission of the publisher, the Vanguard Press, Inc. From *The Adventures of Augie March* by Saul Bellow, © 1949, 1951, 1952, 1953 by Saul Bellow; from *Seize the Day* by Saul Bellow, © 1951, 1954, 1955, 1956 by Saul Bellow; from *Henderson the Rain King* by Saul Bellow, © 1958, 1959 by Saul Bellow; from *Herzog* by Saul Bellow, © 1961, 1963, 1964 by Saul Bellow; from *Mr. Sammler's Planet* by Saul Bellow, © 1969, 1970 by Saul Bellow; and from *The Last Analysis* by Saul Bellow, © 1962, 1965 by Saul Bellow, all reprinted by permission of the Viking Press, Inc., and with acknowledgment to Saul Bellow and Weidenfeld & Nicholson.

TO THE MEMORY OF MA AND PA

Acknowledgments

I wish to express my gratitude to Ernest Samuels, Harrison M. Hayford, and Donald T. Torchiana for their encouragement and useful criticism. To Keith M. Opdahl and George Scouffas, whose perceptive comments caused me to realize the serious implications of Saul Bellow's comedy and its progressive sophistication, I owe a great deal.

Saul Bellow kindly permitted me to read the manuscripts of *Henderson the Rain King*. Ida Gradolph acted as a most deft and dependable intellectual midwife. Bette Howland was an invaluable source of confidence and sound editorial advice.

I am especially grateful to the English department of the State University of New York at Albany for providing me with a genial and stimulating atmosphere in which to complete my book. My thanks also go to the Levie Foundation for financial assistance during the early stages of my research and to the Research Office of the State University of New York at Albany for helping to defray part of the publication costs.

Above all, I am indebted to my parents, Mary and Louis Blacher, for giving me a firsthand knowledge of Yiddish humor, and to my husband, Gary, for his comic sense and critical judgment.

SARAH BLACHER COHEN

State University of New York
Albany

Contents

The one offense . . . which comedy cannot endure is that a man should forget he is man.

—William F. Lynch, *Christ and Apollo*

Introduction

1

Saul Bellow has expressed his preference for the use of the comic in his works: "Obliged to choose between complaint and comedy, I choose comedy, as more energetic, wiser and manlier." [1] Abhorring the "hollow man" conception of character and the tone of "elegy" which has prevailed in modern literature, he has, in his essays and novels [2] alike, inveighed against such exponents of unearned wretchedness. To maintain that existence is "nauseous," that life is a "plague," that we have no chance of winning the "endgame" is, according to Bellow, to convey only partial truths. It is to fail to give a comprehensive account of reality. The fact that he attacks such doomsday writers for expressing a "bitterness to which they . . . have not established clear title" [3] does not mean that his own writing concentrates only on the genial aspect of things, that it overlooks the contemptible and the rancorous. While his

1. Gordon L. Harper, "Saul Bellow—The Art of Fiction: An Interview," *Paris Review* 37 (Winter, 1965): 62.
2. The following editions of Bellow's novels are the ones cited in the text: *Dangling Man* (New York: Vanguard, 1944); *The Victim* (New York: Vanguard, 1947); *The Adventures of Augie March* (New York: Viking Press, 1953); *Seize the Day* (New York: Viking Press, 1956); *Henderson the Rain King* (New York: Viking Press, 1959); *Herzog* (New York: Viking Press, 1964); *Mr. Sammler's Planet* (New York: Viking Press, 1970).
3. Saul Bellow, "Some Notes on Recent American Fiction," *Encounter* 21 (November, 1963): 26.

heroes both yearn and ingeniously scheme for the coming of messianic times, he makes it all too clear that the beatific age has not yet arrived. In his novels the damnable is still rampant and, for the most part, in-eradicable. Thus any study of Bellow's comedy which concludes that his leading principle is "all is well in this most perfect of worlds" is not only to misconstrue the import of his work, but also to undermine the complexity of his vision. With no attempt to gloss over low facts, he unsparingly exposes what is enervating, corruptive, and brutalizing in modern life. Indeed, the question that recurs through most of his novels is how man can discover who he is as well as maintain his dig-nity when he must contend with so many inimical and debilitating forces.

While there is much to brood about in Bellow's novels—the deterio-rating city with its foul air and foul influences, its stampeding hordes overrunning the individual, unpredictable catastrophes, senseless wars, restriction of choice through heredity, abrupt cessation of endeavor through death, emotional bankruptcy, and "poverty of soul"—there is never a total capitulation to despair. Bellow continually retaliates with comedy. Although he realizes the opposition is formidable and that he may never fully vanquish hopelessness, he uses comedy to interrupt, resist, reinterpret, and transcend adversity. The strength of his comedy and the function it performs varies in each novel. In the sullen *Dangling Man* and *The Victim* it acts as a shaky defense which ineffectually staves off distrust and melancholy. Except for providing an uneasy moratorium from the gloom, it does not free the heroes from their long-term hostilities. In *The Adventures of Augie March* comedy serves not only as a tonic for the dispirited, but also as a miraculous al-chemizer which transforms the common into the precious. Although Augie recognizes the disfigurement of the present, his antic sense en-ables him to re-create a golden age out of the "dwarf-end of times." In *Seize the Day,* a compassionate treatment of the beleaguered little man, comedy is a shield, employed more by Bellow than by Tommy Wilhelm, to protect him against his ubiquitous harassers. It is also used as a subtle cosmetic to cover up Wilhelm's blemishes and make him more endearing. In *Henderson the Rain King* the comedy resem-bles a flashing saber brandished by Henderson, the mock *miles glorio-sus,* both to defend and undercut his vaunted image of himself and to attack his brute opponents. While it does not succeed in eliminating

Henderson's self-lionizing or in slaying the iniquitous lions of the world, his nimble and clumsy thrusting and parrying are alone worth the price of admission. In *Herzog* comedy acts as a "balance and a barricade" [4] which the morose hero introduces to counter and combat his own depressive tendencies and the apocalyptic pronouncements of the reigning cognoscenti. It is also a boomerang which ultimately returns to strike him with the knowledge that man does not live by wisdom alone. In *Mr. Sammler's Planet* comedy appears as a confectionery to accompany the bitter views of an angry old man. While Bellow does not think these bitter views need sweetening, he assumes not all of his readers will be able to swallow them without being given his customary jocular treats.

No matter what particular form Bellow's comedy takes, his underlying comic vision is there to oppose his pessimistic outlook. This is not to say that his comic vision is unwaveringly cheerful. When his heroes experience intense frustration and disenchantment, it becomes tinged with the dour and the morbid. During such dark moments it is overwhelmed with the same perplexity at the world's absurdity and entertains the same suspicion of its malicious intent that struck Melville's Ishmael when he remarked: "There are certain queer times and occasions in this strange mixed affair we call life when a man takes this whole universe for a vast practical joke, though the wit thereof he but dimly discerns, and more than suspects that the joke is at nobody's expense but his own." [5] But Bellow's comic vision only seldom regards life as a cruel joke. While not exultingly prophesying the happy ending, it most often holds out the possibility of a hard-won delight in the temporal. Although acknowledging evil, it affirms the prevalence of good. This good, however, is not to be equated with the *summum bonum* as discussed by the philosophers and touted by the preachers. All too aware of the impossibility of having untarnished virtue, Bellow accepts the actual with its mixture of dross and purity. Like Augie March, he cannot go along with "the Reverend Beecher telling his congregation, 'Ye are Gods, you are crystalline, your faces are radiant!'" (76). Much less idealistic in his assessment of humanity, Bellow defines us as "not gods, not beasts, but savages of somewhat damaged but not

4. Mary Lee Allen, "The Flower and the Chalk: The Comic Sense of Saul Bellow" (Ph.D. diss., Stanford University, 1969), p. 62.
5. Herman Melville, *Moby-Dick* (New York: Bobbs-Merrill Company, 1964), p. 302.

extinguished nobility." [6] In his novels he therefore refrains from using the tragic mode, since it assumes that man has an exalted nature which, though sorely tested, will ultimately reassert itself. He likewise avoids the mode of strict naturalism which holds that man, no matter how hard he tries to uplift himself, remains essentially brutish. Instead, Bellow chooses the comic mode, since it does not depict man in either extreme. Because it is able to capture the subtleties of man's composite makeup, Bellow finds it best suited to illustrate his hybrid conception of human nature.

The comic element receiving the most extensive treatment in Bellow's novels is comedy of character. With the candor of untempered realism, it amply exposes man's damaged nature. If the person is mindful of this damage and struggles, though unsuccessfully, to make his internal repairs, the laughter evoked is sympathetic. If he is unaware of the damage and thus exerts no effort to eliminate it, the laughter evoked is unsympathetic. Yet it is never so merciless as to consign him to ash cans or so virulent as to deride him to death like the cruel and devastating laughter flourishing in contemporary black humor. As Bellow states in his play, The Last Analysis, "To disown the individual altogether is nihilism, which isn't funny at all . . . suppose we look again for the manhood we are born to inherit." [7] Accordingly, his comedy of character does not abandon the flawed individual but continually looks for his saving manhood or nobility. Sometimes this nobility lies just below a giddy surface or grotesque exterior and can be easily uncovered. At other times it remains hidden beneath accumulations of wrongdoing and layers of self-deceit, requiring a drastic shock to dislodge it or a vigorous ferreting out to locate it. But once found, it is duly recognized and granted an ecstatic or contained welcome, depending upon the context in which it appears.

The most readily discernible kind of character damage which modern comedy reveals, according to Bellow, is affectation:

> It is not so much the full-fledged bourgeois who is the theme of modern comedy, as the little man—the little man who apes the dignity and refinements of the leaders of society. . . . The comedian of the twen-

6. Presumably written by Saul Bellow, though unsigned, in "Arias," The Noble Savage 4, ed. Saul Bellow and Keith Botsford (New York: Meridian Books, 1961), p. 5.
7. Saul Bellow, The Last Analysis (New York: Viking Press, 1965), p. 97.

tieth century has made much of the private, shabby person who plays the gentleman. Joyce's Leopold Bloom in *Ulysses* is one such figure— 'How grand we are this morning!' . . . the petty individualist of common origins and gentlemanly pretensions.[8]

It is not surprising, therefore, that the most obvious source of the ridiculous in the Bellow hero is his affectation. Finding himself deficient in certain admirable qualities, he cultivates the outward manifestations of them so as to persuade himself and others that he is what he would like to be. If he is an intellectual dilettante and wants to be regarded as a professional scholar, he exaggerates the extent of his knowledge and makes a conspicuous show of it. If he is an economic failure and wants to camouflage the fact from disinterested spectators, he struts about in his most expensive shirt and talks about the business deals he is about to consummate. If he is depressed by middle age and in doubt of his sexual powers, he dresses and acts the part of a youthful lothario. But after a while outward circumstances or his own inner promptings force him to become more authentic. Disgusted with his pose, he is compelled to deflate his own pretensions. If he lacks a penchant for self-correction, Bellow steps in as omniscient author and wryly unmasks his disguise. Once divested of his ostensibly more flattering though ill-fitting borrowed identity, and freed from the need to flaunt it, he accepts or is on the way to accepting his own inadequate and unimpressive self. Initially mocked for being a vain dissembler, he is subsequently commended for becoming a man of humility and integrity.

An equally obvious comic trait of the Bellow hero is his excessive involvement with self. The best description of this trait is provided by Bellow himself:

> The exploration of consciousness, introspection, self-knowledge, and hypochondria, so solemnly conducted in twentieth century literature, is, in books like *The Confessions of Zeno* by Italo Svevo, treated ironically and humorously. The inner life, the 'unhappy consciousness,' the management of personal life, 'alienation'—all the sad questions for which the late romantic writer reserved a special tone of disappointment and bitterness are turned inside-out by the modern comedian.

8. Saul Bellow, "Literature," *The Great Ideas Today,* ed. Mortimer Adler and Robert M. Hutchins (Chicago: The Encyclopedia Britannica, 1963), pp. 163–164.

Deeply subjective self-concern is ridiculed. *My* feelings, *my* early trauma, *my* moral seriousness, *my* progress, *my* sensitivity, *my* fidelity, *my* guilt—the modern reader is easily made to laugh at all of these.[9]

So, too, the reader is made to laugh at the Bellow hero who is constantly exploring his consciousness, sounding its depths and testing its well-being. Like such drolly miserable Jewish characters as Bruce Jay Friedman's Stern, Philip Roth's Portnoy, and Karl Shapiro's Edsel, he is committed not to practicing his faith but to religiously discovering and perpetuating his neuroses. If he cannot find any recent injuries to wince at, he picks at healed psychic scars to open up old wounds. In addition to reviving old feelings of outrage and paranoia, he is able to relish both nursing himself and re-experiencing the pain. When he is not exacerbating and tending his wounds, he assiduously employs his moral Geiger counter to determine the level of his depravity. Since he seldom detects a large concentration of it, he seizes upon any noticeable peccadilloes and magnifies them out of proportion. But unlike Nabokov's amoral Humbert Humbert, he is not convinced of the nobility of his perversity; unlike J. P. Donleavy's unconscionable Sebastian Dangerfield, he is not proud of his scandalous sensual indulgence. He is too overwhelmed with guilt as well as the struggle to expiate that guilt to enjoy his vices, let alone to seek applause for them. Although he may want to engage in dialogue with his fellow man, he is so taken up with self-scrutiny and, afterward, self-reviling that he manages to talk only to himself. Instead of fulfilling himself in a meaningful vocation, all he does is make a career of ascertaining and then advertising his personality disorders. He thus suffers from what Bellow in *The Last Analysis* calls "the Pagliacci gangrene! Caused as all gangrene is by a failure of circulation. Cut off by self-pity. Passivity. Fear. Masochistic rage."[10] Bellow, however, does not permit such a condition to remain untreated. He allows the hero with a capacity for self-diagnosis and a desire to be cured to administer doses of antidotal humor to improve his circulation. The extent to which he improves depends on his ability to fight off the toxic elements. He may arrive only at the intellectual realization that "goodness is achieved not in a vacuum but in the company of other men, attended by love" (*DM:* 92) and

9. *Ibid.,* p. 164.
10. Bellow, *The Last Analysis,* p. 78.

have yet to implement this realization. Or, if he already is in the company of other men, he may vacillate from generously giving of himself to stingily guarding his independence. Or, if he becomes disgusted with his habitual personal pronoun misuse, he may through strenuous trial and error gradually learn to substitute "they want" for "I want." This is not to say that he ever becomes an abnegating saint, totally sacrificing his concerns for others. If, however, his *animal ridens* remains intact, there is no danger of his becoming absorbed with his "inner life" to the point of ludicrous satiety.

There *is* a danger of the Bellow hero's becoming oppressed by his physical being, particularly if he is heavy-set and middle-aged like Asa Leventhal, Tommy Wilhelm, and Eugene Henderson. Henderson expresses their common plight when he exclaims: "Oh, my body, my body! Why have we never really got together as friends?" (182). Indeed, there is a long-standing breach between these characters' minds and their bodies which interferes with the realization of their respective goals. For them the body is "a heavy and cumbersome vesture, a kind of irksome ballast which holds down to earth a soul eager to rise aloft." [11] It causes them to lag behind in the economic race. It impedes their acquisition of the social graces and prevents them from soaring into the higher realm of contemplation and humanitarianism. However, Bellow does not view his heroes' encumbrance by the corporeal as being in any way tragic. Since they are never repulsively disfigured or seriously incapacitated, he continually makes sport of their being tripped up or grounded by the physical. He thus applies Bergson's formula that the comic is produced whenever the soul is *"tantalized by the needs of the body: on the one hand, the moral personality with its intelligently varied energy, and on the other, the stupidly monotonous body, perpetually obstructing everything with its machine-like obstinacy."* [12] Although Bellow capitalizes on the humor springing from the tug-of-war between the spiritual and the somatic in his characters, he does not reject the somatic. He does not consider man's creatureliness repugnant, nor does he deem it inconsequential and focus exclusively on man's higher faculties. Bellow holds, as did Aristotle before him, that the body is not merely a useless repository

11. Henri Bergson, "Laughter," in *Comedy,* ed. Wylie Sypher (New York: Doubleday & Co., 1956), p. 92.
12. *Ibid.,* p. 93.

for the soul, serving only to obstruct it. Rather, he sees the body as essential to the functioning of the soul, since only through it can the soul exercise its powers. Therefore Bellow never reduces his characters to disembodied essences; if anything, he endows them with a surplus of not only distinctive, but often grotesque physical features. Just as Shakespeare both laughs at and adores Falstaff for being a "swoll'n parcel of dropsies" and a "stuff'd cloakbag of guts," so Bellow ridicules and cherishes his characters for their "enormities and deformities."

From making subversive fun of his characters' bodies, Bellow goes one step further and compares some of them to animals. His comparisons, however, do not resemble the prolonged animal analogies of the naturalistic novelists, nor do they serve the same function of eliciting sympathy for man's dumb, impassive nature, or arousing horror at his impulsive, predatory acts. Neither are they similar to the full-scale metamorphoses of Aesop's fables and the medieval beast tales, whose chief intent is to enforce a useful truth. Following rather the primarily comic traditions of animal imagery, Bellow briefly transforms his bipeds into quadrupeds for the sake of levity. By drawing unlikely parallels between untamed beasts and his domesticated heroes, he allows us to guffaw at momentary incongruous reversals. Like Swift, he wryly undercuts the biblical notion that we are vastly superior to every "creeping thing." By occasionally removing the distinctions between man and animal, he drolly but not didactically checks our tendency to deify ourselves.

But most of the time Bellow's heroes are rational animals with the fixed ideas of rational animals. This stubborn adherence to certain dominant theories also renders them comic in a less immediately perceptible way. Bellow has called such dominant theories "ideal constructions," "obsessive devices," and "versions of reality." In his first novel, *Dangling Man,* he enumerates and offers a rudimentary explanation for the many kinds of obsessions which consume man and indeed consume many of the heroes in his subsequent novels:

. . . for study, for wisdom, bravery, war, the benefits of cruelty, for art; the God-man of the ancient cultures, the Humanistic full man, the courtly lover, the knight, the ecclesiastic, the despot, the ascetic, the millionaire, the manager. I could name hundreds of these ideal constructions, each with its assertions and symbols, each finding—in conduct, in God, in art, in money—its particular answer and each proclaiming: 'This is the only possible way to meet chaos' (140).

In his most recent novel, *Mr. Sammler's Planet*, Bellow continues to hold a similar view; only he now associates the chaos which man must confront as "the end of things-as-known" (278). To cope with the departure from a familiar planet to an unfamiliar one, he claims that "each accented more strongly his own subjective style and the practices by which he was known" (278). In both novels he describes his heroes as seizing upon one scheme to avert a troubled life, or mapping one strategy to circumvent the unknown instead of experimenting with many courses of action to achieve their desired end. This dogged clinging to one solution, along with the cavalier dismissal of every alternative, causes them to become laughable, since their bodies mechanically heed the dictates of their minds. Such conduct thus bears out Bergson's view that mental as well as physical rigidity is the proper object of mirth, a view which Nathan Scott enlarges upon:

> . . . the comic is a contradiction in the relation of the human individual to the created orders of existence which arises out of an overspecialization of some instinct or faculty of the self . . . in some special direction, to the neglect of the other avenues through which it ought also to gain expression. And it is this predilection of the self to identify itself too completely with some special interest or project (cf. Aristophanes' Socrates or Jonson's Volpone or Moliere's Tartuffe or Sterne's Walter Shandy or Shaw's Professor Higgins)—it is this by which the self is blinded to the integral character of its humanity and thus thrown out of gear with the fundamental norms and orders of human existence.[13]

Not every Bellow hero hastens to swear allegiance to one exclusive policy and inflexibly execute it. A few try to resist committing themselves and, like Dostoevsky's Underground Man, foster their capriciousness to avoid being turned into robots. They embrace no single point of view, but flirt with many. They try to maintain their protean selves despite the temptation to restrict their elusiveness and settle for a fixed set of values. Yet even they do not remain footloose for long. In their

---

[13.] Nathan A. Scott, Jr., "The Bias of Comedy and the Narrow Escape into Faith," *The Christian Scholar* 44 (Spring, 1961): 30.

attempt to evade confinement, they eventually become enslaved to their own ploy of evasion.

It goes without saying that a considerable amount of energy is required to stay harnessed to a single course of action. Still at times the Bellow hero expends more energy than is necessary so that he often resembles a silent film character, caught up in frenetic activity yet going nowhere. Bellow has, for example, commented on the folly of Henderson's excessive "movement and random action"[14] used to realize his obsession. Henderson is not the only Bellow hero in perpetual motion; he has others to keep him company. Yet it is this same perpetual motion or energy which also prevents these Bellow heroes from becoming marooned in their own "desert places" and enables them to skirt the pitfalls all around them. Their irrepressible vigor, which often insures their very survival, suggests Susanne Langer's view of comedy: "the image of human vitality holding its own in the world amid the surprises of unplanned coincidence."[15] Unlike many of Barth's inert, feckless characters and Beckett's progressively immobile figures, Bellow's kinetic heroes can never be dismissed as lackluster nonentities. Their dynamism forces others to take notice of them and, if not to consider them important, then at least to reckon with them.

Despite the energy of Bellow's active minority, they and the more passive majority are still blind to a large portion of reality because of their total involvement with their "ideal constructions." Consequently, their perception of themselves is impaired. This impairment constitutes another source of the comic in them, for, according to Bergson, an individual is "generally comic in proportion to his ignorance of himself."[16] Bellow's heroes are especially ignorant about their own strengths and weaknesses. They mistake one for the other and excessively chide or praise themselves for the wrong reasons. However, many of them come to realize that their original assessments have been incorrect and become more discriminating judges of themselves. For the few who do not revise their thinking, Bellow ironically points up their miscalculations. Except for this common error of perception, each

14. Nina A. Steers, " 'Successor' to Faulkner?" *Show* 4 (September, 1964): 38.

15. Susanne K. Langer, *Feeling and Form* (New York: Charles Scribner's Sons, 1953), p. 331.

16. Bergson, "Laughter," p. 71.

Bellow hero has his own peculiar lapses of vision and is subject to his own kind of comic misconceptions and inconsistencies.

Although Bellow's protagonists are similar to those characters of English literature whom Taine described as "unruly creatures whose life blood pulses richly, whose features are odd, and whose opinions, gestures, vices, and habits control the mechanism of the plot in which they happen to be cast," [17] Bellow also places his protagonists in comic situations beyond their control. That is, the situations are rendered funny not because of the particular characters involved, but because of the comic aspects of the situations themselves.

Occasionally acting upon the post-existentialist impulse of inventing imaginative alternatives to this world, Bellow creates his own special kind of whimsically fantastic situations. But unlike Barth's strained retreats into antiquarianism or Vonnegut's creaky flights into futurism, his episodes are more of this time and of this place. Even if they are set in an outré Mexico or a fictive Africa, they are never far removed from the realm of the possible or entirely outside the range of the ordinary. Indeed, part of their humor stems from the surprise appearance of the familiar within the context of the farfetched and from the deliberate inclusion of fact to dispel illusion. No matter how much Bellow's fantastic situations exceed the bounds of plausibility, they are never life-escaping. Whether involving fabulous adventures with Metro-Goldwyn-Mayer lions and medicine-men kings or bizarre iguana-hunting expeditions with friendly eagles and unchaste Dianas, prosaic reality ultimately interrupts the myth-making in progress and summons them back to their sordid cities and far less tantalizing responsibilities.

Even within the confines of prosaic reality Bellow sometimes produces situations of sexual farce to disrupt the tedium. This humor rests not so much on the pandemonious clashes between male and female as on the laughable nature of sex itself. Bellow reveals how funny we animals are in the act of mating, what with the devious stratagems and the awkward positions we must adopt to attain so ephemeral a bliss. Moreover, by portraying copulation as a perfunctory, self-indulgent, biological affair, he makes a mockery of the romantic feelings with which we generally endow it. By mentioning

17. Taine quoted in Wylie Sypher, "Our New Sense of the Comic," in *Comedy*, ed. Wylie Sypher (New York: Doubleday & Co., 1956), p. 211.

unmentionable physiological details, he also flaunts our moral code of keeping reticent about sexual practices. Whether his characters are young or old, crippled or able-bodied, he does not shy away from frankly describing their surrenders to lust, their capitulations to the "hedonistic joke of a mammoth industrial civilization" (*H: 166*).

Another kind of comic situation Bellow has dallied with is the burlesque. In no way approaching the intricacy of construction and cleverness of innuendo found in Nabokov's perfection of this type of episode, he still succeeds in ridiculing, through ludicrous imitation of literary forms, whatever smacks of the grandiose, the sentimental, and the morbid. Although he makes sport of the elaborate rites his characters devise to hunt for meaning, to discover love, and to accept death, he never undermines the importance of their ventures or the value of what it is they are seeking. Unlike the less profound comic writer who can express himself only in mocking echoes, Bellow never becomes so shackled to the artifices of burlesque that he hinders himself from ultimately projecting his "own unique metaphor of experience."[18]

The comic situation which best projects Bellow's "metaphor of experience," and the one which he most frequently employs, fits (with some qualification) Stephen Leacock's Aristotelian-inspired definition of the comic situation: "The humor of situation arises . . . out of any set of circumstances that involve discomfiture or disaster of some odd incongruous kind, not connected with the ordinary run of things and not involving sufficient pain or disaster to over-weigh the pleasures of contemplating this incongruous distress. . . ."[19] In keeping with his own dictum that "modern comedy has to do with the disintegrating outline of the worthy and humane Self,"[20] Bellow fashions situations which reveal disintegration in action. Since he is such a master of grotesque realism, the disintegration he depicts is of the odd and incongruous variety. But what differentiates his comedy of situation from

18. The chief fault that Earl Rovit finds with John Barth's *The Sot-Weed Factor* is that its parodic form "denies him the chance to project his own unique metaphor of experience, and denies his novel the necessary illusion of engagement in human affairs which it must have in order to live." See "The Novel as Parody: John Barth," *Critique* 4 (Fall, 1963): 84.

19. Stephen Leacock, *Humour and Humanity* (New York: Henry Holt & Co., 1938), p. 79.

20. Bellow, "Some Notes on Recent American Fiction," p. 28.

Leacock's conception of it is that his portrayal of disintegration generally *does* involve "sufficient pain or disaster to overweigh the pleasure of contemplating this incongruous distress." The response evoked is one of agony and amusement. What Bellow finds to be the distinguishing trait of Yiddish stories can also apply to his own comedy of situation: "Laughter and trembling are so curiously mingled that it is not easy to determine the relations of the two." [21]

Bellow's forte, however, does not lie in producing ingeniously wrought comic situations. Since his muse is more adept at engendering thought than at generating action, he is especially skillful at creating comedy of ideas. This form of the comic occurs, according to Wylie Sypher, "whenever a society becomes self-conscious about its opinions, codes, or etiquette," with the author acting as the "intellectual conscience" of this "self-scrutinizing society." Through "sanity and verbal wit" the author is able to magnify "comedy of manners to the dimensions of a criticism of life." [22] Bellow permits his protagonists to be his "intellectual conscience." How penetrating their criticism is depends upon their intellectual capacities, their powers of perception, and the degree of their articulateness. The less astute do not seek or find explanations for the egregious conduct of their contemporaries. Viewing it as expressly intended to infuriate or unnerve them, they do nothing more than fulminate at the outward effects of this conduct. Their reactions never go beyond private pique. Even the presumably wiser protagonists occasionally cannot differentiate between their own personal troubles and impersonal issues, since they tend, when highly distraught, to transfer the former onto the latter. Only when they have regained their composure are they able to dissociate the two and constructively deal with each. Those who have any kind of historical sense are able to regard the prevailing injustices not merely as isolated phenomena peculiar to present-day America, but as repetitions with only slight variations of the abuses which have outraged upright men through the ages. But such a perspective is not the only prerequisite for ideological comedy. These same protagonists have, after long years of wrestling with life's anomalies, formulated a clearly defined set of

[21]. Saul Bellow, "Introduction," *Great Jewish Short Stories*, ed. Saul Bellow (New York: Dell Publishing Co., 1963), p. 12.
[22]. Sypher, *Comedy*, pp. 211–212.

moral norms and standards against which to judge the grotesque and the absurd. This capacity for keen judgment, along with the ability to express this judgment trenchantly, makes the resultant comedy of ideas similar to what Northrop Frye terms "militant irony" [23] or satire. While Bellow's comedy of ideas does not accomplish the purported aim of conventional satire—the reform of the corrupt or inane status quo through ridicule—it does accentuate and clarify the nature of the corruption or inanity. The high degree of distortion it contains functions very much like "a dye dropped onto the specimen to make vivid the traits and qualities that otherwise would be blurry or invisible to the naked eye." [24]

Even though Bellow's "militant irony" accomplishes its intended purpose, he does not extensively develop it or employ it in any systematic way. Unlike Philip Roth in *Our Gang,* his full-length mockery of President Nixon and his policies, Bellow is not willing to sacrifice subtle character portrayal and thematic profundity merely to "lilliputianize public figures" [25] and then inflate them into execrable monsters. He refuses to permit madcap satire to determine the course of his literary vehicle. Only when it is in accord with the demands of his narrative does he allow the wittiest of his protagonists to hurl scornful superlatives at villains who are not so extravagantly caricatured. And then they do not wage a full-scale campaign, but cease fire after venting their spleens.

In *Herzog* Bellow states that "there is something funny about the human condition and civilized intelligence makes fun of its own ideas" (271). While Bellow is that civilized intelligence who indicates what is funny about each of the worlds in his novels, he has evidently been schooled in this area by very distinguished instructors. From his Jewish background there are traces of the exhortative kind of satire and irony unique to the Prophets, especially Amos and Isaiah, who with matchless skill lay bare the weaknesses and follies of the stiff-necked Israelites. His often circuitous way of ascertaining what is ludicrous is akin to the tortuous wit found in the *Talmud* and *Midrash,*

23. Northrop Frye, *Anatomy of Criticism* (New York: Atheneum, 1965), p. 223.
24. Alan Lelchuk, "On Satirizing Presidents: An Interview with Philip Roth," *Atlantic* 228 (December, 1971): 84.
25. *Ibid.,* p. 82.

the commentaries on Jewish oral law. His defiant topical satire resembles that of the "affected Jewish minority" whom Goebbels denounced for originating "jokes that cease to be jokes when they touch the holiest matters of national life." [26] From his American literary heritage there are strong suggestions of Melville's heady speculative comedy and Twain's sardonic indictments of the "damned human race." Bellow has obvious ties with the masters of world literature as well. His acrimonious outbursts against imperious "reality instructors" and fraudulent powers of authority are like the derision which Dostoevsky's embittered *eirons* level at the fatuous *alazons* or blocking figures in control of society. His exuberant forays into vast stretches of often unexplored learned territory call to mind the lively "encyclopedic comedy of knowledge" [27] of Rabelais, Burton, Sterne, and Joyce. Despite such echoes and affinities, Bellow is a comedian of ideas who strikes out on his own. In contrast to many twentieth-century American novelists who have been ashamed to think and have depicted what he regards as "passionate activity without ideas," Bellow is that rare writer who not only values but also produces "miracles, born of thought" [28] which at once reveal how ridiculous and sublime we are.

In dealing with comedy of language, Bergson writes that there may be "something artificial in making a special category for the comic in words since most of the varieties of the comic . . . are produced through the medium of language." He goes on to distinguish between the "comic expressed" and the "comic *created* by language":

> The former could, if necessary, be translated from one language into another, though at the cost of losing the greater portion of its significance when introduced into a fresh society different in manners, in literature, and above all in association of ideas. But it is generally im-

[26.] Quoted in Albert Goldman, "Boy-man, schlemiel: The Jewish Element in American Humour," in *Explorations,* ed. Murray Mindlin and Chaim Bermant (London, 1967), p. 6.

[27.] Robert Shulman incisively relates Bellow's erudite and expansive style in his three "open form" novels, *The Adventures of Augie March, Henderson the Rain King,* and *Herzog,* to the baroque style of such creators of "encyclopedic comedies of knowledge" as Rabelais, Burton, Sterne, Melville, and Joyce. See "The Style of Bellow's Comedy," *PMLA* 83 (March, 1968): 109–117.

[28.] Saul Bellow, "Where Do We Go from Here: The Future of Fiction," in *To the Young Writer,* ed. A. L. Bader (Ann Arbor: University of Michigan Press, 1965), p. 144.

possible to translate the latter. It owes its entire being to the structure of the sentences or to the choice of the words.[29]

In *The Adventures of Augie March, Seize the Day, Henderson the Rain King, Herzog,* and *Mr. Sammler's Planet* one can readily detect the comedy *created* by Bellow's language. Unlike the recent literature of exhaustion, whose language and characters are drained of vitality, the verbal response of Bellow's heroes to comparable despairing circumstances is an energetic and feisty one. Unlike the literature of the absurd, whose language has been reduced to mechanical phrases, nonsense syllables, incoherent grunts, and even silence in reaction to the banal and the baleful, Bellow's discourse is highly articulate and innovative. While he never succeeds in verbally routing the banal and the baleful, he refuses to lose faith in the cognitive power of his language to expose them for what they are. In the process he animates, loosens up, and coins words and phrases to make for a comic style which entertains as well as elucidates.

In a highly suggestive review of Sholom Aleichem's *The Adventures of Mottel the Cantor's Son,* Bellow makes certain observations about Yiddish conversation in the ghetto which seem particularly relevant to his own comic style:

> The most ordinary Yiddish conversation is full of the grandest historical, mythological, and religious allusions. The Creation, the Fall, the Flood, Egypt, Alexander, Titus, Napoleon, the Rothschilds, the sages, and the Laws may get into the discussion of an egg, a clothes-line, or a pair of pants. This manner of living on terms of familiarity with all times and all greatness contributed, because of the poverty and powerlessness of the Chosen, to the ghetto's sense of the ridiculous. Powerlessness appears to force people to have recourse to words. Hamlet has to unpack his heart with words, he complains. The fact that the Jews of Eastern Europe lived among menacing and powerful neighbors no doubt contributed to the subtlety and richness of the words with which they unpacked.[30]

Similarly, Bellow's prose is crowded with the most farfetched mock-heroic allusions. These obviously serve to point up the humorous discrepancies existing between his all too fallible characters and the

[29.] Bergson, "Laughter," pp. 127–128.

[30.] Saul Bellow, "Laughter in the Ghetto," *Saturday Review of Literature* 36 (May 30, 1953): 15.

grand figures of Bible, myth, and history with whom they are compared. But in a more subtle way such lofty associations sometimes ennoble these same fallible characters, since they call to mind hitherto unrecognized honorific qualities. Bellow's prose is also glutted with words. Those "destiny molders" and "heavy-water brains" who persistently arise before the Bellow heroes with their "life counsels and illumination" are voluminous word-spinners. Yet the heroes themselves do their fair share of talking as well. Some are compelled to be garrulous because they feel powerless, while others choose to be garrulous because they feel the full extent of their powers. The former resemble their constrained Old World ancestors who "unpack" their hearts with words, whereas the latter resemble the unbridled Walt Whitmans and Thomas Wolfes who celebrate themselves and their new world with their bountiful and rambling catalogues.

In addition to being delightfully allusive and profuse, Bellow's prose contains the comic juxtaposition of many levels of discourse. He has undoubtedly picked up this stylistic feature from both American and Yiddish sources. According to Richard Chase, the common denominator of Melville, Emerson, Thoreau, Dickinson, and Whitman is the "tendency of [their] language to shift rapidly from the homely and the colloquial to a rhetoric at once highly self-conscious, highly abstract and highly elaborate." "Such shifts of ground" Chase regards as the "essence of wit."[31] Maurice Samuel makes similar observations about Jewish writing: "The fusion of the secular and the sacred in Yiddish . . . makes possible a charming transition from the jocular to the solemn and back again. Well-worn quotations from sacred texts mingle easily with colloquialisms and dignified passages jostle popular interjections without taking or giving offense."[32] So, too, in *The Adventures of Augie March, Seize the Day, Henderson the Rain King, Herzog,* and *Mr. Sammler's Planet* there is the risible coexistence of polished English and fractured English, reputable euphemisms and their disreputable four-letter equivalents, ostentatious diction and unassuming diction, philosophical obscurity and gutter clarity.

Another stylistic device which Bellow seems to have borrowed from

[31.] Richard Chase, *Walt Whitman Reconsidered* (New York: William Sloane Associates, 1955), p. 74.

[32.] Maurice Samuel quoted in Irving Howe, "Introduction," *A Treasury of Yiddish Stories,* ed. Irving Howe and Eliezer Greenberg (New York: Viking Press, 1953), p. 47.

Yiddish literature is what Maurice Samuel calls "the humor of verbal retrieval, the word triumphant over the situation." [33] He finds this kind of humor especially prominent in the works of Sholom Aleichem: "Not what happens to people is funny, but what they themselves say about it. There is nothing funny about Tevyeh the diaryman as a character, and nothing funny ever happens to him. What Tevyeh does is to turn the tables on tragedy by a verbal ingenuity; life gets the better of him, but he gets the better of the argument." [34] So it is with the heroes of Bellow's last five novels. Although, unlike Tevyeh, they have their comic traits of character, they, too, often undergo harrowing experiences. But they also have at their command sprightly metaphors and agile wit which temporarily enable them to spring free of their troubles.

In *The Last Analysis* the protagonist, Philip Bummidge, attempts to present an accurate description of himself—a description which can also apply to Bellow. ". . . I formed my own method. I learned to obtain self-knowledge by doing what I best know how to do, acting out the main events of my life, dragging repressed material into the open by sheer force of drama. I am not solely a man, but also a man who is an artist, and an artist whose sphere is comedy." [35] Throughout most of his novels Bellow has either directly occupied the sphere of comedy or gravitated toward it. He has populated it with his own moral and physical grotesques, whose hidden excellences have sometimes emerged to redeem them. He has cast these characters in mirthful fantasies, ribald sexual farces, clever burlesques, and ruefully incongruous disintegrations. He has allowed the more sophisticated ones and those with a talent for acidulous social criticism to be his comedians of ideas. He has adopted as the official language of his comic sphere his own Yiddish-accented prolix and polyglot native tongue. Yet with all of these amusing features, Bellow's comic sphere is not a utopia free of inequity and despair. He is ever mindful of the brute impersonality of physical nature and the calculated treachery of human nature threatening to overwhelm his heroes. Nevertheless, Bellow does not give way to nihilism. He endows his heroes with a phoenix-like hope

33. Maurice Samuel, *The World of Sholom Aleichem* (New York: Schocken Books, 1943), p. 186.

34. *Ibid.*, p. 184.

35. Bellow, *The Last Analysis*, p. 74.

which leads them to think they can defeat the agents of their destruction. Bellow does not reveal the easy triumph of either side but dramatizes the ongoing "comical-tearful" tension between the two. Or, as Augie March describes it, "Is the laugh at nature—including eternity—that it thinks it can win over us and the power of hope? Nah, nah! I think. It never will. But that probably is the joke, on one or the other, and laughing is an enigma that includes both" (536).

A Bureaucratic Comedy

2

Dangling Man,[1] Bellow's contribution to the civilian war novel, records the failure of a man to win his separate peace. The hero Joseph,
awaiting his induction into the army and possible annihilation, rails
at the Fates for snatching away his time for self-exploration. He plain-
tively asks: "Who can be the earnest huntsman of himself when he
knows he is in turn a quarry?" (119). Yet he also rails at himself for
his failure to employ his intellect meaningfully during his stay of execu-
tion. Assuming he can learn who he is during his imposed exile from
the world, he discovers what he thought was a rare opportunity to manage his freedom to be just another form of bondage. Overwhelmed by
his impotence, he indulges in the Dostoevskian humor of the insulted
and the injured. He becomes the clown who, offended at not being the
main attraction of the show, screws up his face and sheds crocodile
tears merely to gain attention. In Joseph's case, he advertises that he
already is a "moral casualty of the war" (18) and eagerly exhibits his
psychic scars. When this behavior elicits no sympathetic response,
Joseph becomes "a human grenade whose pin has been withdrawn"
(147) and sputters his venom at innocuous bystanders. While Joseph's
rage at being arbitrarily assigned a role in an "eternally fixed plot" is
understandable, his luxuriating in self-pity and his gleeful lashing out

1. Citations from this novel are to *Dangling Man* (New York: Vanguard, 1944).

22

at chance spectators is excessive and therefore perversely comic. As Bellow himself remarked about novels extolling wretchedness "thoroughly pleased with itself": "There is grandeur in cursing the heavens, but when we curse our socks we should not expect to be taken seriously." [2]

At the outset of the novel, Joseph has for seven months been ensnared in "a bureaucratic comedy trimmed out in red tape" (10). Even though he has spent eighteen law-abiding years in this country, the army still regards him as a suspect Canadian alien who must be thoroughly investigated before final conscription. Thus he is like Kafka's Joseph K, who "without having done anything wrong" [3] suddenly finds himself under arrest and under constant summons by a menacing system. Once Joseph's draft notice releases him from his duties as a petty clerk, he, too, is subjected to protracted examinations with ever-changing regulations, misplaced records, tedious interviews, and endless reclassifications. It is during this period of frequent external harassment that Joseph attempts to engage in sustained intellectual pursuits, to write biographical essays on the philosophers of the Enlightenment. But since he finds himself in an age of general irrationality, he becomes powerless to write essays on the Rationalists. He therefore languishes at home, participating in domestic farce and minor intrigue which, unlike the bureaucratic comedy, is of his own creation.

To underscore the absurdity of his present existence, he intricately describes the day's inane ritual: his three hours of reading the newspaper, Hurstwood fashion, his frequent feedings, and his afternoon of listening to the housewives' favorite soap operas. Like Dostoevsky's Underground Man who revels in abuse, he boasts of the real and imaginary indignities which befall him. According to his increasingly paranoiac view of things, Marie the maid regards him as a nonentity and does not hesitate to smoke in front of him. Vanaker, an alcoholic neighbor, not only steals his socks and his wife's perfume, but leaves the bathroom door ajar just to annoy him. His mother-in-law purposely drops a chicken feather in his orange juice to show her contempt for his inactivity. Moreover, his peculiar dangling status prompts him to

---

2. Saul Bellow, "The Writer as Moralist," *Atlantic* 211 (March, 1963): 61.

3. Franz Kafka, *The Trial*, trans. Willa and Edwin Muir (New York: Alfred A. Knopf, 1964), p. 3.

be highly devious. Certain that people in the outside world regard him as "something unlawful in being abroad, idle in the middle of the day" (14), he rarely leaves the room, and when he does go out he patronizes no one establishment too regularly. He takes unfamiliar streets to escape familiar faces. Although he realizes that his elaborate ploys of subterfuge are wasted on an indifferent public, all he can do is amuse himself with his foolish ingenuity.

It is obvious that Joseph's predicament is an odd and incongruous one. For no sane reason at all an upright man whose movement has been unencumbered is caught in the grip of the hangman's noose. His anguish is justified, for the rope is surely around his neck. Yet he increases his torment by wildly thrashing about and fretfully tugging at the rope. This wild thrashing and fretful tugging is responsible for whatever grim humor there is in the situation. For the most part, however, Joseph's circumstances are monotonously trying. Were his dangling rendered in a variety of more fully dramatized situations rather than having him brood about it in his room or philosophize about it in his journal, the reader could become more involved in his dilemma. There might then be more entanglements and extrications and hence more diverse and strongly felt comic and tragic effects. As it is, the reader is just as impatient for Joseph to be cut down as he is.

There are, however, certain benefits resulting from Joseph's suspended position. Temporarily disengaged from the world, he enjoys an excellent vantage point from which to assess its flaws. Although he occasionally gives the "impression of a man who screams out in laughter to see his guts dangling from his belly,"[4] his brains are still pretty much intact; his intellectual powers can still generate an adequately charged comedy of ideas. It is not, to be sure, the high voltage satire of a Herzog, which totally demolishes the ossified beliefs and Stone Age practices of society. Herzog, a fictional creation some twenty years older, has at his ready command an accumulation of wit and erudition for his ammunition, whereas Joseph is first amassing his stockpile. His wit is just beginning to assert itself, and his intellectual references are just starting to become an integral part of the narrative. Instead of Herzog's strategically placed and massively launched attacks, Joseph's formless journal is filled with haphazard shots at any target which

4. Ihab H. Hassan, *Radical Innocence: Studies in the Contemporary American Novel* (Princeton: Princeton University Press, 1961), p. 299.

happens to cross his mind. Instead of Herzog's denunciation seasoned with drollery, there is for the most part Joseph's pure denunciation.

Imbued with the uncompromising idealism of youth and an inflexible notion of the way things should be, Joseph begins his "record of . . . inward transactions" (9) by angrily noting the great divergence between individual desire and mass expectation with respect to human conduct. The present age, he finds, is permeated with a new asceticism, embodied in the Hemingway code. It advocates the use of verbal and emotional restraint, the abandonment of introspection as mere indulgence, and the adoption of the active, violent life as the only good life. Such a code, however, totally ignores one of the most vital facets of a human being: man has feelings and the need to express them; he has an inner life and the need to examine it. But unlike Robert Cohn, Joseph knows he cannot singlehandedly abolish such a firmly entrenched code. Because he is filled with the " 'yellow humor' . . . of those on the verge of despair, but not yet altogether immersed in it," [5] all he can do is weakly flaunt its dictates and wryly dismiss its adherents as "unpracticed in introspection, and therefore badly equipped to deal with opponents whom they cannot shoot like big game or outdo in daring" (9).

In addition to attacking the age for its disparagement of the inner life, Joseph derisively comments on its inconsistent attitude toward life as a whole, particularly during wartime. "With all the respect we seem to have for perishable stuff, we have easily accustomed ourselves to slaughter . . . and yet we have small pity for the victims" (83). To call attention to such a disparity of values, Joseph, possessing some of Herzog's and Sammler's sensitivity to the ridiculous in the quotidian, describes the elaborate measures people adopt to preserve life on the home front: "Pet cats are flown hundreds of miles to be saved by rare serums; and country neighbors in Arkansas keep a month's vigil night and day to save the life of a man stricken at ninety" (83–84). Yet these same people, Joseph bitterly observes, are oblivious to the fact that young men in full possession of their powers are being butchered in a dubious carnage. If they were asked to justify the waging of war, they would be quick to supply all the noble motives. Joseph punctures such inflated motives when he all too knowingly remarks: "Certain blood will be given for half-certain reasons, as in all wars" (84).

[5.] Jean Collignon, "Kafka's Humor," *Yale French Studies* 16 (Winter, 1955–56): 60.

Not only does Joseph indict the age for its scant regard for life during war; he also chastens humanity for its self-interest, operative at all times. In the "megalopolis" he finds that the law of supply and demand is the convenient rationalization employed to camouflage all kinds of debasement. To corroborate his generalization he cites the same kind of acerbic evidence which Sammler is so inventive at compiling:

> For every need there is an entrepreneur, by a marvelous providence. You can find a man to bury your dog, rub your back, teach you Swahili, read your horoscope, murder your competitor. . . . There was a Parisian cripple . . . who stood in the streets renting out his hump for a writing desk to people who had no convenient place to take their transactions (110).

With tongue in cheek Joseph declares that as long as these arrangements prove mutually advantageous, they are not wrong. If for some reason all cannot benefit, so his comically specious Jewish shopkeeper argument runs, is it not advisable that at least a few should profit? Joseph cites the case of the suitor Luzhin in *Crime and Punishment* to illustrate this "unimpeachable conclusion." Luzhin has been reading the English economists, or claims he has. " 'If I were to tear my coat in half,' " he says, " 'in order to share it with some wretch, no one would be benefited. Both of us would shiver in the cold.' And why should both shiver? Is it not better that one should be warm?" (112).

In the same mordant fashion Joseph exposes mankind's self-aggrandizement as well as its self-interest. Since "we have been taught there is no limit to what a man can be" (88), we resort, he maintains, to the most ruthless means to realize our potential. Not only do the Napoleons have a compulsive need for significance, but also the "schoolboys and clerks who roared like revolutionary lions" (89), and the "pimps and subway creatures, debaters in midnight cafeterias" (89) fanatically scheme for a distinguished personal destiny. Just as Sammler notes the havoc caused by man's "fantasies of vaulting into higher states" (93), so Joseph sees the dire consequences of such insane striving: "The fear of lagging pursues and maddens us. The fear lies in us like a cloud. It makes an inner climate of darkness. And occasionally there is a storm and hate and wounding rain out of us" (89).

These are some of Joseph's scathing observations about the contemporary scene which emerge from his random musings. While he does, in part, correctly diagnose certain genuine ills of society, his findings more accurately reflect the ills of the diagnostician. A man whose "endowment of generosity and good will" (12) is being corroded by bitterness and spite sees the world as more vicious than a man whose good will is intact or is being restored. There is the contrast between the debilitated Joseph who resignedly owns, "This would probably be a condemned age" (25) and the revived Herzog who defiantly asserts, "We must get it out of our heads that this is a doomed time" (317–318). This contrast explains the presence of such a dark comedy of ideas in *Dangling Man*.

Joseph also has an excessively dim view of his immediate associates; hence his analysis of their behavior is deprived of the full-scale levity found in Bellow's subsequent character portrayal. Whereas the later high-spirited protagonists are entertained by the foibles of their contemporaries and relish embroidering their antics, Joseph can only grimly conclude, "There is an element of the comic or fantastic in everyone. You can never bring that altogether under control" (28). The more adventurous protagonists seize every opportunity to mingle with the eccentrics, but only during rare escapes from his prison does Joseph grudgingly discover the ways in which his friends and relatives are uncontrollably comic and fantastic. The most conspicuous source of the ridiculous he witnesses is affectation. However, he does not provide any elaborate description of it or censure it with the satiric gusto of a Herzog or a Sammler. Although Joseph's mother-in-law, Mrs. Almstadt, is just as foolish and vain as Madeleine's Aunt Zelda, he does not offer a prolonged character assassination of her. Rather, he peremptorily dismisses her as just another unkempt housewife who "powders herself thickly," paints her lips "in the shape that has become the universal device of sensuality for all women" (19), and dresses her unassuming husband "like a mandarin or a Romanoff prince" (20). In like fashion Joseph curtly describes Jimmy Burns, the other flagrantly pretentious individual he recalls. Although Burns resembles Valentine Gersbach in his feigned commitment to causes and his wearing of costumes appropriate to them, Joseph, unlike Herzog, does not heap ingenious animus upon him. Rather, he tersely

denounces Burns as a has-been communist who "still wears that prole-
tarian bang on his earnest forehead and dreams of becoming an
American Robespierre" (35).

But affectation is a fairly innocuous vice compared to the more
destructive element of the comic which Joseph is perceptive enough to
discern: "the ideal construction," or what Pope called the "ruling passion." There are men Joseph notices who have so exclusively subju-
gated themselves to a single tyrannical claim that they have closed off
all other avenues for self-expression. With the strictest of obedience
they ceaselessly march along the narrow path leading to what they
adamantly believe is significance. They are "willing to pursue [their]
ideal until [their] eyes burst from [their] head and [their] feet from
[their] shoes" (140). They cannot see that they are slaves in a self-
created bondage. In Joseph's diary, however, there is not much of an
opportunity to see them in their bondage and to observe the ludicrous
consequences ensuing from that bondage. They are not like the full-
bodied ideal constructionists of Bellow's later novels who vigorously
ride their hobby horses and are vigorously toppled from them. In
Dangling Man they have no vivid existence apart from Joseph's speculation about them; they function merely as object lessons in his enforced
education. Joseph only superficially informs us about his brother Amos,
who, obsessed with becoming a plutocrat, is transformed into an adding machine, registering worth strictly in monetary terms. Like Augie's
brother Simon, Amos serves as a negative model whom Joseph stub-
bornly refuses to imitate. Whereas Amos is a beneficiary of the war,
Joseph vows to be its victim. Joseph is likewise determined to be the
opposite of his intellectual friend Morris Abt, who, unable to realize
his self-imposed rigorous standards of excellence, must lord it over a
defenseless neurotic woman, since he is "continually in need of being
consequential" (86). Nor does Joseph wish to become like the confirmed vagrant, Alf Steidler, who strains to be indolent in the grand
manner, or like the enterprising Alsatian tailor, Mr. Fanzel, who, because he is consumed with taking care of "number one," can afford to
show no concern for his neighbors. Perhaps the ideal constructionist
whom Joseph most dreads resembling is a zealously dedicated faith-
healer who desperately tries to convert him to Christian Science, even
though her own health is rapidly declining. By persisting in her evan-
gelism and thus aggravating her condition, she gives full vent to the

self-destructive tendencies which Joseph possesses but has struggled to check.[6]

Although Joseph finds these ideal constructions—for affluence, for intellectual eminence, for sloth, for self-preservation—to be a source of the comic, he realizes that they are also a source of the near-tragic. He refers to them as parasites which "eat us, drink us and leave us life-lessly prostrate." Yet, he ruefully observes, "We are always inviting the parasite, as if we were eager to be drained and eaten" (88). More-over, once these monomaniacs are "lifelessly prostrate" from relent-lessly pursuing their separate goals, they want an audience, if not to share their obsessions, then at least to applaud their performance. Amos urges Joseph to emulate him; Abt craves praise for his brilliance; Steidler wants appreciation for his life style; and the sick woman seeks fellow Christian Scientists. Yet these attempts to recruit others not only fail to win the allegiance and admiration of their peers; they actually incur their ridicule and (what is even more objectionable) their wrath or pity.

The talent Joseph has for detecting the comic in others he can in some measure apply to himself. Although he lacks Herzog's in-depth awareness of his own foibles, much of his journal is concerned with the disclosure of the foolish aspects of his character. "Very little about the Joseph of a year ago pleases me," he initially remarks. "I cannot help laughing at him, at some of his traits and sayings" (26). While these "traits and sayings" recalled in Joseph's present state of "narcotic dull-ness" (18) are unavoidably tinged with this dullness, they are still in their colorless way wryly amusing. In his former appearance, for instance, Joseph admits to having been just as ridiculously affected as those he has criticized. At the age of twenty-seven he selected dark conservative suits to suggest the reflective, mature man, and he wore "pointed, dandyish" shoes to avoid being considered too old—that is, in his middle thirties. Moreover, apparel that was unkempt or in poor taste did not suit him as the proper attire for the truly sophisticated in-dividual. Very deliberate in his choice of clothing, he strained to be inconspicuous by wearing " 'the uniform of the times' " (28). Although

---

[6.] Keith Opdahl, commenting more fully on the significance of the Christian Science Lady, views her as an example of "too human deadness" as well as the individual who "invests his life in death." See *The Novels of Saul Bellow: An Introduction* (University Park: Pennsylvania State University Press, 1967), pp. 34–35.

he was a nonconformist, he did not feel the need to dress like one; rather, he took a perverse delight in having his outer appearance belie his inner nature.

Joseph was affected about his avocation and vocation, too. Essentially a dilettante, he liked to think of himself as a scholar. Not surprisingly, he chose studies that corresponded to various stages of his psychological development. He first became preoccupied with "Romanticism and the child prodigy"; he then became immersed in the early ascetics; most recently, priding himself on being a rationalist, he became consumed with the Enlightenment. His job was another matter. Although he did not find it particularly absorbing, he purposely overextended himself "simply to prove that 'visionaries' can be hard-headed" (29). Hence he could boast of functioning in two worlds—the contemplative and the practical—and could accordingly adopt the airs of a philosopher-king.

Joseph also recognizes that he was " 'on the funny side' " (28) because he had his own "ideal construction." "In the last seven or eight years he has worked everything out in accordance with a general plan" (29). He fervently believed that culture, defined generally as the "enlightenment and excellence of taste acquired by intellectual and esthetic training," [7] was ultimately the only influence which could civilize humanity. The Joseph of the present, however, realizes how foolish this plan was. It had caused him to make "mistakes of the sort people make who see things as they wish to see them, or for the sake of their plans *must* see them" (39). And, just like the other ideal constructionists, the Joseph of the past had tried to enlist others to adopt his particular obsession. He had tried to civilize his niece Etta through exposure to his precious learning. Like the other converters, he succeeded not in winning her cooperation, but in provoking her long-term hostility. Similarly, he had tried to dominate his wife's intellectual and aesthetic taste. For years he had sought to transform her into one of "Burckhardt's great ladies of the Renaissance" or the "no less profound Augustan women" (98). Here, too, he encountered resistance. "Clothes, appearance, furniture, light entertainment, mystery stories, the attractions of fashion magazines, the radio, the enjoyable evening" (98) constituted an opposition which he could not conquer. He was forced to admit that his wife could not figure in his savant's pipedreams. The

7. *Webster's Seventh New Collegiate Dictionary*, 3rd ed., s.v. "culture."

now enlightened Joseph realizes how frenetic and thus how laughable his zeal to spread the gospel of culture had been.

Although Joseph is deft at revealing the comic elements of his former self, he is inept at discovering the humorous inconsistencies of his present self. Totally unaware of the many contradictions in his current behavior, he possesses the "unconsciousness" of the Bergsonian comic person who is "invisible to himself while remaining visible to all the world." [8] This "unconsciousness" makes Joseph an object of Bellow's mockery, just as society's "unconsciousness" has made it an object of Joseph's mockery. Moreover, just as Joseph has used irony to expose the folly of others, so Bellow uses irony to expose Joseph's folly. When Joseph acts as the strident commentator on the decadent times, he expresses Bellow's own views; there is then no distance between author and protagonist. But Bellow is also detached from Joseph, and from his authorial perch he makes us aware of Joseph's disparate attitudes by wry indirection.

For one thing, Bellow causes us to see Joseph's conflicting views regarding privacy and recognition. Early in the journal he insists that he desires a withdrawal from society to cultivate new insights. Grateful for the public's utter disregard, he welcomes his newly achieved anonymity. But a while later he desperately seeks acknowledgment of his identity. So forsaken does he feel that, like Dostoevsky's buffoonish Underground Man, he prefers "embarrassment or pain to indifference" (82). Hence Joseph creates a painfully funny scene in a restaurant when he encounters Jimmy Burns, once a close friend and fellow comrade. When Burns, who undoubtedly regards him as an apostate, purposely ignores him, Joseph is incensed. On an ideological level he is offended that a cause which supposedly dedicated itself to effecting the brotherhood of man was forbidding one individual to communicate with another. But it is on the personal level that Joseph is most crucially affected. Almost a case of Berkeleian metaphysics, it is as if his existence depended upon Burns's recognition of it. Just as Dostoevsky's Underground Man forces his company on former classmates whom he despises, so Joseph directly insults Burns to provoke some kind of reaction from him. Eliciting no response, all he succeeds in doing is attracting the crowd's attention, when only the day before he

8. Henri Bergson, "Laughter," in *Comedy,* ed. Wylie Sypher (New York: Doubleday & Co., 1956), p. 71.

wished to remain inconspicuous, to luxuriate in splendid isolationism.

Bellow also points up Joseph's humorously discrepant feelings about the army. On a theoretical level he admits that no man is totally self-sufficient. He even appears highly intoxicated with the belief (undoubtedly acquired through his reading) that "goodness is achieved not in a vacuum, but in the company of other men attended by love" (92). But on a very practical level, when he is faced with the actual possibility of induction, a situation which would allow him to be in the company of other men, he rebels. Although he consents to be a "member of the Army," he is not willing to be "a *part* of it" (133–134). Always a person "greatly concerned with keeping intact and free from encumbrance a sense of his own being" (27), he is determined once again to withhold himself, to prevent his treasured individuality from being usurped by the vulgar mass.

Bellow reveals Joseph's contrary notions about his own importance as well. These notions proceed not so much from Joseph's quirky personality as from his being a captive rider on the merry-go-round of war. The result, in any case, is two diametrically opposed self-images. In one respect Joseph has the grandiose view that he is "an inestimable prize" (119). Created to have dominion over the beasts of the earth, he presumes he has dominion over himself and the events which affect him. He likes to think that his opinions on the war will influence its outcome, that it is an issue of "personal morality and private will" (84). In another respect he regards himself as the lowliest of creatures whose fate is completely determined, "one of a shoal, driven toward the weirs" (119). He therefore believes it is his lot to "accept the imposition of all kinds of wrongs, to wait in ranks under a hot sun . . . to be those in the train when it is blown up, or those at the gates when they are locked, to be of no significance, to die" (119).

Joseph's chameleon shifts of mind are not as laughable as his mindlessness when it comes to recognizing evil within himself. Although he readily admits that the next man might be "full of instinctive bloody rages, licentious and unruly from his earliest days, an animal who had to be tamed" (39), he rather self-righteously claims that he "could find in himself no such history of hate overcome. . . . He believed in his own mildness, believed in it piously" (39). But his mildness exists only when he resides within his anchorite's cell or imaginatively dwells within the "heavenly cities" of the eighteenth-century philosophers. When he is in the company of others on this earth, he, like Henderson, excels at losing friends and alienating strangers. While Joseph's hassles with those who baffle his "cyclonic wishes" (133) are not as flamboyantly bellicose as Henderson's, they are still charged with their own inflammatory rage. Like many of Bellow's other heroes whose most heated wrangles are with relatives, Joseph's fiercest rage is directed at his niece Etta, an over-indulged teenager who has absorbed her parents' nouveau riche disdain for impoverished intellectuals. The point of contention between Joseph and Etta at a family gathering concerns who shall have the use of the phonograph. Joseph wants to play a Haydn divertimento over and over again because it enables him to realize that he is still "an apprentice in suffering and humilia- tion" (67), and that only "with grace, without meanness" (67) will he be able to lead an exemplary life. Etta, on the other hand, wants to play Xavier Cugat conga records. Just as Henderson refuses to allow his children to win at checkers, Joseph refuses to allow Etta to have her way. But it is not only a matter of needing to assert his supremacy over a juvenile opponent. What is of even greater importance to Joseph is that he, a refined humanist, and not Etta, a crass philistine, have control of the phonograph, that mechanical Pied Piper with its power to sway the populace. The fact that Joseph resorts to brute force—dragging Etta by the hair and savagely spanking her—to be- come master of the machine, whose music should soothe the savage beast, never strikes Joseph as being in any way ironic. Nor does he see the comic irony in the fact that the divertimento which had recently given him instruction in emotional maturity was also the cause of a quarrel which had reduced him to the level of a spiteful child. Writing about the incident in his journal, Joseph claims that Etta and her parents are solely responsible for the fracas and that he will have to protect himself from their baseness in the future.[9] Although Joseph remains unaware of his culpability, Bellow causes us to recognize the humorous discrepancy between Joseph's holier-than-thou intentions and his unholy actions.

Joseph is the same kind of "pharisaical stinker"[10] in his dealings with those outside his family. He continually sees himself as the un-

9. Keith Opdahl's discussion of *Dangling Man* first called my attention to the ironies proceeding from Joseph's encounter with Etta. See *The Novels of Saul Bellow*, pp. 38–39.
10. *Time* 43 (May 8, 1944): 104.

justifiably abused party when he himself has been the abuser. For example, he accuses an overly cautious bank clerk of being distrustful and patronizing when it is he who acts as if he were an imperious patrician demanding special treatment from a plebeian servant. Joseph also feels slighted when a mistress with whom he has abruptly severed relations is entertaining another gentleman caller and is unwilling to admit him. Like Leventhal, boorishly interrupting the love-making of Allbee and his lady-friend, Joseph insists that his former mistress halt her amours to look for a book he has lent her. When she refuses, he views her as inconsiderate and fickle. Even more unreasonable is Joseph's harsh treatment of Vanaker. Just as Dostoevsky's Underground Man attributes his own sadistic traits to his fairly innocuous servant Apollon, so Joseph attributes his own perversities to the harmless antics of the old drunk. When the landlady's son-in-law fails to differentiate between the two men and accuses both of them of "rowdyism" in the house of a dying woman, Joseph is provoked to fight him as well. In his present "dishevelment of mind" (37) he is unable to see that, by scolding Vanaker for "raising hell" and by pugnaciously asserting his innocence, he has been the chief rowdy.[11] Instead it is Bellow who ironically points up this fact.

Joseph's outbursts against such self-created foes serve several functions in *Dangling Man*. They convince us of Joseph's total ignorance of his waywardness. Further, the more violent and unprovoked they are, the more they indicate Joseph's progressive disintegration and underscore the gap between his former highly restrained nature and his present wildly uncontrollable one. His outbursts also provide some comic relief to dispel the tedium of a journal devoid of "changing phenomena" (18). More specifically, such amusement comes from Bellow's subtle depiction of Joseph's hypocritical qualities. Early in the journal, for example, Joseph prides himself on being a "sworn upholder of *tout comprendre c'est tout pardonner*" (29), but later he cannot pardon even the slightest offense. At the outset he grudgingly admires the Hemingway "closemouthed straight-forwardness" (9), but with the constant "derangement of days" (81) he becomes openmouthed to the point of incessant whining. Initially impressed by the

---

11. Keith Opdahl views Vanaker as another ideal constructionist who "represents the evils which the dangling man has consciously rejected but still retains." See "The Crab and the Butterfly" (Ph.D. diss., University of Illinois, 1961), p. 55.

Hemingway grace under pressure, he eventually becomes graceless under the least stress.

A stress particularly intolerable to Joseph is the overhanging threat of death. So distraught is he that he cannot indulge in the gallows humor which so many of the condemned heroes in contemporary literature resort to. Nor is he mature enough to have the sublime comic perspective of a Herzog who can accept his mortality with equanimity. One way Joseph handles his anxiety about death is to simulate the Hemingway bravado in the face of extinction, a way which he has previously ridiculed. In colloquies with himself he melodramatically declares that he is ready to be a hostage to fortune, to embrace the annihilation awaiting him. The other way Joseph copes with his anxiety about death is to engage in knotty philosophical disquisitions on its nature. Although Joseph is not one of those German existentialist necrophiles whom Herzog deplores, Joseph loves ruminating about the topic of death and human choice. Both ways, strained heroics and tortuous intellectualizing, serve as diversionary tactics, for they prevent Joseph from acknowledging the certainty of his own death. They so preoccupy him that he ceases to interact with others. Instead of hiding from death, he ironically ends up buried alive in his own self-erected crypt. Like the entombed Bartleby, Joseph's "perspectives end in the walls" (92).

To rouse Joseph from his death in life, Bellow creates a mocking alter ego during the last part of the journal. Since there are no other fully realized characters to offer opposing viewpoints, Bellow has to personify one part of Joseph's divided self to remove certain errors in his vision. In one respect the "Spirit of Alternatives," as this alter ego is called, is Bellow's thinly developed comic characterization of the non-directive therapist who is maddeningly parsimonious with his interpretations. So evasive and cryptic are the few comments he does make that Joseph, acting out the fantasies of many an exasperated patient, furiously throws orange peels at him and accuses him of making him sick with his "suave little, false little looks" (141). But like Dr. Tamkin who, despite his suspect methods, helps Tommy Wilhelm, the "Spirit of Alternatives" does get Joseph to arrive at particular truths about himself through a kind of whimsical Socratic questioning. He first suggests that man is a creature not only of reason, but also of instincts and feelings. Joseph, finding this view simple-minded, attempts to ridicule it by devising the argument which he thinks the "Spirit of Alternatives" would have used to reach this conclusion: "Reason has to conquer itself. Then what are we given reason for? To discover the blessedness of unreason" (136). Although "the Spirit of Alternatives" denies having such an argument in mind, he does succeed in causing Joseph to formulate its terms and in the process weigh its implications.

Another view which the "Spirit of Alternatives" circuitously gets Joseph to accept is that an individual "can't banish the world by decree" if it is in him; indeed, his "very denial implicates" (137) him further. No matter what escapist stratagems he employs, Joseph, like Bellow's other solitaries, knows that he will not be allowed to remain undisturbed in his cocoon of privacy. But unlike Herzog or Sammler, who actually experience rude invasions of their privacy, Joseph only imagines what it will be like. Because he is so callow, he envisions it as more alarming than it is: "The world comes after you . . . shunts you back and forth, abridges your rights, cuts off your future, is clumsy or crafty, oppressive, treacherous, murderous, black, whorish, venal . . ." (137). However, right after he denounces the world for ruining his life, the "Spirit of Alternatives" causes him to admit that the fault may lie with him as well and to blame only the world is "too narrow, too cowardly" (137). A month and a half passes before Joseph begins to comprehend what the nature of his fault has been. Although he earlier conceded that "alienation . . . [is] a fool's plea" (137), he now realizes he has led a foolishly alienated life and, like Augie March making a fetish of his "independent fate," has ignored the "whole question of [his] real and not superficial business as a man" (166). On a theoretical level he now believes that the " 'highest ideal construction' is the one that unlocks the imprisoning self" (153), that we should "stop living so exclusively and vainly for our own sake, impure and unknowing, turning inward and self-fastened" (154). Yet such noble reasons are not what finally cause Joseph to hasten his induction into the army. He turns outward only because he cannot turn inward in any meaningful way.[12]

12. Opdahl likens *Dangling Man* to Sartre's *Nausea*, since both authors end their novels by having their heroes rejoin society. The reasons for their return differ, however. Roquentin, according to Opdahl, "feels that he can define himself only by action within a social context; Joseph volunteers because he fails to find the self which exists separately from its actions." See *The Novels of Saul Bellow*, p. 31.

The most disturbing insight which the "Spirit of Alternatives" compels Joseph to acknowledge is the same one which the Grand Inquisitor demonically conveys to the tortured Ivan Karamazov: "Nothing is more seductive for man than his freedom . . . but nothing is a greater cause of suffering." [13] Joseph welcomes his temporary reprieve "to do all the delightful things" (11) he had always wanted to do. But as he ruefully discovers, "The worlds we bargained for were never the worlds we got" (26). Instead of thriving in the blissful absence of constraint, he is immobilized by the terrifying presence of freedom. Like Jacob Horner in John Barth's *The End of the Road,* he suffers from his own kind of "cosmopsis" or paralysis of will. Experiencing the same "weatherless" days, he can neither activate his creative powers nor control his fractious self. Painfully vacillating between wanting to rejoin society and wanting to retreat from it, he also resembles the murderer Barnadine in *Measure for Measure,* who, Joseph recalls, refused to leave his cell to be executed because his "contempt for life equaled his contempt for death" (19). Ravaged with the same conflicting desires, Joseph remains in his cell and, like the rigid half-cleaned chicken in Mrs. Almstadt's sink, can do nothing but examine his "entrails." In such a demoralized state Joseph cannot help but reach the same disheartening conclusion as Ivan Karamazov: although man is eager to attain freedom, once he has it he is oppressed by it and quickly gives it up. Or, as Joseph sardonically observes, "And soon we run out, we choose a master, roll over on our backs and ask for the leash" (168). Not surprisingly, a week and a half later Joseph chooses the army for his master. With self-directed irony he claims to be grateful that he is "in other hands, relieved of self-determination, freedom canceled" (191). He further undercuts his momentous decision by histrionically announcing that he is "off to the wars" (184) before an indifferent bartender and a tavern full of servicemen who are not at all concerned about him or the military.

Joseph recognizes that he has lost the battle for self-possession. Although he can cite some abstract reasons for his defeat, he has not been able to adopt any successful course of action. As for his rushed submission to the army, he knows he is giving up one kind of imprisonment for another; hence his false enthusiasm. Since he is not a

[13]. Fyodor Dostoevsky, *The Brothers Karamazov,* trans. Constance Garnett (New York: Random House, 1950), p. 302.

tragic character, he does not have a total anagnorisis. What he does not discover at the end of the novel is that there was a satisfactory answer to his question, "How should a good man live?" (39) The answer lay within his immediate grasp, yet he was blind to its existence. Just as Isabel Archer in her passionate search for experience remains unaware of the real experience she is having in the process of searching, so Joseph in his zealous quest for the good life overlooks the miracles of the commonplace. One such miracle is the comforting presence of a loved one. But like those writers who, Bellow claims, are so consumed with the morbid that they ignore the "revelations" of an ordinary "baker's daughters," [14] Joseph, obsessed with thoughts of death, forgets his ordinary wife's selfless care of him when he is sick and the happiness he derives from her devotion. He likewise forgets the pleasure he receives from the miracle of nature. Unlike Henderson, who feels permanently enriched by the splendors of an African dawn, or Herzog, who acquires abiding tranquillity from his pastoral refuge, Joseph soon forgets the ecstasy he experiences from a certain winter day which "held its own beauty and was engaged with nothing but itself" (119). What Joseph has been looking for is already in his possession: the joy of life itself, which need be "engaged with nothing but itself." As Keith Opdahl rightly concludes, had Joseph prized the "full measure of his own" and another's existence and appreciated "the value that simple fact provides," his "quest for a basis for life—for an identity— should have ended before it began." [15]

Early in the journal Joseph fiercely resists his brother's advice that he use the army to advance himself. To justify his desire to be a private, he likens himself to Socrates, who was "a plain foot soldier, a hoplite" (64). But the Joseph we see in the entire novel more closely resembles the Socrates of Aristophanes' *The Clouds* "who, in his contempt of the common world of human experience and in his consuming passion for the clear and distinct idea, lives ridiculously suspended in a basket high up in the air. . . ." [16] Aristophanes brings this Socrates down from his basket so that he will "not be allowed to

14. Saul Bellow, "Where Do We Go from Here: The Future of Fiction," in *To the Young Writer*, ed. A. L. Bader (Ann Arbor: University of Michigan Press, 1965), p. 145.

15. Opdahl, *The Novels of Saul Bellow*, p. 41.

16. Nathan A. Scott, Jr., "The Bias of Comedy and the Narrow Escape into Faith," *The Christian Scholar* 44 (Spring, 1961): 27–28.

get away with this pretense that he lives above the relativities of history" and so that he will "be made to confront some of the elemental facts of life." [17] Similarly, because Joseph strives to be of only mind, to give all to reason, he becomes the target of Bellow's irony. Like Aristophanes' Socrates, Joseph is "ridiculously suspended," not in a basket but in his "six-sided box" (92). Closeted with his loathings, he scorns the brutish world and thus remains oblivious to the "pleasurable mainsprings of our earthly life" (187). At times he also forgets the most alarming event of his history—the war. Socrates has his "consuming passion for the clear and distinct idea"; Joseph is consumed with leading a culturally enriched life. Finally, just as Aristophanes makes Socrates "confront some of the elemental facts of life," so Bellow causes Joseph to realize that he is "an incomplete and conditioned creature of a particular time and a particular space," [18]—in other words, a comic man. This is not to say that Joseph is pleased with such a self-concept; in fact, he is ashamed of it; hence his wry self-deprecation. It remains for his fictional descendants to accept this definition of themselves and even to revel in it.

The humor of Bellow's first novel is as dangling as its protagonist. It oscillates between rueful smiles at private flaws and exaggerated scoffings at public vices. It fluctuates between roiling self-victimization and riotous victimization of others. But what most distinguishes this humor is that, like its protagonist, it sorely lacks the maturity of Bellow's later comedy. Its "intellectual onanism" [19] has not been sufficiently corrected by Bellow's antic muse. Its querulousness has not been leavened with enough mirth. Its gibes have been muffled with too few jests. As Bellow has observed about other excessively despairing literature, *Dangling Man,* "naggingly conscious of the absurd, is absurdly portentous, not metaphysically 'absurd.' " [20]

17. *Ibid.,* p. 28.
18. *Ibid.,* p. 19.
19. Jonathan Baumbach, "The Double Vision: *The Victim* by Saul Bellow," *The Landscape of Nightmare* (New York: New York University Press, 1965), p. 37.
20. Bellow, "The Writer as Moralist," p. 61.

Countering Absurdity with Absurdity

3

Just as the war precipitated Joseph's dangling and his foolish and profound reactions to it, anti-Semitism sparked the explosive battle of wits between Gentile and Jew in *The Victim*.[1] Such a subject was by no means original in 1947, a few short years after Buchenwald, Dachau, and Auschwitz, but Bellow's treatment of it is original. While most authors wrote excessively earnest novels resembling ponderous tracts from the Anti-Defamation League, Bellow introduces comic relief in his examination of the problem. Although he regards bigotry as a serious matter, he views it as a diabolically funny matter as well. More specifically, he exposes the outrageous nonsense of the anti-Semite's spurious accusations and the comparable folly of the Jew's exaggerated attempts at self-justification. He employs grotesque humor to reveal how each of them, so caught up in his game of mutual recrimination, not only fails to gain any advantage, but almost forfeits his humanity as well.

The player through whose eyes we see most of the game is Asa Leventhal, inconsequential editor of a minor trade journal. To a great extent he embodies that comic sense of Bellow's which Alfred Kazin describes as "a human being's diffidence before the superior forces of life, a Chaplinesque sense of himself as the accidental and paltry vessel

[1.] Citations from this novel are to *The Victim* (New York: Vanguard, 1947).

on which life has been conferred." [2] Leventhal is not just diffident before the "superior forces of life"; he positively cowers before them. Even though his employers find his work most satisfactory, he continually fears that he will be dismissed at any moment. Unable to enjoy his modest good fortune, all he manages to do is tread cautiously, maintaining a delicate balance on what he sees as the hazardous vocational tightrope. Unlike Joseph, who can bitterly laugh at the wild behavior and eccentric beliefs which his difficult position force upon him, Leventhal is so intent on retaining his poise in a precarious situation that he is not aware of how ridiculous his exaggerated efforts at keeping upright make him appear. Joseph at least can grin and bear it; Leventhal can only grimace and bear it. It is this grimace, unwarranted and out of place, which invites mockery.

Leventhal is also insecure because he is a Jew compelled to live in an alien world of Gentiles who, he thinks, are hostile to him. His ancestors, the Jews of the Eastern European ghetto, the *shtetl,* were forced to assume the guise of *dos kleine menschele,* the little man, who in the face of real danger resorted to ingenious methods of survival. However, the contemporary world is not a reduplication of the ghetto world. Leventhal cannot recognize this fact, for he is consumed with being a transplanted version of *dos kleine menschele* who feels he must also be constantly watching for ubiquitous persecutors and priming himself to cope with equally numerous and awful perils. Engrossed with bigot-hunting and survival tactics, Leventhal is not only a disturbed man, but also a comically obsessed man. He has identified himself "[so] completely with some special interest or project . . . [that he] is blinded to the integral character of [his] humanity and thus thrown out of gear with the fundamental norms and orders of human existence." [3] Like Bruce Jay Friedman's Stern, he changes from being a trusting person, expecting to receive fair treatment from his fellow man, to an abnormally suspicious character, always anticipating the worst from those around him. While Leventhal does not go to Stern's ludicrous extreme of imagining a "squadron of voyeurs" watching him perform his conjugal intimacies, he does paranoically believe that dur-

2. Alfred Kazin, "The World of Saul Bellow," *Contemporaries* (Boston: Little, Brown & Co., 1962), p. 221.

3. Nathan A. Scott, Jr., "The Bias of Comedy and the Narrow Escape into Faith," *The Christian Scholar* 44 (Spring, 1961): 30.

ing the Depression he was on the "black list," that he alone was the victim of a "secret process, passing through many connections, private and professional" (47). Even now, when he is comfortably situated, he suspects that Williston, the man who was instrumental in getting him his job, may have helped him because he "disliked him unfairly and wanted to pay for [his] prejudice" (95). In his own family he is certain that his brother's Catholic mother-in-law despises him just because he is Jewish; after the death of her grandson, he imagines she regards him with "spite and exultation as though he were the devil" (178). Unlike Bellow, who in a *Commentary* symposium stated that the "pain of Shylock" is no greater than the pain of Job or Lear,[4] Leventhal feels that he has been singled out for the most excruciating agony. It is fairly obvious that much of this agony is self-induced, and therefore Leventhal's plight evokes more smiles than sympathy.

Because Leventhal's energies have been mobilized for injustice-collecting, he no longer has the capacity to see himself clearly. This lack of self-knowledge serves to make him laughable also, since Bergson would say he is unable to eliminate his ridiculous defects because he is not "fully conscious of [who] he is" and what he does.[5] In particular, Leventhal, like Joseph, fails to recognize his own depravity. For one thing, he is unaware of his most glaring fault—his religious prejudice. It is highly ironic, Bellow indicates, that the Jew who accuses the Christian of intolerance is oblivious to his own intolerance of the Christian. Yet Leventhal finds it difficult to accept his brother's marriage to an Italian Catholic, since he assumes she will be superstitious and temperamental. He is angered and saddened by the fact that his nephew will receive a Catholic funeral: "It was peculiar, after so many generations, to have this. . . . Never mind, thanks, we'll manage by ourselves" (180). Nevertheless, he condemns the Gentiles in his office for being devoid of compassion, for not having the decency to express their condolences on the death of his nephew: "It showed the low quality of the people, their inferiority and meanness" (198). He accuses Williston, a Kentucky Protestant, of paying only lip service to his "Anglo-Saxon [notion] of fairness" (89). He views his victimizer,

---

4. Saul Bellow, "The Jewish Writer and the English Literary Tradition," *Commentary* 8 (October, 1949): 366.

5. Henri Bergson, "Laughter," in *Comedy,* ed. Wylie Sypher (New York: Doubleday & Co., 1956), p. 71.

Kirby Allbee, the dissipated wretch who has given free reign to all his animal desires, as the prototype of all Gentiles.

Leventhal is almost as anti-Semitic as he is anti-Christian. He has no use for the ethical, cultural, and religious traditions of Judaism. Ironically, Allbee, the Jew-hater, has from his family's ministerial background a greater interest in Jewish learning than does the Jew, whereas the only Jewish concern Leventhal has is for the six million Jews killed in the holocaust. As for the Jews who were not martyrs, he has contempt for them. He is ashamed of his money-grubbing father and finds all Jewish vendors to be unduly gross. He even accuses the eminent Disraeli of exploiting his Jewishness to gain fame. By discriminating against his own people, Leventhal unwittingly becomes what Sartre calls an "inauthentic" Jew in that he has allowed himself "to be poisoned by the stereotype that others have" [6] of him. Consequently, he can see his fellow Jews only as stereotypes.

In addition to bigotry, Leventhal has other unacknowledged sins. Mental infidelity is one of them. Witnessing a scene of a cuckolded husband apprehending his cheating wife, Leventhal self-righteously claims that "he really did not know what went on about him, what strange things, what savage things. They hung near him all the time in trembling drops, invisible, usually, or seen from a distance. But that did not mean that there was always to be a distance, or that sooner or later one or two of the drops might not fall on him" (94). Apparently some "drops" have fallen on him, for Bellow insinuates that during his wife's absence Leventhal secretly desires his landlady, Mrs. Nunez, and also covets the woman Allbee has brought to his apartment.

Along with regarding himself as a faithful husband, Leventhal likes to think of himself as a refined, sensitive individual, always considerate of other people's feelings. He is unaware that he has been "peculiarly aggressive" in job-hunting, heartless in shattering Mrs. Williston's illusions about the no longer brilliant Allbee, and brutal in embarrassing Allbee's lady friend. Similarly, Leventhal professes to have a great aversion to all kinds of violence. Yet he almost strikes a woman in the theater for an anti-Semitic remark and actually does manhandle Allbee for intruding upon his privacy. He complains of

---

[6.] Jean-Paul Sartre, *Anti-Semite and Jew,* trans. George J. Becker (New York: Schocken Books, 1965), p. 95.

Allbee's dogged pursuit of him while all the time he has been likewise badgering Williston. He drinks himself senseless at the home of his friend Harkavy, even though he claims to abhor drinking, especially Allbee's despicable alcoholism. Bellow suggests here that all men, including Leventhal, no matter how vehemently they argue to the contrary, contain "something inhuman that didn't care about anything human" (51). To deny this fact is to persist in comic self-deception.

Not only is Leventhal's defective vision subject to ridicule; his inordinate self-absorption evokes a similar reaction. As Bellow has noted elsewhere, "Writers may not wholly agree with Bertrand Russell that 'I' is no more than a grammatical expression, but they do consider certain claims of the 'I' to be definitely funny." [7] Leventhal has such funny claims. He is so preoccupied with safeguarding his already guaranteed position, so involved with battling imaginary Jew-baiters that he cannot be troubled with anyone else. When his sister-in-law seeks his aid to care for her sick child, he views it as a most unreasonable request, a presumptuous infringement on his valuable time. And when the doctor mistakes him for the father, he is vexed by the error, wishing to assume no more responsibility than is absolutely essential. Moreover, when Allbee initially accosts him, claiming restitution for the injustice done him, Leventhal peremptorily dismisses him with the remark, "I haven't thought about you in years, frankly, and I don't know why you think I care whether you exist or not. What, are we related?" (29). It is not surprising, Bellow ironically implies, that Leventhal should feel no obligation to an almost total stranger when he finds fulfilling his duties to his own kin so onerous. Bellow further accentuates Leventhal's selfishness by having him rationalize: "Well, the world was a busy place. . . . You couldn't find a place in your feelings for everything, or give at every touch like a swinging door, the same for everyone . . ." (98).

Aside from keeping an excessively close watch on his feelings, Leventhal suffers from hypochondria. Just as Molière viewed the imaginary invalid as comic, so Bellow finds the chronic complainer of nonexistent ailments to be the worthy subject of laughter. Although Leventhal is not nearly as inventive as Henderson in manufacturing

<hr/>

7. Saul Bellow, "Some Notes on Recent American Fiction," *Encounter* 21 (November, 1963): 28.

his ills, nor nearly as eloquent as Herzog in publicizing them, he does tell anyone who will listen about how nervous he has become since his wife's temporary absence. He feels threatened by a vague presence while he sleeps. He imagines he sees mice darting along the walls. He has "begun to jerk his head around at the suspicion of a movement" (25). Adding all of these disorders together, he convinces himself that he is unwell and in no time at all credibly plays the part of a sick man.

Not only does he worry about his own present condition, but he also broods about the affliction of his deceased mother. According to his father's explanation of her illness, she had died insane. Although Leventhal has never corroborated this fact, he still dreads the manifestation in himself of any resemblance to his mother. Indeed, he is so disturbed by this unfounded knowledge that he sees evidence of madness in others. He is especially alarmed by the striking similarity between his sister-in-law and his mother. But what he foolishly mistakes for insanity is actually intense anxiety for her gravely ill child, and later overwhelming grief for his death. Greatly distressed, Leventhal projects his own darkest fears about himself onto anyone whose behavior is the least bit abnormal.[8] And although we should pity him, we are still prompted to laugh at the little man who continually spooks himself with his own huge distortions.

Leventhal is also bothered by his huge body. Joseph is mostly depicted as a disembodied spirit embarking upon metaphysical flights in a vacuum, while Leventhal is often seen as a spiritless body squeezing through a crowded universe. Although he eventually struggles to ascertain what his obligations are, his ungainly body vexes him and distracts him from his loftier aspirations. Yet, paradoxically, Bellow implies, it is only through the corporeal that we meet our obligations. Leventhal's body could be instrumental in furthering meaningful relations with others—or at least Bellow indicates there is more of a possibility for the physical wreck, Leventhal, than for the intellectual wraith, Joseph, to make vital connections with society. But this possibility does not fully materialize. As it happens in the novel, Leventhal's body is more of an impediment than an instrument. Admittedly, he does not

8. For a fuller treatment of Leventhal's fears of irrationality and sensuality as well as the ways in which he projects these fears onto others, see Keith M. Opdahl, "The Crab and the Butterfly" (Ph.D. diss., University of Illinois, 1961), p. 78.

possess the gross physical defects of a Henderson, nor does he experience his riotous collisions with all kinds of people. Still, his body is humorously conspicuous enough to take attention away from the soul. And so throughout his summer trial he is "embarrassed by his body, looking round for some convenient cloak-room in which to deposit it." [9] But he is unable to deposit it and therefore laments, "Dear God, am I so lazy, so weak, is my soul fat like my body?" (169). While his lamentation may be justified, Bellow still makes light of it. To be sure, he does not make as much sport of Leventhal's body as he does of Henderson's; yet he cannot avoid treating it as just another funny claim of the "I."

From focusing on Leventhal's fat body and restrainedly mocking his excessive concern about it, Bellow further jests at his expense by calling attention to his animal characteristics. But since Leventhal does not run the zoological gamut of a Henderson, Bellow's jests are half-hearted and scarcely developed. Any humor there is arises from Leventhal's resemblance to a bear. Like a bear, he is clumsy and lumbering, unable to keep pace with his more agile fellow creatures. Not coincidentally, Bellow has him envyingly remark, "Some men behaved as though they had a horse under them and went through life at a gallop. . . . He was not that way" (38). Also, with his coarse black hair, his overgrown eyebrows, his large head, and his surly uncouth ways, Leventhal appears to be more of a droll bear than an eccentric human. But the greatest similarity between Leventhal and the bear is in their refusal to become involved with anyone outside themselves. Leventhal, engrossed in his own difficulties, is described as "a bear in a winter hole," "not wanting to be bothered" (98).

Despite Leventhal's animal characteristics, he has the ability to think like a human being. Although he does not possess Joseph's powers of lucid inner reflection or his handy assortment of appropriate intellectual theories, he is prompted to make semi-profound observations about the comic anomalies of life, observations expressed in the simple, familiar language of a man who is too aware that he doesn't "know all that he needed to know . . ." (54). Torn between detachment and involvement in his own life, he generalizes about man's conflicting desires, for anonymity and fame: ". . . if you shut yourself up . . . you were like . . . a mirror wrapped in a piece of flannel. And like such a

9. Bergson, "Laughter," p. 94.

mirror, you were in less danger of being broken, but you didn't flash either. But you had to flash. . . . Everybody wanted to be what he was to the limit" (98). Joseph discusses a comparable idea, only he develops it more intricately and abstractly, tracing its implications through history and employing such high-flown expressions as "We suffer from bottomless avidity" and "The fear of lagging pursues and maddens us" (88–89).

Essentially unaccustomed to philosophizing, Leventhal is sometimes amused by the excessive ingenuity of his own speculations. Especially ingenious is his examination of another idea which Joseph has explored: man's contradictory inclination both to destroy and to preserve himself. Joseph mordantly attacks the utter irrationality of such ambivalent behavior, but Leventhal, dreading its manifestation in himself, is perplexed by it and attempts to explain its strangeness through a commonplace analogy he can understand:

> We were all the time taking care of ourselves, laying up, storing up, watching out on this side and on that side, and at the same time running, running desperately, running as if in an egg race with the egg in a spoon. And sometimes we were fed up with the egg, sick of it, and and at such a time would rather sign on with the devil and what they called the powers of darkness than run with the spoon, watching for the egg, fearing for the egg. Man is weak and breakable, has to have just the right amounts of everything—water, air, food. . . . That, you might say, was for the sake of the egg. There was also the opposite, playing catch with the egg, threatening the egg (99).

Through the use of a simple yet apt comparison, Leventhal succeeds not only in making a degree of sense out of nonsense, but also in mitigating his own anxiety.

Another set of opposing views which Leventhal tries to clarify with his low-keyed wit concerns the markedly differing attitudes of the immigrant Jew and his first-generation American offspring toward the American Christian. Once again, Leventhal's most reliable reference book proves to be his own experience. He points out that his immigrant father was not at all concerned about having amicable relations with the Christians. He did not even care if he were the object of their scorn. All that mattered to him was earning money from his transactions with them. His attitude was reflected in the comic verse: "Call me Ikey, call me Moe, but give me the dough" (111). With money he could be self-sufficient; he did not have to rely on anyone's good opinion of him. This is not the case, however, with the immigrant Jew's offspring. For the younger Jew, Leventhal sagely observes, money is no longer the only compensation. He has to live in the outer-directed age where a man's good name is just as precious a commodity as his bank account. Accordingly, an individual's worth is determined by the next fellow's estimation of it. If he intentionally or unintention-ally alienates his Christian neighbor, he almost of necessity feels alienated from himself; that is, "another man's words and looks could . . . convert him into his own worst enemy" (121). So Leventhal concludes that his father, with his attitude of indifference toward the Christians, was essentially a free agent, whereas his offspring, desper-ately wishing the Christians to accept him, cannot say he was the "master of [himself] when there were so many people by whom [he] could be humiliated" (149).

Despite Asa Leventhal's paranoia, egocentricity, self-deception, hypo-chondria, and odd physical features—his bearishness and rotundity—it would be inaccurate to place him in the ranks of Bellow's full-blown comic characters. While he does possess many of their same flaws, Bellow is not yet ready to loosen the reins of solemnity in his handling of these flaws. Still not allowing his comic imagination to go unbridled, his tongue is more in cheek than it is wagging impishly at us. He ironically indicates Leventhal's imperfections rather than humorously dwelling upon them. Nor does he permit Leventhal any notable aware-ness of the ridiculous aspects of his own character. Unlike a Henderson or a Herzog, he cannot endear himself to us with an amusing recital of his foibles. Nor does Bellow endow him with a resilient sense of humor to assuage his ills. Asa—whose name in Hebrew means "healer" —cannot heal himself, for Bellow does not provide him with the necessary anodyne of laughter.

If there is any adept funny man in *The Victim*, it is Kirby Allbee, whose repertoire includes all kinds of impersonations—comic, demonic, and pathetic. Just as Leventhal appears as a transplanted version of *dos kleine menschele*, Allbee first crops up as another ghetto import, the *schnorrer* or professional beggar who preys upon those of better means. In the Eastern European *shtetl* the *schnorrer* felt no shame in living off the resources of others; since giving charity to the poor was considered a most sacred duty, the beggar did not even feel the need to express any kind of gratitude to his benefactor. On the contrary, the donor was usually made to feel indebted to the beneficiary, because the latter gave the former the opportunity to attain great religious merit. In many anecdotes the *schnorrers* treat their benefactors as if the roles were reversed—as if they were doing them a favor in accepting their money. As Bernard Schilling points out, such anecdotes are especially comic because they contain "the incongruous picture of a beggar who so behaves as to seem superior to the very people from whom he begs; it is they who must defend themselves for their actions and their high place in the world and to show cause why, in actual fact, the beggar is not more to be praised than the man who just happens to have the money." [10] So it is with Allbee. Instead of shamefacedly or even humbly asking Leventhal for aid, he presumptuously demands recompense from him. He acts as if Leventhal owes him hospitality. Enviously scrutinizing his comfortable apartment, he concludes that Leventhal, not excelling "in brains and personality," does not deserve such good fortune; he merely was "handed a bucket when it rained" (71). Were it not for a stroke of ill luck, he, too, might be enjoying similar prosperity. Regarding himself as infinitely superior to Leventhal, he therefore has no compunction in forcing him to become his benefactor. Allbee deems it his right to wear Leventhal's clothes, eat his food, sleep in his bed, read his mail, and even use his oven in a suicide attempt. Like the *schnorrer,* he feels he is giving Leventhal not only the privilege of his company, but also the opportunity to do a good deed.

Another humorous role which Allbee convincingly portrays is that of the sham aristocrat. Hailing from an old New England family who boasts Governor Winthrop as one of its ancestors, he melodramatically declaims that he has been dispossessed of his birthright in the modern competitive world, that he and his refined Anglo-Saxon brethren have been forced to abdicate their power to the vulgar hordes of invading immigrants. He neglects to mention that his own behavior has for many years been even more vulgar. Nevertheless, he goes on to insist that the present age no longer contains any patrician honor, the kind that does not "ask for damages" (141) for any slight or unintentional wrong. Yet this is exactly how he acts toward Leventhal. Although he

10. Bernard N. Schilling, *The Comic Spirit* (Detroit: Wayne State University Press, 1965), p. 148.

self-righteously asserts that he can never bring himself to practice the brute ethic of the metropolis, he actually hits back at Leventhal "in any way and anything goes" (141). Bellow ironically implies that Allbee is not only a comic Miniver Cheevy who, cursing "the commonplace," longs for the days of old and keeps on drinking, but is also a violent Miniver Cheevy who cruelly lashes out at the commonplace.

In addition to the *schnorrer* and the aristocrat *manqué,* the part with which Allbee is most consumed and the one which is the most monstrously funny is that of the anti-Semite. Sartre comments on the nature of the bigot's humor:

> Never believe that anti-Semites are completely unaware of the absurdity of their replies. They know that their remarks are frivolous, open to challenge. But they are amusing themselves, for it is their adversary who is obliged to use words responsibly, since he believes in words. The anti-Semites have the *right* to play. They even like to play with discourse, for by giving ridiculous reasons, they discredit the serious-ness of their interlocutors.[11]

Allbee is often aware of the absurdity of his remarks; yet he still utters them, both to bolster his shaky esteem and to derive amusement from disconcerting Leventhal. His constant use of "you people," for instance, succeeds in piquing Leventhal, since it is only a polite way of saying that the Jews are naturally outside the larger refined Gentile community and that he, Allbee, although temporarily down on his luck, will always have a place in it. For the most part, however, Allbee's insinuations are not that veiled. He openly accuses the Jews of con-temptuously regarding the Gentiles as "born drunkards" (34), "the veritable sons of Belial" (76), when in truth he hates himself for his own drinking, especially since his was a family of abstinent ministers. It is far easier to view the Jews as life-denying than to acknowledge his own lack of control. He even goes to the extreme of picturing the Jews as being entirely devoid of compassion, of making no allowances for human frailty. Fashioned in the image of the stern, retributive God of the Old Testament, they, in his view, fanatically believe that an individual deserves any punishment he receives. Such hard-hearted pharisaical Jews could never understand what would make a man drink, since they would never allow themselves to become that vulner-

11. Sartre, *Anti-Semite and Jew,* p. 20.

able. Allbee would agree with Irving Howe's description of the stereo-
typed Jew as a person who is "highly self-conscious and calculating,
never able to 'let himself go,' always measuring the advantages to be
gained from personal relations." [12] He seems to have such a stereotype
in mind when he hurls his most cunning insult at Leventhal: "You
keep your spirit under lock and key. That's the way you're brought up.
You make it your business assistant, and it's safe and tame and never
leads you toward anything risky. Nothing dangerous and nothing
glorious. Nothing ever tempts you to dissolve yourself. What for?
What's in it? No percentage" (146). Leventhal, in turn, reacts as Allbee had intended him to react. He is so unnerved by Allbee's malicious
frivolity that he can scarcely say anything in his own defense. All that
he can muster is the foolishly irrelevant comment, "Millions of us
have been killed. What about that?" (147). Allbee's ridiculous accusations have succeeded in completely unsettling and thereby "discredit-
ing" his adversary.

Equally absurd is Allbee's conviction that there is a Jewish conspiracy
taking over the country. A latter day Paul Revere, he feels it is his duty
to alert everyone to this clear and present danger. He even tries to
convince Leventhal, a member of the enemy camp, of the alarming
inroads the conspiracy has already made in New York City: "You
know yourself how many Jewish dishes there are in the cafeterias,
how much of the stage—how many Jewish comedians and jokes, and
stores, and so on, and Jews in public life, and so on" (73). But like
many other magnanimous bigots, he hastens to assure Leventhal that
he would not deprive Jews of their lawful rights; he merely believes
they should not trespass on territory that doesn't belong to them, especially in the area of culture. Thus he objects to Leventhal's Jewish
friend Harkavy singing old American ballads since he was not "born
to them" (40). Instead, he insists that Harkavy sing a psalm or any
Jewish song like the "one about the mother" (40). He is equally upset
at seeing a "book about Thoreau and Emerson by a man named
Lipschitz" (145), and indignantly comments, "After all, it seems to
me that people of such background simply couldn't understand . . ."
(145). In this respect Allbee is a comic version of Sartre's native
Frenchman who has spoken the language for a thousand years and
therefore claims he possesses Racine, whereas he adamantly believes

12. Irving Howe, "The Stranger and the Victim," *Commentary* 8 (August, 1949): 151.

that the Jew, even though he may be very learned, can never grasp the true import of Racine because he has been and always will be a stranger on French soil.[13]

Allbee is not always obsessed with playing the anti-Semite; he occasionally acts as a lay philosopher who is responsible for some of the novel's ideological comedy. Even though he is described by Chester Eisinger as "one of Bellow's . . . eccentrics, a madman loosed upon the world with a perfectly straight face and an unencumbered right to pursue his peculiar fantasy," [14] what he says is sometimes provocative, especially his views on man's bondage in a mechanistic environment.[15] Like Joseph in *Dangling Man*, he believes that "personal choice does not count for much these days" (125), only he develops the idea with a half-crazed "speculative earnestness." Recalling his abortive attempts to master his own destiny, and his many unprovoked upsets, he concludes that "now it's all blind movement, vast movement, and the individual is shuttled back and forth" (70). But it is not only mysterious forces which enthrall the individual and impede his wishes; it is also "a hundred million others who want the very damn same thing" (194) which ultimately obstructs self-gratification. The Catholic catechism which states that the world was made for man, "for every last mother's son" (194), Allbee regards as patently farcical. According to his way of thinking, a more accurate assessment of the world is revealed in his own intentionally shocking observation: "Hot stars and cold hearts, that's your universe!" (195). While this is clearly not Bellow's own view of the world, he permits it to be expressed, no matter how at odds it may be. Toward the end of the novel, however, he will counter it with an opposing view that admits the possibility of warm hearts gladly accepting responsibility "for every last mother's son."

In his role of philosopher Allbee also resembles the "Spirit of Alternatives," Joseph's alter ego. The "Spirit of Alternatives" mockingly exposes lapses in Joseph's vision; so Allbee, when he is not tormenting Leventhal, wryly corrects his errors of perception. Prior to his forced

---

13. Sartre, *Anti-Semite and Jew*, p. 24.

14. Chester E. Eisinger, *Fiction of the Forties* (Chicago: University of Chicago Press, 1963), p. 352.

15. See Keith M. Opdahl, *The Novels of Saul Bellow: An Introduction* (University Park: Pennsylvania State University Press, 1967), p. 54.

encounter with Allbee, Leventhal had always believed in a highly individualistic and moralistic philosophy which held that people were accountable for the quality of their actions. He had little patience with weakness and scant compassion for failure. But Allbee's incessant claims of unearned wretchedness batter away at Leventhal's resistance. Disagreeing with Job's friends, Allbee movingly argues, "We do get it in the neck for nothing and suffer for nothing, and there's no denying that evil is as real as sunshine" (146). Again and again he offers himself as living proof of this fact so that Leventhal cannot long remain impervious to his appeal. Subjected to repeated bombardments of Allbee's environmentalist philosophy, he is at last forced to admit that such a belief exists and has validity. When Allbee chooses to deal with the man and not the stereotype, he makes some headway in clearing and enlarging Leventhal's field of vision.

Allbee is not always able to clarify his own thinking, however. Like Joseph, he passionately adopts a given philosophical position at one time and, shortly thereafter, unwittingly contradicts himself. On one hand, he espouses a strictly deterministic philosophy which absolves him of all responsibility for his failure. He believes that people have a destiny forced upon them, so "they'd better not assume they're running their own show" (71). On the other hand, he subscribes to a doctrine of free will which holds that Leventhal, a vindictive Jew, intentionally caused his ruin.[16] Somewhat later Allbee becomes an even more zealous exponent of free will. He is confident that he doesn't have to be next year what he was last year. If he so chooses, there is no limit to what he can become. Such drastic reversals make Allbee an amusingly suspect commentator on his own life.

Bellow has claimed that he did "nothing very original by writing another realistic novel about a common man and calling it *The Victim*."[17] In one sense it is but another faithful and detailed rendering of ordinary flawed human beings existing in a fully specified, recognizable world. Yet *The Victim* is not a purely realistic novel. It incorporates many of the aspects of a Gothic romance: "the shimmering atmosphere," the sudden nightmarish appearance of grisly villains,

16. I am indebted to Keith Opdahl for revealing Allbee's specious doctrine of free will which holds Leventhal accountable for his ruin. *Ibid*.

17. Gordon L. Harper, "Saul Bellow—The Art of Fiction: An Interview," *Paris Review* 37 (Winter, 1965): 61.

"mysteriously compelling relationships," and the "quality of often unnamable horror." [18] These Gothic features are responsible for much of the dark humor in *The Victim* and allow it to lapse into what Northrop Frye designates as the "final or sixth phase of [comedy]," encompassing "the world of ghost stories, thrillers and Gothic romances." [19] In this phase the comic cast is reduced to a few bizarre members, inextricably bound together. The settings are secret and guarded. The story is permeated with the "occult and marvellous, the sense of individual detachment from routine existence." [20] Far from the realm of lambent mirth, only audible shudders and uneasy laughter prevail.

Bellow immediately suggests Leventhal's grisly comic plight by citing an epigraph from "The Tale of the Trader and the Jinni" in *Thousand and One Nights*. Like the merchant who is charged with intentionally killing an Ifrit, Leventhal is accused of willfully murdering Allbee's opportunities. The merchant had no idea that his cast-off date stones would strike the Ifrit; so Leventhal never entertained the possibility that his offensive behavior toward Allbee's irascible boss, Rudiger, would cause him to fire Allbee. When Leventhal is suddenly asked to pay for his heinous crime, a crime he never knew he committed, he is shocked beyond belief. He feels that he has "been singled out to be the object of some freakish, insane process" (31). The senselessness of the accusation is what most disturbs him. When he is not so flabbergasted, however, he can concede that there "was a wrong, a general wrong" (80), for it was unfair that one man be blessed with the comforts of life while another be deprived of them. But to be directly blamed for another's misfortune he finds utterly preposterous. Nevertheless, Allbee, resorting to a "devious 'logic' that would do credit to *Mein Kampf*," [21] spends his time trying to make Leventhal believe the preposterous. A master of non sequiturs, he blames Leventhal not only for the loss of his job, but also for his alcoholism, his wife's leaving him, and her eventual death in an automobile accident.

18. For an elaboration of this interpretation, see Mary Lee Allen, "The Flower and the Chalk: The Comic Sense of Saul Bellow" (Ph.D. diss., Stanford University, 1968), p. 129.

19. Northrop Frye, *Anatomy of Criticism* (New York: Atheneum, 1965), p. 185.

20. *Ibid*.

21. Richard Match, Review of *The Victim* by Saul Bellow, *New York Herald Tribune Weekly Book Review* 24 (November 23, 1947): 10.

Bizarre as it seems, Leventhal is soon taken in by this specious reasoning. Because of his own gullibility and the diabolical power of his persuader, he at once accepts as plausible what he previously regarded as highly implausible. He becomes so intimately acquainted with absurdity that for the time being he can no longer distinguish between fact and fiction.

In such a nightmarish situation it is difficult to discern identities. Who is the victim and who is the victimizer? It is one of the macabre ironies of the novel that Allbee passes himself off as the grievously wronged innocent all the while he fastens himself onto his alleged oppressor, gradually burrowing into his life until he has almost consumed him. But Leventhal is not entirely more sinned against than sinning. He, too, is guilty of dismissing Allbee as an unholy barbarian and of trying his utmost to shield himself from his contaminating presence. In addition to demonically victimizing each other, each man victimizes himself. Plagued with an intense fear of the world which has rejected him, Allbee creates an imaginary adversary whom he can censure for his unjust treatment. He can also displace some of his corrosive self-hatred onto such a readily available scapegoat. Leventhal, too, fears that the world will find him all too expendable. Every man he meets (and especially Allbee) he suspects of scheming to take his place so that he can scarcely afford to be unwary, let alone generous. Both men are forced to become anxiety-ridden chameleons, always ready to change their colors to protect themselves against real and fancied dangers.

The weird state of affairs makes impossible the unity and continuity of personality, and it often causes a bizarre fusion of personalities. In the course of *The Victim*'s grim farce Allbee becomes Leventhal's perversely comic double. In physical appearance he is described by Jonathan Baumbach "as Leventhal's reflection, as seen in one of those freakishly distorting Coney Island mirrors . . . a kind of stretched out version of Leventhal." [22] During their first meeting, moreover, the possibility is suggested that they might be related in some fundamental

---

22. Jonathan Baumbach, "The Double Vision: *The Victim* by Saul Bellow," *The Landscape of Nightmare* (New York: New York University Press, 1965), p. 41. My discussion of other aspects of the double relation in *The Victim* has, in part, been influenced by Jonathan Baumbach's perceptive analysis of it. See "The Double Vision," pp. 41–44.

way. Why would Leventhal, who had not received Allbee's request for an appointment, come to the designated spot at the designated time if he were not somehow physically attuned to Allbee? Further intimacy is established by Allbee's ludicrous jack-in-the-box appearances until Leventhal imagines he sees him lurking everywhere. He is even tempted to force Allbee to come out in the open, but he temporarily restrains himself, since that would be "countering absurdity with absurdity and madness with madness" (108). Yet absurd as it seems, he cannot remain apart from Allbee for long. Just as Petrovitch Golyadkin, the disturbed petty official of Dostoevsky's *The Double*,[23] has a strange fascination for his pretender self, Golyadkin, Jr., so Leventhal is helplessly attracted to Allbee. Both Golyadkin and Leventhal, devoid of self-confidence, exhibit a sneaking regard for their alter egos, who possess qualities which they themselves lack. Golyadkin, Jr., gifted with social ease, is able to ingratiate himself with those superiors whose commendation Golyadkin, Sr., has failed to obtain. Allbee, still a New England gentleman beneath his frayed collar and "five o'clock shadow," can yet win the respect of the Willistons, whose approval Leventhal desperately seeks. At the same time that both men grudgingly admire their doubles, they are also contemptuous of them. They nevertheless commit the greatest folly of all by allowing them to reside in their quarters. Although Golyadkin, Jr., just stays the night, Allbee all too readily extends his visit, welcoming the opportunity to insinuate himself further into Leventhal's life. The longer Allbee remains with him, the more he becomes his psychic twin. Subject to frequent weird sensations of "intimate nearness," Leventhal soon has a "particularly vivid recollection of the explicit recognition in Allbee's eyes which he could not doubt was the double of something in his own" (169). Through forced association with Allbee, Leventhal grows so attached to him, his reputed enemy, that he treats him as if he were his most intimate confidant. He even alienates one of his friends by his heated defense of Allbee. These are not the only absurd consequences of Leventhal's nightmarish involvement with Allbee. Golyadkin, Sr., reproaches himself for his double's misconduct with women; so Leventhal is overwhelmed with guilt when discovering Allbee in his bed

23. Fyodor Dostoevsky, *The Double*, in *Three Short Novels of Dostoevsky*, trans. Constance Garnett, rev. and ed. Abraham Yarmolinsky (New York: Doubleday & Co., 1960).

with a whore. Insane as it seems, Leventhal feels so completely identified with Allbee that it is as though he himself had been unfaithful to
his wife. Leventhal's insanity is short-lived, however, for his guilt
feelings prove stronger than his fascination for Allbee. Repulsed by
Allbee's gross behavior, he is compelled to sever his relationship with
him. Fortunately, his severance occurs just in time. As a separate individual he is able to prevent himself from being implicated in the
cruelest joke of all—Allbee's mutual death pact without his prior
consent.

In addition to depicting a grotesque double, Bellow succeeds in
evoking a grotesque *mise-en-scène*. Its nature is suggested in the
second epigraph to the novel, a description of a hallucinatory vision
from De Quincey's *The Pains of Opium* in which "the sea appeared
paved with innumerable faces, upturned to the heavens; faces, im-
ploring, wrathful, despairing; faces that surged upward by thousands,
by myriads, by generations . . ." (1). Leventhal, frantically clinging to
his little corner in the inimical milieu, sees comparable throngs of
people. To him they appear as "barbaric fellahin," ready to cut his
throat without the slightest provocation. Even if most of them are not
malicious, he still feels suffocated by their presence. "There was an
overwhelming human closeness and thickness, and Leventhal was pene-
trated by a sense not merely of the crowd in this park but of innumerable millions, crossing, touching, pressing" (183–84). These are the same
multitudes whom Allbee names as his opponents, the millions of people wanting "the very damn same thing" (194). An indispensable
part of Bellow's city-scapes, these crowds are sources of delight and
wonder for his later heroes and sources of dread and contempt for his
earlier ones. Especially to Leventhal it seems as if Hell itself had
cracked open and that all the souls packed together were straining to
break free and engulf him. Imagining their faces to be "wrathful and
despairing," he views them as endless duplications of Allbee, all bent on
wringing his sympathies and wrenching his conscience.

Leventhal also feels overwhelmed by the noxious elements of his
environment, though there is no slapstick humor in the physical injuries he sustains. Unlike Augie March, who quickly rallies from his
urban buffets, Leventhal helplessly reels from the inimical thrusts of
the city: bus doors ruthlessly evict him; subway turnstiles painfully
jab him; the trains bombard him with their "charges of metal dust";

and the cars nearly asphyxiate him with their carbon monoxide gases. Leventhal is so oppressed by the mechanical that the metaphor which Bellow most frequently employs to characterize him is "of a human being imprisoned in and made to function as part of a machine. The machine itself functions in an unnatural element; the machine and the human being within wear out, become exhausted together." [24] During his Staten Island ferry trips to visit his sister-in-law, he is associated with a constricted descending elevator, a barge smothered with "the slow, thick cloud" of orange paint, and a tanker, "the huge thing rolled in a sweat of oil, the engines laboring . . . a repeated strain on the hearts and ribs of the wipers" (51). On land, Leventhal is most often linked with his refrigerator, whose function declines within All-bee's deleterious presence. Its mechanical exhaustion is directly related to the progressive depletion of Leventhal's inner resources: "Even before he unlocked the door, he heard the refrigerator panting as though it were trying to keep up a charge of energy in the air of the empty flat" (158).

Equally unbearable is the relentless tyranny of the sun which, like an evil wizard, distorts Leventhal's once familiar world almost beyond recognition. New York becomes Bangkok. "The whole continent seems to have moved from its place and slid nearer the equator, the bitter gray Atlantic to have become green and tropical . . ." (3). Streets become "deadened with heat and light" and buildings "smoulder" (36). From his vantage point on the Staten Island ferry, he sees "the towers on the shore [rise] up in huge blocks, scorched, smoky, gray, and bare white where the sun was direct upon them" (51). On land he watches the new tides of evening heat roll in, "thickening the air, sinking grasses and bushes under its weight" (108). Thus there could not be a more perfect infernal setting for the diabolic comedy going on.

Not only is physical nature visibly altered by the malignant powers of the sun; human nature is also affected. The sun, like "the flame at the back of a vast baker's oven" (22), flares up Leventhal's temper and exacerbates his discomfort. It makes his body all the more cumbersome and physical contact all the more undesirable. Just as the sun provokes Camus's Meursault to murder the Arab, so Leventhal mentally

---

[24]. Hugh Hartman, "Character, Theme and Tradition in the Novels of Saul Bellow" (Ph.D. diss., University of Washington, 1968), p. 96. Hartman also mentions the particular machines with which Leventhal is identified.

kills anyone who jostles him. The sun brings to consciousness the evil impulses he has tried to suppress, causing him to see the light "akin to the yellow revealed in the slit of the eye of a wild animal, say a lion, something inhuman that didn't care about anything human and yet was implanted in every human being too, one speck of it, and formed a part of him that responded to the heat and glare" (51). Crazed by this "heat and glare," he cannot escape from his midsummer madness.[25] No wonder, then, that Leventhal, goaded by his feverish psyche, hemmed in by menacing crowds, exposed to mechanical hazards, and tormented by the fiendish sun, should go about in a dazed state, unable to account for what is happening to him. Understandably, the world appears to him a fusion of the real and the fantastic, the bizarre and the conventional.

Bellow's grotesque humor in *The Victim* is far from uproariously funny. The absurd situations, freakish doubles, and distorted milieus arouse a mixture of laughter, horror, and perplexity, with laughter serving to diminish the horror and perplexity and so to enable us to survive the nightmare. Our response is like the one Wylie Sypher describes: "We laugh in self-defense and bare our teeth to recruit our sinking spirits [and] to ease our aching sense of . . . danger."[26]

To convey the central truths of the novel, Bellow does not rely on such a mongrel breed of humor. Instead, he appoints Schlossberg, an aging theater critic for the Jewish papers, as the chief spokesman for his comedy of ideas. His Yiddish-flavored cafeteria discourses define the follies of Leventhal and Allbee. Before a small but attentive audience, he states his opinion on what constitutes good stage-acting and, by extension, good living: "It's bad to be less than human and it's bad to be more than human. . . . Good acting is what is exactly human. And if you say I am a tough critic, you mean I have a high opinion of what is human. This is my whole idea. More than human, can you have any use for life? Less than human, you don't either" (133). Yet Schlossberg knows that most people underestimate the worth of the purely human. They feel compelled to clothe it in illusion, to con-

---

[25.] In my discussion of the sun's effects on human nature and physical nature in *The Victim*, I rely in part on Opdahl's treatment of the subject. See *The Novels of Saul Bellow*, p. 64.

[26.] Wylie Sypher, "Our New Sense of the Comic," in *Comedy*, ed. Wylie Sypher (New York: Doubleday & Co., 1956), p. 204.

ceal its defects in an attractive package. They do the same with death. They desperately try to camouflage it out of existence by having "paper grass in the grave to cover up the dirt" (255). But this is not Schlossberg's way. Possessing what Martin Buber calls "joy in the world as it is," he is able to discover value in existence because he chooses to attach value to it:

> I am as sure about greatness and beauty as you are about black and white. If a human life is a great thing to me, it *is* a great thing. Do you know better? I'm entitled as much as you. And why be measly. Do you have to be? Is somebody holding you by the neck? Have dignity, you understand me? Choose dignity. Nobody knows enough to turn it down (134).

Realizing he's "not too good for this world" (133), he is able to accept himself with all of his imperfections. Most important, he is able to choose dignity even though he knows he will die soon, that "there's a limit" to him. Determined to lead as rich a life as possible, he asserts, "But I have to be myself in full" (255).

Illumination in the Jewish tradition is often received on a mountain. Schlossberg, Bellow's "castle-mountain," reveals all we need to know about Leventhal's and Allbee's "bad acting." Like Caesar, who pretends he never sweats or has wax in his ears, Leventhal regards himself as a paragon of Hebrew righteousness and thus behaves "more than human." Similarly Allbee, taking refuge in his Christian aristocratic origins, thinks himself infinitely superior to the lowly Jew. Both men also "behave less than human." Since fear and distrust are "holding [them] by the neck," they are not able "to choose dignity," "to be [themselves] in full." Buttressed by his many defenses, Leventhal hibernates in his "recalcitrance" and "indifference." Consumed with self-loathing, Allbee values neither his nor anyone else's life.

The ordinary Jews of limited perception never fully understood the messages from the mountain. So it is with Leventhal, who is after all *dos kleine menschele* and not a *Moses* Herzog. Allbee's parting explanation of his attempted suicide—"When you turn against yourself, nobody else means anything to you either" (293)—is insightful, but he doesn't seem to understand the full implications of this insight. Nor does Leventhal have an accurate realization of his faults; like Tommy Wilhelm, he has faint clues throughout his ordeal. As he says, he felt "like a man in a mine who could smell smoke and feel heat but never see the flames" (258). One signal he receives is from a dream he has just after he grudgingly provides Allbee with hospitality. In the dream he sobs uncontrollably when excluded from a train. John Clayton provides a likely interpretation of its latent content:

> . . . Asa is able to identify himself with the runner unable to catch his train (or with Allbee, who often asks for a place on 'the train'), with the rigid enforcer of the 'rules' who prevents him from succeeding, and with the helpless workman (Asa's self-righteousness and conscience, his pity and sense of helpless responsibility). All are inside Asa, and thus the truth is formed: 'It was supremely plain to him that everything, without exception, took place as if within a single soul or person' (169).[27]

This uplifting sense of union with others, this removal of distinctions between victim and victimizer, is not long-lasting. Leventhal soon "knew that tomorrow this would be untenable" (169). On still another occasion he is "bewilderingly moved" by the feeling that "there was not a single part of him on which the whole world did not press with full weight" (257). But unlike Tommy Wilhelm, he does not discover the meaning of this pressure. Even a few years after his ghastly comedy of errors he has not acquired any abiding self-knowledge. While he does appear less tense, less guarded, less resistant to life's pleasures, Bellow ironically intimates that this change is brought about not by any sustained insights from his previous harrowing experience, but by the recent improvement in his external circumstances: a more lucrative position at a better trade journal. Yet Leventhal is still humorously devoid of affectation, for he continues to feel guilty about his new prosperity and thus repeats his former justification for his success: "It was a shuffle, all, all accidental and haphazard" (285). Moreover, when he meets Allbee again after several years, he is still obsessed with hating Christians and, as usual, is unaware of the fact. Right after Leventhal admits that Allbee has "gone places" (290), he is immediately repelled by the flower he wears, regarding it "as a mark of something extraordinary, barbaric, rich, even decadent" (290). He is again quick to detect Allbee's drinking and again silently condemns it as a noxious

---

27. John J. Clayton, *Saul Bellow: In Defense of Man* (Bloomington: Indiana University Press, 1968), p. 163.

trait of a Gentile. When Allbee earnestly claims that he never intended to hurt him while trying to gas himself, Leventhal, still distrustful, laughs outright and accuses Allbee of telling another "funny lie" (293). Finally, when Allbee maintains that he has come to "terms with whoever runs things" (294), Leventhal, still "the accidental and paltry vessel on which life has been conferred," [28] is anxious to know who is in control. Unlike Joseph, he does not allow a specific puppeteer to pull the strings. Instead, he tries to rely on his own shaky self. Just as the insecure Jews of the *shtetl* looked to the Messiah to usher in a higher order of existence blessed with more than material prosperity, Leventhal clings to the possibility of there being a promise to "more important things" than choice seats in a theater, desirable economic and social positions in life. Joyful, unconditional commitment to "all beings" is undoubtedly the promise Bellow has in mind. Yet at the novel's end Leventhal does not have a firm grasp of what the promise entails. Still not sufficiently roused from his stupor as the victim, he achieves only a "kind of recognition" (26). Total recognition of the promise is reserved for Bellow's more fully awakened heroes.

The humor of *The Victim* is also not fully awakened. Like Leventhal, it is sluggish and slow to gain momentum. Yet when it does make its appearance, it is not as inhibited as the choked Mephistophelean laughter of Joseph. There is a more ready flow of both high spirits and evil spirits. Joseph's is a one-man show with a fairly monotonous patter, while Leventhal and Allbee often resemble a zany vaudeville duo with many unpredictable quips. The most devastating ones, of course, involve what Irwin Stock describes as the "maddening paradox of anti-Semitism, in which the Jew is forced to be better than others at the same time that he is being called worse, or is accused of betraying human values precisely by those who are inhumanely tormenting him." [29] In this routine Leventhal functions as Allbee's "fall guy and is reduced by his wit and his exaggerated postures into a position of powerlessness." [30] But in the next act Leventhal, even though he is essentially a straight man, wounds Allbee with his own vitriolic

28. Kazin, "The World of Saul Bellow," p. 211.

29. Irwin Stock, "The Novels of Saul Bellow," *Southern Review* 3 (Winter, 1967): 20.

30. Allen, "The Flower and the Chalk," p. 164.

mockery. We are more terrified than amused by such caustic perfor-mances, even though they enliven an otherwise grim novel. If we desire a more genial humor, unadulterated by horror, we must look to the promise of *Augie March*.

The *Animal Ridens*

4

If Augie March is depicted as a "Columbus of those near-at-hand" (536), then the novel which contains him is the logbook, bursting with the marvels of the New World. Unlike Joseph, who seldom leaves his bleak room and the companionship of his rarefied thoughts, or Leventhal, who never escapes from his cheerless ghetto and the terrifying creatures of his imagination, Augie is forever exploring new facets of America and listening to the varied carols of her people. But Augie is not an entirely new breed of Bellow hero. Although he is more mobile and open to experience, he still has some of the same concerns as his antecedents. Like Joseph, he yearns to discover his purpose, to ascertain the worthiest contribution he can make. Yet, like Leventhal, he is wary that his contribution to others might involve too great a sacrifice for himself. Nevertheless, these concerns do not weigh Augie down for long. Soon departing from the wailing wall to which Joseph and Leventhal permanently cling, he resumes his "pilgrimage," looking for and creating his own merriment. The humor of Bellow's first two fretful novels emerges primarily from his subtle mockery of the *animal lacrimans,* who feels overwhelmed by the maddening incongruities and grotesqueries of the outer world. Conversely, most of the humor in *The Adventures of Augie March* [1] is initiated by Augie himself, the

1. Citations from this novel are to *The Adventures of Augie March* (New York: Viking Press, 1953).

"animal ridens" (536), who is more diverted than disturbed by the same unfathomable and meaningless occurrences.

As a resilient young picaro, Augie is not greatly stunned by the blows of fortune. Leventhal is constantly wincing from real or fancied anti-Semitic verbal attacks, while Augie, living in the midst of the hostile Polish neighborhood, is actually "chased, stoned, bitten and beat up for Christ-killers" (12). Yet he is not in a state of perpetual anguish over his persecution; rather, he insouciantly claims, "But I never had any special grief from it, or brooded, being by and large too larky and boisterous to take it to heart" (12). Unlike Leventhal, fleeing from the city's "barbaric fellahin," or Joseph, shunning inquisitors, Augie associates freely with them and savors their idiosyncrasies. As Irving Kristol expresses it, Bellow struggled with fiends in his first two novels; in *Augie March* he "jumped in their midst, bussed them, and inquired if they had read any good books lately."[2]

. Moreover, as a rogue hero occupying a marginal position in society, Augie is eminently qualified to be an astute observer of human foibles and pretensions. Unlike the dangler Joseph, who, detecting comparable absurdities, lashes out at them with his sardonic humor, Augie is entertained by mankind's follies, feeling no need to expose them stridently. In this respect Augie resembles an earlier picaresque hero, Gil Blas, whose ironies "are not bitter or cynical" and "whose faculty for compassion is continuous with his satirical consciousness."[3] Similarly, Augie invites the reader to join him in his benign laughter at the many comic figures he encounters. Since these figures play such an important part in his life, Bellow allows Augie as "the hero of an episodic novel," requiring little "character development,"[4] to present initially more information about them than about himself. As he states, "All the influences were lined up waiting for me. . . . which is why I tell you more of them than of myself" (43).

In *The Adventures of Augie March,* an autobiographical tale told in retrospect by a nostalgic expatriate, the scenes and characters of youth are amply and endearingly sketched. Just as Joseph fondly re-

2. Irving Kristol, Review of *The Adventures of Augie March* by Saul Bellow, *Encounter* 13 (July, 1954): 74.

3. Robert Alter, *Rogues' Progress: Studies in the Picaresque Novel* (Cambridge: Harvard University Press, 1964), p. 23.

4. Keith M. Opdahl, *The Novels of Saul Bellow: An Introduction* (University Park: Pennsylvania State University Press, 1967), p. 78.

members his early years in Montreal's St. Dominique Street as "the only place where [he] was ever allowed to encounter reality" (86), and Herzog realizes that "his heart was attached with great power" to his boyhood Napoleon Street (140), so Augie pays tribute to his early West Side Chicago neighborhood. As is the case with reminiscences by highly active imaginations, the grotesque features and droll actions of former acquaintances multiply and become even more pronounced. Similarly, in the first half of *Augie March* Bellow provides us with a vast procession of excessively flawed individuals who not only establish the humorous mood of the novel but also reinforce his view that all men are but patched creatures. Although they may at first glance resemble Dickensian caricatures, Bellow's method of characterization is his own. True to his anthropological training, he precisely notes their physical abnormalities and their likenesses to primitive man. It is as if the more data he can amass, the more authentic his findings will be considered. Five Properties is described as "long-armed and humped, his head grown off the thick band of muscle as original as a bole on his back, hair tender and greenish brown, eyes completely green . . . Eskimo teeth buried in high gums . . ." (19–20). Mrs. Einhorn is said to have "strong hair bobbed with that declivity that you see in pictures of the Egyptian coif, the flat base forming a black brush about the back of the neck" (64). Yet Bellow does not exhibit the usual scientific detachment of an anthropologist commenting on a peculiar species. Attached to the most imperfect of his creations, he invariably mentions their redeeming qualities as well.

Anna Coblin, endowed with the novel's most conspicuous anatomical distortions, is such a cursed and blessed creation. Although Augie enumerates all of her unsightly growths—her "moles, blebs, hairs, bumps in her forehead, huge concentration in her neck," and her "spiraling reddish hair . . . cut duck-tail fashion in the back and scrawled out high above her ears" (16–17)—he still expresses respect for her "great size and terrific energy of constitution" (16). Bellow's comic treatment of Anna Coblin does not rest solely upon the depiction of her grotesque outward appearance. He is most laughable in his disclosure of her inner defects, her mental excesses. She functions as the leading lady in the novel's finest Jewish comedy of manners. As Bellow's caricature of the Jewish mother, she gives free reign to all her emotions. When she is not wildly mourning the absence of her Marine son or virulently cursing the fiends who spirited him away, she is anxiously priming her nine-year-old daughter for marriage and melo-dramatically alerting her greenhorn brother to the dangers of marrying an exploitive American woman. Yet she still manages to provide Augie with her macaronic account of the Old Testament's unabridged stories. Most important, she does not neglect to overfeed her brood to compen-sate for any rough treatment they might receive outside her kosher nest. Although Anna Coblin commits some of the same maternal offenses as the Yiddishe mommas of Philip Roth's *Portnoy's Complaint* and Bruce Jay Friedman's *A Mother's Kisses,* she is not the target of a vindictive satire. Since Bellow has not made her out to be the calculating Jocasta of a private Oedipus tragedy, she is not devastated with merciless laughter, but playfully tweaked for her incorrigible ways.

The novel's other scene of Jewish comedy of manners focuses not so much on the values and actions of a single individual within the group—Anna Coblin, the matriarch within the immigrant family—as on the entire Magnus clan. Bellow had already attempted social satire in his treatment of the Servatius party in *Dangling Man,* but his description of the decor, manners, and talk was so lifeless that his guests resembled drab mannequins propped against an artificial back-drop. In *Augie March* Bellow's satiric talents have improved. Although his vignette of nouveau riche Jews is not as cleverly drawn as Philip Roth's *Goodbye Columbus,* he captures what is peculiarly amusing about them. Candidly photographed are all the "ungainly" Magnus relatives with their matching oversized furnishings, their gross table manners, their randy talk, their contempt for economic inferiors, and their equation of intellectuals with "starving Pentateuch peddlers" (221). But unlike Philip Roth, Bellow does not want to hoot the Magnuses out of existence. Since they are capable of displaying real affection toward each other, he makes room for them in his world. As Augie concludes, "Finding yourself amongst warm faces, why, there's many objections that recede . . ." (218).

Augie withholds the most objections about the "Machiavellis,"[5] those would-be shapers of his destiny. Although they are manipulative and diabolical, he does not dwell on their villainous qualities. This is especially so with Grandma Lausch and William Einhorn, the rulers

[5]. The original title of the novel was *Life among the Machiavellians.* An excerpt of it first appeared in *Partisan Review* 16 (November, 1949): 1077–1089.

of his early age. They loom in his memory as benevolent despots whose comic traits are more prominent than their malicious ones. Thus we smile rather than sneer at Grandma Lausch's affectation—her pose as the vindictive Juno, punishing the errant Mama March; as the female Castiglione, making courtiers out of the bastard March brothers; and as the queen of the Russian intelligentsia, dazzling the gerontocracy with her multilingual skills and "Murad" cigar. Similarly, we overlook Einhorn's sins of pride and are diverted by the vanity of a cripple who dresses like a dandy, yet whose bathroom habits are not as tidy as they could be—an inconsistency made even more humorous by Augie's Rabelaisian defense of Einhorn: "I understand that British aristocrats are still legally entitled to piss, if they should care to, on the hind wheels of carriages" (65).

Even funnier is Einhorn's view of himself as an irresistible lady's man. When he works his "wicked, lustful charm" (77) and tries to convince women that he is not disabled where it really matters, the comic incongruity is intensified. Most amusing is the disparity between Einhorn's intellectual pretensions and preoccupations, a disparity accentuated by Augie's enumerating Einhorn's zany projects and hodge-podge knowledge, followed by the ironic observation that Einhorn "lived by Baconian ideas of what makes the man this and that, and had a weakness for complete information" (66).

Our reaction to Grandma Lausch's and Einhorn's hypocrisy is just as mirthful. We do not censure the *grande dame* for advising Augie "to be honest, *erlich*" (9) and, at the same time, coaching him in the devious strategy of obtaining free glasses from the county dispensary. Nor do we upbraid Einhorn for being both comforter and exploiter of the lame as well as a Father Flanagan, rehabilitating wayward youth while he is committing the most outrageous thievery himself. Since Grandma Lausch and Einhorn have undoubtedly become more quaint through Augie's far-removed recollection of them, what would otherwise be despicable behavior is transformed into delightful, quirky ways.

But Augie cannot laughingly excuse Grandma Lausch's comic rigidity, or what Bergson characterizes as a machine-like fixation with certain ideas, preventing "the wideawake adaptability and the living pliableness of a human being." [6] Augie cannot subscribe to the old

6. Henri Bergson, "Laughter," in *Comedy*, ed. Wylie Sypher (New York: Doubleday & Co., 1956), p. 67.

lady's determining principle of life: "The more you love people the more they'll mix you up. A child loves, a person respects" (9). When she acts upon her belief and does not allow love to deter her from committing Georgie, Augie's idiot brother, to an institution, she does irreparable damage to her prestige and unwittingly seals her own doom—the eventual consignment to a like institution. Once Georgie is banished, the household union is not only destroyed, but it is as though the "chaste, lummoxy, caressing, gentle and diligent" (9) part of Augie himself has been driven out. So deprived, he can no longer heed the counsel of such a cruel mentor.

Nor can Augie accept with levity Einhorn's prevailing view that people can be divided as to "whether they screwed or were screwed, whether they themselves did the manipulating or were roughly handled, tugged, and bobbled by their fates" (73). When Einhorn becomes obsessed with being the arch-manipulator and regards Augie not as a son, but only as a mindless implementer of his scheming, Augie becomes disillusioned with the "first superior man" (60) he had ever known. It is not that he ceases to marvel at Einhorn's sizable victory over his infirmity or his Franklinesque way to wealth, but that he refuses to adhere to a philosophy foreign to his own.

By the time Augie is in his late teens and has become acquainted with the seamy Chicago of Farrell's *Studs Lonigan* and has had his taste of "deep city vexation" (84), his euphoria is somewhat subdued. He is not nearly as lavish in his humorous evocation of the other Machiavellians in his life. While Mrs. Renling, the Evanston sporting goods owner who wants to fashion Augie in her aristocratic image, is just as vain and derisive as Grandma Lausch, her flaws are more outlined than substantially developed. In place of Augie's highly embellished account of Grandma Lausch's character assassinations, he sparingly describes Mrs. Renling's "damnation chats" (137). In place of Grandma Lausch's "wit and discontent" (7), he focuses on Mrs. Renling's discontent. The difference in impression is explainable. Seen through the magnifying glass of fanciful childhood, Grandma Lausch appears as "a pouncy old hawk of a Bolshevik" (7), while Augie's new protectress, viewed through the more objective eyes of young manhood, appears no more formidable than a nitpicking social (w)renling. But when her "paleface concentration" (131) is directed not at schooling Augie in every grace, but toward coercing him to "consolidate what she affirmed she was" (151), she becomes just as devouring as Grandma Lausch. Augie, no longer amused, also flees this bird of prey.

Claiming that he has "family enough to suit [him]" (153), Augie next allows himself to be recruited by his older brother Simon. He is the least comically conceived of the Machiavellians in that we are permitted to see the many complex shades of his character and not just his colorful eccentricities. Since Simon is the novel's most fully realized character next to Augie, he serves as Bellow's man with commitments to contrast to the unattached Augie, whom Robert Penn Warren has pejoratively called "the man with no commitments." [7] But inasmuch as Simon's commitments are so base and have such adverse consequences, Bellow seems to approve of Augie's way—his cutting loose of all binding constructions.

The Simon Augie remembers as a youth is not that objectionable. He appears as a ridiculously affected though inoffensive Tom Sawyer figure who absorbs his "English schoolboy notions of honor" (4) from books and wages imaginary battles with villains of history. But as Simon grows older, his pretensions are not as harmless; he demands that Augie acknowledge the superiority of his ways and pattern his behavior after him. Just as Amos, the thorough-going materialist in *Dangling Man,* urges his younger brother Joseph to marry into money and become the enterprising businessman, so Simon, having practiced the "simony" of selling himself to the wealthiest bidder, insists that Augie wed his wife's rich cousin, Lucy Magnus. His dynastic fantasies can then become a reality: the March brothers commanding a vast financial empire. Simon thus becomes consumed not only with playing the tycoon, but also with transforming Augie into the ideal suitor. So exacting are his standards that even the usually agreeable Augie complains, "It was getting so that I had to undergo an examination of almost brass-hat severity when I appeared before him" (223). Simon's self-aggrandizement is a source of the near-tragic as well as the comic in his character. Augie soon observes that Simon has paid an exorbitant fee to become a plutocrat, since he must face the "task of doing bold things with an unhappy gut" (217) which took its toll in the "mental wounds of his face, the death of its color, and the near insanity of his behavior" (226). Understandably, Augie does

---

[7.] Robert Penn Warren, Review of *The Adventures of Augie March, New Republic* 129 (November 2, 1953): 23.

not wish to become a duplicate of Simon; yet he does not want to abandon him, either. As it turns out, it is Simon who forsakes Augie because he has not been a very apt imitator. Instead of being the attentive squire of Lucy Magnus, Augie is discovered helping Mimi Villars get an abortion, and it is automatically assumed that he is the father. Fearing that Augie's failure to measure up to the Magnuses' conception of the proper son-in-law might endanger his position with them, Simon hastily severs fraternal ties.

An Esau abandoned by a Jacob, Augie leaves the Chicago tribe and goes into the Mexican wilderness, where he worships the pagan goddess. Thea Fenchel. Like Madeleine Herzog, she is endowed with a more distinctive personality than other women in Bellow's fiction— the assortment of absent or vaguely present wives and the indistinguishable bevy of alluring though ephemeral mistresses. Moreover, like Madeleine, she exerts a more profound impact upon her partner than the other consorts who merely graze the hero's consciousness. Yet Bellow cannot resist the temptation to comically reduce the stature of his two female giants, not only for the sport of it, but to make sure that they never overshadow his protagonists and to justify their being eventually cast off by his freedom-seeking heroes. Thus Thea is made out to be a ludicrous combination of Diana, goddess of the hunt, and Circe, who, instead of transforming her captive admirers into tamed animals, changes her lovers into animal-tamers. Having ensnared Augie with her charms, she enlists him to realize her bizarre ambition: to hunt gigantic iguanas *"with* an eagle trained in falconry" (319). The practical justification she gives for such a venture is equally farfetched. Soon to be penniless, she hopes to make money by selling articles about her eagle-hunting to the *National Geographic,* although she has no writing ability whatever. Yet during her Chicago stay she is hilariously inconsistent regarding financial matters. Like most of Bellow's female characters, she is both extravagant and slovenly, only more inventively so. She carelessly stashes all her money in the refrigerator, where it mixes freely with the rotting salad leaves and rancid bacon grease which she is too frugal to discard. She shops at the dimestore, which she believes "gave her the best sense of the innermost relations of pennies and nickels and expressed the real depth of money" (315); yet she lavishly outfits Augie for the expedition. Thea's other inconsistencies are just as silly. She professes to love animals yet has no compunction about abandoning a pet cat. She trembles in the dark but evidences no fear in milking the poison from a diamondback snake. She claims to be impervious to people's opinion of her, yet she bribes clerks and maids to think well of her.

Thus Bellow shatters our reverence for his goddess by exposing her mortal follies, though he does not minimize her destructive powers, or make her any less Machiavellian. Ironically, she cautions Augie to guard himself against those people who might seek to absorb his life, while she casts him as the Leicester to her Elizabeth. Moreover, she is consumed with the dominant idea that "there must be something better than what people call reality" (316). She believes that love is not an end in itself, but the means of enabling man to engage in significant action, thereby transcending pedestrian reality. For her, the ancient and venerable act of falconry constitutes such significant action. She therefore insists that Augie adopt her view, and for a time he is a willing convert. But when Thea's attempt to prove her theory has ridiculous consequences—that is, when the venerable falcon turns into a craven raven—Augie cannot conceal his amusement. Shocked by his levity in such a grave undertaking, she doubts his faith in her sacred endeavor. And when he refuses to hunt rare snakes, which she regards as a meaningful alternative to falconry, she is certain he is a total disbeliever and excommunicates him from her fold. Although there are grounds for reprimanding Augie for his short-lived devotion, he is not entirely blameworthy. Thea is made out to be so grotesque that Augie cannot possibly love her; rather, he can only be fascinated by her freakish novelty.

The two remaining Machiavellians in Augie's life are just as freakish though not as novel. Since their eccentricities are but forced imitations of the earliest, most antic of Augie's influences, and since their advice proceeds more from the demented head than from the throbbing heart, their hold on him is not that binding. The quirky millionaire Robey, who wishes Augie to help him write a "survey of human happiness from the standpoint of the rich" (438), is but an anemic version of the full-blooded intellectual systematizer Einhorn. Although he, too, has an impediment (stuttering painfully whenever he discusses his scrambled ideas) and is ridiculously hypocritical (professing reverence for life, yet gleefully killing cockroaches), his oddities do not captivate Augie for long. World War II prompts him to enlist in the Merchant Marine, where he is soon shipwrecked with another crazy theoretician, Hymie Basteshaw. Just as Thea fancied herself an erotic goddess pursuing a higher calling, Basteshaw claims to be an intellectual god who has not only created life, but investigated the cellular origins of boredom in higher organisms. While his explanation of boredom is ingenious and his condemnation of it has Bellow's sanction, his monomaniacal desire to perfect a serum to eradicate boredom and thus refashion man makes him another of Bellow's zany "heavy-water brains" (524). The more Basteshaw raves about his project, the more he becomes a caricature of a zealous redeemer and his crazed language becomes a travesty of inspired biblical discourse. When he insists that Augie remain with him in the lifeboat—his ship of fools—and then continue his research on some remote island, Augie cannot take him seriously. Refusing to "tamper" with humanity, Augie escapes from the redeemer and chooses to go back to a marred civilization where everyone is not "a poet" or "saint" (509).

Although Augie can appreciate the humor arising from the psychic inelasticity of these Machiavellians, he never allows himself to be cast in their rigid image. He preserves his flexibility at all cost. As Einhorn has perceptively noted, Augie has *"opposition"* (117) in him. He doesn't want to be "determined," to "become what other people wanted to make" (117) of him. He therefore refuses the restrictive destinies offered him as Grandma Lausch's reformed urchin, Einhorn's trusty squire, Mrs. Renling's dapper escort, Simon's fellow robber baron, Thea's snake-charmer, Robey's ghost writer, and Basteshaw's sorcerer's apprentice. It seems that Richard Chase's observation is correct: "The plot of *Augie March* is that of Whitman's *Song of Myself*—the eluding of all of the identities proffered to one by the world, by one's past, and by one's friends." [8] Like Whitman, who resisted anything better than his own diversity, Augie prefers being the self-reliant, "varietistic" picaro who proclaims his own declaration of independence: "I . . . go at things as I have taught myself, freestyle and will make the record in my own way . . ." (3). Moreover, like Whitman, he does not attempt to deny his lowly origins. Echoing

8. Richard Chase, "The Adventures of Saul Bellow: Progress of a Novelist," *Commentary* 27 (April, 1959): 325.

the "solitary singer," Augie reflects on "what very seldom mattered with me, namely, where I came from, parentage, and other history, things I had never much thought of as difficulties, being democratic in temperament, available to everybody and assuming about others what I assumed about myself" (147). Unashamed that he is a bastard, Augie jocularly refers to himself as "the by-blow of a traveling man" (125). He mock-heroically describes his mother as one of "those women conquered by the superior force of love . . . whom Zeus got the better of in animal form" (10), when actually she had been a simple-minded, nondescript factory girl who had been ravished and abandoned not by a "marble-legged Olympian" (10), but by a common laundry man. By having Augie humorously advertise his illegitimacy, Bellow, like many novelists of the picaresque, parodies "the mysterious birth of the traditional hero."[9]

In addition to a lack of respectable origins, Augie has a superabundance of enthusiasm, the comic flaw of the picaresque hero from Don Quixote to Felix Krull. This boundless eagerness to penetrate the thicket of reality accounts for the versatile jobs Augie readily accepts. Thus we initially laugh at the sheer variety of roles he assumes as welfare defrauder, shoplifter, valet, boxing trainer, sporting-goods model, dog-groomer, paint salesman, union organizer, professional student, coal-yard worker, iguana hunter, Merchant Marine counselor, and black marketeer. In no other Bellow novel are we permitted to witness such a diversity of occupational spheres and such chameleon shifts of outward identity. Moreover, we are tickled by the lack of orderly progression and logical connection between Augie's adventures. If comedy involves, as Bellow suggests, a burst of rebellion against mental restraints,[10] then Augie's "catch-as-catch-can"[11] adventures allow us to break free momentarily from the compulsion to lead well-ordered sensible lives. We can vicariously revel in his haphazard and improbable experiences.

What amuses us most is Augie's total absorption in the parts he plays. As he admits, "Those days whatever touched me had me entirely" (315). What touches him earliest is the excitement of

9. Alter, *Rogues' Progress*, p. 110.

10. See David Galloway, "An Interview with Saul Bellow," *Audit* 3 (Spring, 1963): 21.

11. Saul Bellow quoted in Harvey Breit, "Saul Bellow," *The Writer Observed* (New York: World Publishing Co., 1956), p. 273.

thievery. Even as a child he "loved a piece of strategy" (5) and relishes executing Grandma Lausch's devious schemes. Years later, when he engages in petty embezzlement at the neighborhood department store, he is still more thrilled with acting the thief than he is with his added income. Imagining himself "a Roger Touhy, Tommy O'Connor, Basil Banghart, or Dillinger" (44), he wildly imagines what it will be like after he is apprehended: "jail sentence, head shaven, fed on slumgullion, mustered in the mud, buffaloed and bossed" (45). Augie's fantasies are so diverting that we overlook the actual crime; we even secretly wish he would continue his thievery so that he would continue weaving his fantasies about it.

Augie is equally consumed with being a lover. Bellow, however, mocks Augie's romances by exposing the shortcomings of his lady loves while he reveals Augie's excessive ardor for them. The first object of his affections, Hilda Novinson, is described as "small-faced with pallor and other signs of weakness of the chest" (47). Yet Augie views her as the fairest damsel and, in true courtly love fashion, bristles "with an idiot desire to fall before her" (47). Before the more sensual Esther Fenchel, pampered virgin and inaccessible rich girl, Augie realizes this desire; he actually does faint before her when she spurns his attentions. Bellow also humorously undercuts Augie's sexual initiation. Unlike a Tom Jones who chances upon ready sexual gratification, Augie must first hoist Einhorn on his back, walk up a tortuous flight of icy stairs in the dark, deposit Einhorn, before an astonished whore, choose a nameless woman himself, and then seek his own pleasure, which *"didn't* have the luster it should have had" (124). Even when he has a known partner like Sophie Geratis, Bellow mentions the funny noises she makes when aroused rather than dwelling upon the raptures of sex. Nevertheless, such distractions do not deter Augie from making further contacts, professing his undying love to every desirable woman he meets and each time believing that he is the true servant of Eros.

With the outbreak of World War II Augie abruptly terminates his amours to become the super-patriot, the rabid activist. In retrospect, he mocks his own fanaticism: "I was a madman in the movies and yelled and clapped in the newsreel" (457). Getting up on his "hind-legs like an orator" (458), he becomes inflamed with rallying his countrymen to defend America from the superhuman monsters who

would gobble her up. So frenzied is he that he sounds like Dostoevsky's Underground Man, alerting everyone to "the universal ant heap
the enemy would establish if they won" (457). But as it is with
most picaros, whose intensities die a quick death only to give birth
to new ones, so it is with Augie. Once he becomes the staunch protector of his country, he is filled with the even stronger yearning to
be protected again within its borders.

Along with the ridiculous enthusiasm of the picaro, Augie possesses his laughable amorality. As Meade Harwell observes, "Rabelais' antimonastic injunction, 'Do what you will,' an ideology that
explains much of *Gargantua,* becomes concretely the civil liberties
assumed in Augie's program of growth. . . ."[12] Unlike the Machiavellians, Augie has no hypocritical illusions about his morality. With
comic frankness he admits, "So don't think I'm trying to put over
that, if handled right, a Cato could have been made for me, or a young
Lincoln who tramped four miles in a frontier zero gale to refund
three cents to a customer. I don't want to pass for having such legen-
dary presidential stuff" (23). Nor does Augie have any ethical qualms
about his illegal activities. Humorously enough, he views them as
normal free-enterprise undertakings. When he graduates from petty
theft and armed robbery to stealing books, he sees no wrong in taking
duplicate copies, since he hopes to educate himself by reading the
books his erudite customers order. What's more, he is even proud of
being in the "book business." Even at the close of the novel, when he
earns his living by selling pharmaceutical goods on the black market,
he is still not stricken with guilt. In "times of special disfigurement
and world-wide Babylonishness" (76), he is the comically amoral
picaro who does only what he must to survive.

In keeping with the amorality of the picaro, Augie also shares
his essentially anti-heroic stance. He "refuses the 'heroic' in favor of
what he believes the heroic destroys, a complete humanity."[13] It is "in
this formulated, programmatic rejection of the heroic will" that Lionel
Trilling believes *"Augie March* is most specifically and essentially

12. Meade Harwell, *"Picaro* from Chicago," *Southwest Review* 39 (Summer, 1954):
275.
13. Lionel Trilling, "Introduction," *The Adventures of Augie March* (New York:
Modern Library, 1965), p. xi.

comic." [14] Just as Yossarian of *Catch-22* values his imperfect men more than the accomplishment of the allegedly lofty objectives of his crazed superiors, so Augie values the unexceptional eagle, Caligula, more than the success of the iguana-hunting expedition and the realization of Thea's perverted definition of glory. But Augie, unlike Yossarian, does not immediately reach this conclusion. At first he is greatly intimidated by Caligula, who appears to be a creature of wanton cruelty. Augie even facetiously calls to mind all the eagles he has ever read about as a way of lessening his dread of the real thing. Further acquaintance with the bird soon dispels his fear. And just as Poe's student eventually grows fond of his uninvited raven, Augie gradually becomes friends with Caligula and even identifies with him in his defeat. As Trilling observes,

> [Augie's] emblematic beast is that eagle . . . which accepts its training for a heroic function and then, at the great moment of test, refuses the heroic role with the calmest comic indifference—to all appearance a perfect Hotspur of a bird, he flaps away from the conflict with a Falstaffian imperviousness to what is required of one of his breed, careless of what is expected of a being so manifestly noble and so fiercely armed." [15]

Both Augie and Caligula, retaining what Whitman called "the pride and centripetal isolation of a human being in himself," ultimately balk at accepting the fate decreed for them by another. In spite of the romantic assumptions, they prefer to view the world through a single pair of eyes and insist on their place in nature, no matter how ignoble it may be.

Augie's choice of the anti-heroic causes Leslie Fiedler to remark that the novel "is a strangely non-Jewish book in being concerned not with a man's rise, but with his evasion of rising." [16] Yet when the anti-heroic posture is forced upon Augie, he is very much the Jewish *schlimazl,* the butt of a painful comedy of situation. If he were to suffer one or two disasters, he would elicit well-deserved sympathy. But since he experiences a rash of calamities, he becomes the object of laughter. When Augie loses his first important job by being

14. *Ibid.*
15. *Ibid.,* p. xii.
16. Leslie A. Fiedler, "Saul Bellow," *Prairie Schooner* 31 (Summer, 1957): 107.

repeatedly short-changed, or when he is unwittingly implicated in the illegal scheme of running immigrants into the United States from Canada and is subsequently jailed, he is more to be pitied than ridiculed. But when Mimi Villar's request for moral support ruins his chances with Lucy Magnus, when he is beaten up as a CIO organizer by the very people whom he is helping, when he is thrown from a horse just at the moment of possible triumph in falconry, when his ship is torpedoed and the lifeboat he chooses just happens to contain a dangerous monomaniac, we cannot believe that so many strokes of misfortune could befall one individual—and we are therefore prompted to make light of his misery. Another reason for our amusement at Augie's misadventures is suggested by Henry Popkin: *"The Adventures of Augie March* traces a richly comic pattern of aspiration and disaster. It is a comic pattern because the height of Augie's aspirations and the speed of his recoveries keep us from taking his catastrophies seriously."[17] Indeed, time and again Augie is a Humpty Dumpty who is miraculously put back together again. After he is beaten up by the neighborhood gang, he speedily recovers only to return to the streets to court danger again. Any bruises his conscience receives heal quickly also. After he is sorely denounced for his thievery in Deever's Department Store, he remains the chastened criminal only until he sees an opportunity for another crime. Similarly, Augie's heartaches are short-lived. Almost overnight he is transformed from the swain suffering from the pangs of unrequited love for Esther Fenchel to the Don Juan whose love is very much requited by Sophie Geratis. In fact, love seems to be the most potent medicine for rapidly curing his ills. After Augie is severely trounced by anti-union men, he is soon magically restored to his vigorous self by the all-absorbing love of Thea Fenchel. After he is critically injured in his Mexican escapade, he makes a Lazarus-like recovery to become the healthy lover of Stella Chesney. Possessing the indestructibility of a cartoon character, Augie seems able to survive any "set of circumstances that involve discomfiture or disaster of some odd incongruous kind."[18] In this respect he resembles the buffoon whom Susanne Langer describes as "the indomitable living creature . . . the

---

17. Henry Popkin, "American Comedy," *Kenyon Review* 16 (Spring, 1954): 329.
18. Stephen Leacock, *Humour and Humanity* (New York: Henry Holt & Co., 1938), p. 79.

personified *élan vital* . . . now triumphant, now worsted and rueful, but in his ruefulness and dismay he is funny, because his energy is really unimpaired and each failure prepares the situation for a new fantastic move." [19]

While Augie makes his fantastic moves as the picaro, he is also the meditator attempting to extract meaning from these fantastic moves. Although his "improvised existence has the rhythm of primitive, savage, if not animalian life," [20] he is very much the *homo sapiens* who cannot ignore certain truths which emerge from his adventures. He must explore their implications and assess their worth. Augie is not only the unreflective picaro; he is also Bellow's peripatetic comedian of ideas. As an individual who "refuse[s] to lead a disappointed life" (432) but has no particular specialty, Augie realizes that he appears "funny" (432) to most people. Yet he finds those people equally funny who are energetic specialists first and enervated men afterward. He thus ridicules Clem Tambow, the psychology specialist who facilely analyzes him but has little self-insight. He exposes the folly of Basteshaw, who would use reason to save mankind but is unable to save himself from madness. He "laugh[s] out loud" (205) at the "mixture of pompousness and revolutionist's jargon" (205) of Hooker Frazer, who is a brilliant political science student but is not man enough to stand by the girl due to give birth to his child. Similarly, Augie has little use for the university because it seems to bypass "some of the stages from the brute creation to the sublime mind" (286). Recalling a painting in which a thief robs a venerable sage lost in celestial contemplation, he concludes "that it is earthly power that steals, while the ridiculous wise are in a dream about this world and the next . . ." (191). Unlike Joseph, who regards the rationalist as the highest order of being, Augie all too clearly sees the comic limitations of the thinking man who is not the Emersonian "Man Thinking." Having watched the best-laid intellectual plans of man go awry, he wittily remarks, "After much making with sense, it's senselessness that you submit to" (390).

In addition to senselessness, Augie observes that the all too vulnerable human being falls prey to his imagination and therefore acts

[19]. Susanne K. Langer, *Feeling and Form* (New York: Charles Scribner's Sons, 1953), p. 342.
[20]. *Ibid.*

more foolishly than ever. Augie hyperbolically compares the imagination to "the Roman army out in Spain or Gaul [which] makes streets and walls even if it's only camping for the night" (403). Yet what is even more ridiculous is that each man is trying to superimpose his, own fabrication on the next fellow. As Augie aptly expresses it, "[Humanity is] made up of these inventors or artists, millions and millions of them, each in his own way trying to recruit other people to play a supporting role and sustain him in his make-believe" (402). Assuming that these great pretenders secure a large following to believe in their pretense, Augie points out the greatest absurdity of all. "Nothing genuine is allowed to appear and nobody knows what's real" (401).

In addition to being a perpetrator of comic deeds and an explorer of comic values, Augie is above all the earnest seeker, actively engaged in self-discovery. He belongs to the ranks of those Bellow heroes who, according to Alfred Kazin, are "burdened by a speculative quest, a need to understand their particular destiny within the general problem of human destiny."[21] During the first half of the novel Augie is too caught up in his fantastic adventures and too mesmerized by the spell-binding Machiavellians to feel the full extent of this burden. But when his madcap escapades grow progressively more maddening and he suffers more and more from the adverse effects of the Machiavellians' hypnotic powers, he becomes disenchanted with them and turns inward to find his own powers.[22] Then Augie ceases to be the fleeting two-dimensional picaro who is known only by the peculiar company he keeps. Instead he becomes the more substantial introspective hero who keeps his own company and learns to know himself. As he tells Mintouchian, another Socratic questioner like Joseph's "Spirit of Alternatives," "I suppose I better . . . give in and be [myself]. I will never force the hand of fate to create a better Augie March, nor change the time to an age of gold" (485).

While Augie's quest for a proper fate is treated with due seriousness, his traits as a seeker—his Candide-like optimism and his "too effusive

21. Alfred Kazin, "The World of Saul Bellow," *Contemporaries* (Boston: Little, Brown & Co., 1962), p. 218.

22. According to Opdahl, Augie's "recognition that he is not a man of love" causes him to turn inward, where he hopes to cultivate the ability to love. See *The Novels of Saul Bellow*, p. 89.

and uncritical" [23] acceptance of life's obvious inequities—make him the target of Bellow's subtle mockery. Despite "permanent disappointment, more or less permanent pain, death of children, lovers, friends, ends of causes, old age . . . maybe most intolerable, the hardening of detestable character" (255), Augie still insists that there are "occasions for happiness that weren't illusions of people" (255). This does not mean that Augie is totally oblivious to the evil in his midst. The older he gets, the more he sees those "iron-deep clouds, just plain brutal and not mitigated" and the civilizations which "beget nothing on one another" (159). Perhaps because he has had such a searing glimpse of the "mud-sprung, famine-knifed, street-pounding, war-rattled, difficult, painstaking, kicked in the belly, grief and cartilage mankind" (175), and has been so horrified by the sight, he is excessively hopeful in attempts to mask his despair and sometimes even shrill in expressing his faith in the perfectibility of the human being. For example, he is totally convinced that it is possible for anyone to pick his "own ideal creature in the mirror coastal air and sharp leaves of ancient perfections and be at home where a great mankind was at home" (76). In marked contrast to Joseph, who regards modern society as a bastardization of the venerable communities of antiquity, Augie refuses to admit that "we're at the dwarf end of all times and mere children whose only share in grandeur is like a boy's share in fairy-tale kings, beings of a different kind from times better and stronger than ours" (60). Augie obviously protests too much. While we can sympathetically view his protests as an indication of the "uncertainty and emotional strain that lurked on the underside" [24] of his optimism, we must chuckle at his persistent attempts to offer the most favorable interpretations of what are often the least optimum circumstances.

Even more laughable are Augie's intentions to re-create an Eden. His Eden, however, turns out to be more of a fool's paradise. Given to reading vast quantities of utopian literature, he is inspired to establish his own little utopia—an academy and foster home in some

---

23. Nina A. Steers, "Interview with Saul Bellow—'Successor' to Faulkner?" *Show* 4 (September, 1964): 38.

24. Norman Podhoretz, "The New Nihilism and the Novel," *Partisan Review* 25 (Fall, 1958): 579.

idyllic spot. But his imagination runs away with him. He envisions the school as "one of those Walden or Innisfree wattle jobs under the kind sun, surrounded by velvet woods and bright gardens and Elysium lawns sown with Lincoln Park grass seed" (515). The students would be his own children and orphans; the curriculum would consist of auto mechanics, shoe repairing, bee-keeping, and horticulture; the faculty would include himself, his wife Stella, his blind mother, and his idiot brother Georgie. Unlike other daft reformers, he is not wedded to his farfetched project for long. His common sense soon punctures his inflated idealism and causes him to see that his utopian venture is "only one of those bubble-headed dreams of people who haven't yet realized what they're like nor what they're intended for" (515). Moreover, he realizes that he is just as ludicrous as the Machiavellians, since the academy is but an embodiment of his own obsessive theory. "I wanted simplicity and denied complexity, and in this I was guileful and suppressed many patents in my secret heart and was as devising as anybody else" (402). He recognizes that he has been as comically rigid and self-absorbed in his single-minded pursuit of his goal as those "imposers-upon, absolutists" (524) from whom he has fled. Even more disconcerting is his discovery that, like the others, his ideal construction had been the cause of his comic self-deception. He had convinced himself that he was the selfless devotee of Love, when in truth he selfishly became the lover of anyone who would protect him from the grim world.

Although Augie realizes the folly of establishing such an academy, he does not dismiss as a "featherhead millenarian notion" (516) his conception of the "axial lines" (454), his version of those transcendental laws of nature symbolizing the laws of the spirit. He avidly believes that if he bases his existence on them, he will have the good enough fate he has been earnestly seeking. But to discover them and feel their full impact, he knows he must first curtail his ridiculous evasive movement. "When striving stops, there they are as a gift. . . . Truth, love, peace, bounty, usefulness, harmony!" (454). With such treasures in his possession, he feels he will have access to his own messianic age in which "all noise and grates, distortion, chatter, distraction, effort, superfluity, will pass off like something unreal" (454). At the end of the novel, however, Augie has not yet located the axial lines. He is forced to admit, "And since I never had any place of rest,

it should follow that I have trouble being still, and furthermore my
hope is based upon getting to be still so that the axial lines can be
found" (514). Bellow seems to indicate that Augie has once again become the comic victim of his own hyperactive idealism. As Howard M.
Harper notes, "The point is that striving never stops, that Augie's
hope of 'getting to be still so that the axial lines can be found' is
illusory. We are 'still' only in death. The lines themselves do exist, but
only in our minds as ideals, not in the real world." [25]

Although Augie realizes the axial lines are conspicuously absent
from his life, he does not give way to the paralyzing dejection of a
Joseph or a Leventhal. From all outward appearances he would have
good reason to make brooding a full-time occupation. Stella Chesney,
the woman he finally marries, is more concerned with being a cine-
matic star of the first magnitude than a magnanimous human being
who could give Augie the genuine love he craves. Nor does it seem
likely that the children who inhabit his fancies will ever become ac-
tualities. Rather than cultivating his garden on native ground, he will
undoubtedly have to cultivate himself in foreign lands. No longer
geared to dodging his relentless drafters and blaming them for con-
trolling his life, he will, from all indications, hold himself accountable and attend to the "terribly hard work" taking place within him—
the "excavation and digging, mining, moling through tunnels, heaving, pushing, moving rock . . ." (523). Along with this internal reno-
vation, what will surely remain with him during his "bondage of
strangeness" (523) is his comic sense, "the laughing creature, forever
rising up" (536). This faculty enables him to comprehend the lesson
Schlossberg attempted to teach: what it means to be human. Despite
his many foolish aspirations and his "clownery hiding tragedy" (454),
Augie comes to understand

> that you don't take so wide a stand that it makes a human life impos-
> sible, nor try to bring together irreconcilables that destroy you, but try
> out what of human you can live with first. And if the highest should
> come in that empty overheated tavern with its flies and the hot radio
> buzzing between the plays and plugged beer from Sox Park, what are
> you supposed to do but take the mixture and say imperfection is always
> the condition as found. . . (260).

25. Howard M. Harper, Jr., *Desperate Faith* (Chapel Hill: University of North
Carolina Press, 1967), p. 29.

Thus Augie's comic sense enables him to face the fact that we are not flawless, but limited and conditioned creatures, prone to all kinds of absurdities, interruptions, mishaps, and embarrassments. Yet it still allows him to possess *"amor fati* . . . mysterious adoration of what occurs"* (527). Above all, it permits him not only to scoff at the brute deterministic forces threatening to overwhelm him, but it also inspires him to keep hoping that he can defeat them. At the same time, it ridicules him for hoping to win such an uneven contest. Augie is therefore prompted to laugh both at nature for presuming it will be victorious and at himself for refusing to capitulate and "lead a disappointed life" (536). Since the outcome of the contest is not yet decided, it is impossible to determine who will ultimately be the butt of the laughter. Augie is left with the inscrutable joke, as well as the recurrent hope that his distinctive fate lies within reach.

Although Augie may be a "flop" (536) at discovering the good life, he is certainly a success at discovering the comic style. Whereas Joseph and Leventhal employ a highly restrained and unobtrusive language, overly concerned with adhering to the Flaubertian standards of precision and correctness, Augie uses an uninhibited, overly confident language which hilariously calls attention to itself as it irreverently violates all the rules. So irreverent is the style that Bellow himself later had misgivings about it:

> I think that when I wrote those early books I was timid. . . . I had to touch a great many bases, demonstrate my abilities, pay my respects to formal requirements. In short, I was afraid to let myself go. . . . When I began to write *Augie March,* I took off many of these restraints. I think I took off too many, and went too far, but I was feeling the excitement of discovery. I had just increased my freedom and like any emancipated plebeian, I abused it at once.[26]

Yet this abuse of freedom made possible the release of a nimble, mongrelized, verbose, spontaneous, and above all zestful rhetoric. Although such rhetoric may be accused of being too conspicuous and upstaging other aspects of *Augie March,* it delights us with its novelty. Its maverick quality, catching us unawares, makes us laugh at its unexpected jocularity and thus eases our intense concentration on the more weighty matters of the novel. Once diverted, however, we are

[26.] Harper, "Saul Bellow—The Art of Fiction: An Interview," p. 55.

prompted to return to the source of our diversion, examine it more closely, and in the process gain a fuller understanding of the entire context. Bellow's comedy of language has a triple function: it entertains, it relieves, and it enlightens.

This triple function is most operative in Bellow's encyclopedic wit. Like the droll conversation of his Yiddish forebears which was "full of the grandest historical, mythological, and religious allusions," [27] Augie's speech is brimming with the same kind of wide-ranging and spectacular allusions. Just as the ghetto dwellers were momentarily transported from their restrictive lives by sounding the magic names of the great, Augie is temporarily freed from Chicago's bleak Depression years by invoking the higher deities. These inventive heroic references provide not only escape, but also laughter. They represent the lively creations of an overly active imagination, along with underscoring the comic anti-heroism of the Machiavellians and their actions. When Augie likens Grandma Lausch to Tamerlane, Juno, Pharaoh, Jehovah, and the Praetorian Guard, he stresses how ridiculous she appears in her self-created role of minor tyrant. Or when he places Einhorn in the company of Caesar, Ulysses, Francis Bacon, Pope Alexander VI, Hephaestus, Socrates, Sardanapalus, Anchises, and Croesus, he calls attention to Einhorn's petty thoughts and activities and thereby reduces him to comic stature. Such farfetched comparisons also distract us from Grandma Lausch's genuinely unhappy lot and Einhorn's sorry predicament; for a time we are given respite from empathizing with an old woman abandoned by her sons, compelled to be indebted to strangers. We do not have to gaze continually at a pathetic cripple, straining to be as well groomed and well loved as any able-bodied man. Yet the comparisons have still another purpose. They serve to convince us that, in the final analysis, Grandma Lausch, Einhorn, and all the other little people Augie encounters are made of the same noble stuff as the heroes to whom they are likened. Grandma Lausch, salvaging her pride and exercising her cunning in the worst of straits, has the grandeur of a Juno; Einhorn, in his undaunted refusal to succumb to invalidism, possesses the same dignity as a Hephaestus. Bellow is not jesting when he has Augie remark that "gods [may] turn up anywhere" (260), or "given time, we all catch up

27. Saul Bellow, "Laughter in the Ghetto," *Saturday Review of Literature* 36 (May 30, 1953): 15.

with legends, more or less" (333). These improbable allusions "reflect one of [Bellow's] major themes, that modern man, however ridiculous or ugly he may seem, is as capable of nobility as men of any age, that he is in touch with the legends and is worthy of esteem." [28]

Augie employs many suggestive allusions, and like his ghetto ancestors, whose most precious gift was their rich language, he expresses himself in a surplus of words. As a young autodidact, he is eager to reveal his newly acquired wisdom by using the most impressive language possible. Mark Twain's statement, "I never write 'metropolis' for seven cents, because I can get the same money for 'city,'" [29] does not describe Augie's practice. Having rummaged through Einhorn's fire-damaged Harvard Classics and the scholarly books he has pirated, he likes to dazzle us with his gems of knowledge and high-priced diction. Especially at the beginnings of chapters he exhibits his booty to entice us to read on and discover further treasures.

Moreover, should anyone doubt the keenness and accuracy of his perceptions, he feels compelled to over-modify them. His nouns and verbs are weighted down with excess qualifiers. Mamma, for example, is pictured as "big, gentle, dilapidated, scrubbing and lugging" (10), and the French maid Jacqueline's face is described as "freezing, wavering, mascara-lined, goblin, earnest and disciplinarian, membranous, and yet gorgeous" (535). Should anyone question the inclusiveness of Augie's vision, he readily presents vast Whitmanesque catalogues of everything he sees, significant or not. He enumerates the characters riding up a city hall elevator, the students of his city college, or the habitués of Einhorn's poolroom, including their unsightly tell-tale characteristics:

> . . . the blood-smelling swaggeroos, recruits for mobs, automobile thieves, stick-up men, sluggers and bouncers, punks with ambition to become torpedoes, neighborhood cowboys with Jack Holt sideburns down to the jawbone, collegiates, tinhorns and small-time racketeers and pugs, and ex-servicemen, home-evading husbands, hackies, truckers and bush-league athletes (81).

28. Mary Lee Allen, 'The Flower and the Chalk: The Comic Sense of Saul Bellow" (Ph.D. diss., Stanford University, 1968), p. 178.

29. Quoted in Frances G. Emberson, "Mark Twain's Vocabulary," *University of Missouri Studies* 10 (July 1, 1935): 11.

But like Dreiser, who saw himself as the historian of an era, Bellow is especially intent on grasping the particular facts and spirit of the 1920's and 1930's. Just as Dreiser in *Sister Carrie* provided unduly copious details about the department store, the drummer as social type, and the telephone booth to make sure that they would never vanish from the scene, Augie profusely describes the County Hospital dental dispensary as it appeared during his childhood:

> . . . a multitude of dentists' chairs, hundreds of them in a space as enormous as an armory, and green bowls with designs of glass grapes, drills, lifted zigzag as insects' legs and gas flames on the porcelain swivel trays—a thundery gloom in Harrison Street of limestone county buildings and cumbersome red streetcars with metal grillwork on their windows and monarchical iron whiskers of cowcatchers front and rear (7).

He inadvertently pinpoints the consuming popular interests of the times by endlessly listing all the free literature Einhorn sends away for: "quack hygiene books, advice on bust development, on getting rid of pimples, on longevity and Couéism, pamphlets on Fletcherism. Yoga, spirit-rapping, anti-vivisection . . . [brochures from the] Henry George Institute . . . the Rudolf Steiner Foundation in London, the local bar association [and] the American Legion" (70).

Augie does not continually make a conspicuous display of his highbrow learning, his erudite diction, and his exhaustive impressions. He frequently lapses back into his untutored and unrefined self, and along with his breezy colloquialisms and slang he even slips in those four-letter words which Olivia never permitted Twain to use. Or he mimics the racy patter of the pseudo-intellectual, the genuine thug, the hyphenated Polish-American and the unalloyed Midwesterner. Unable to emancipate himself entirely from his immigrant stock, Augie's "barbaric yawp" becomes all the more "untranslatable" because of his own Yiddish accent and syntax. In addition to including such Yiddish words as *verpitzed, gescheft, gedenk, ipisch,* and *wehtig*,[30] and recording the broken English of his scarcely assimilated Jewish friends and relatives, Augie himself commits some Yiddish-inspired

---

30. Such Yiddish words as *verpitzed* (excessively adorned), *gescheft* (business), *gedenk* (think), *ipisch* (stench), and *wehtig* (pain) occur, for the most part, in Grandma Lausch, Anna Coblin, and Einhorn chapters.

grammatical crimes. Taking many liberties with sentence structure, he occasionally comes up with the inverted word order of Yiddish: "Was she a vain person, or injurious or cynical, it couldn't make any difference now" (474). He also mutilates verb form to sound like the Yiddish equivalent: "As this information came out, which I didn't know how seriously to take, I thought this was like me and my life— I could not find myself in love without it should have some peculiarity" (319).[31] Yet such bastardizations are welcome offenses, for they add still another distinctive strain to the comically hybrid rhetoric of the novel.

Another feature of comedy of language which Augie has inherited from his Yiddish progenitors is the humor of verbal retrieval. Although many of Augie's experiences are agonizing, the metaphoric and hyperbolic expressions he originates to describe them initially take the sting out of them and permit him to recognize what is outwardly funny about them. Through an imaginative use of language Augie is able "to evoke his own and our laughter" and thereby "avoid or absorb his own pain." [32] When, for example, he is first made to wear a gauntlet in preparation for his dreaded eagle-training, he minimizes his anguish by facetiously comparing himself to a "fielder in a demon's game [who] would have to gallop here and there and catch burning stone in the air" (321). Filled with remorse over his penchant for deception, he temporarily eases his conscience by inventing the cleverly exaggerated rationalization: "One day's ordinary falsehood if you could convert it into silt would choke the Amazon back a hundred miles over the banks" (375). Censuring himself for his perpetual credulity, he jocularly insists that he has "holes in [his] head like a colander" (417). The use of such high-spirited language does not permit Augie to be low-spirited for long. More than anything, his talent for innovative articulation enables him to transform disaster into drollery.

The humor of *The Adventures of Augie March* marks a new departure for Bellow. Turning from the mordant lacerations of *Dangling Man* and the fiendish ironies of *The Victim*, its comedy of character

31. I am indebted to Mary Lee Allen for pointing out these examples. See "The Flower and the Chalk: The Comic Sense of Saul Bellow," pp. 175–176.

32. Earl Rovit, *Saul Bellow*, University of Minnesota Pamphlets on American Writers, no. 65 (Minneapolis: University of Minnesota Press, 1967), p. 40.

is now suffused with the tolerant laughter of the "genial" romantics of the early nineteenth century, the laughter Wylie Sypher describes as "an overflow of sympathy, an amiable feeling of identity with what is disreputably human, a relish for the whimsical, the odd, the private blunder." [33] Indeed, throughout his travels Augie is the picaresque apostle who, meeting up with errant humanity, eagerly listens to their confessions and generously pardons their sins, even blessing them for their antic trespasses. And in tranquillity he recalls them and is again amused by them. There is also a change in the novel's comedy of situation. In place of the static, dreary predicament of Joseph or the single macabre ordeal of Leventhal, an incredible variety of happenings befall Augie, each more bizarre than the next, yet no one unduly debilitating. In the midst of Augie's recurrent involvement in and extraction from crises, he is still able to tackle some of the same philosophical issues actively perplexing Joseph and vaguely troubling Leventhal. The only difference is that Augie is not compelled to be so deadly serious or pessimistic in his discussions. By nature and experience more cheerful, he can afford to introduce levity without minimizing the worth of what he is saying. But what most crucially distinguishes Augie from Joseph and Leventhal as a comedian of ideas is the language he uses to formulate these ideas. Whereas Joseph's and Leventhal's discourses are as straitjacketed and colorless as their existences, Augie's expressions are as irrepressible and glowing as his life. His comically aberrant, allusion-studded, and word-congested rhetoric is most responsible for Augie's "kidding his way to Jesus" (302).

33. Wylie Sypher, "Our New Sense of the Comic," in *Comedy*, ed. Wylie Sypher (New York: Doubleday & Co., 1956), p. 204.

Velvel, the Fair-Haired Hippopotamus

5

Unlike Joseph, who can philosophize about freedom while his wife supports him, or Augie, who can exercise his freedom while ever available patrons sponsor him, Tommy Wilhelm, the out-of-commission toy salesman of Bellow's novella *Seize the Day*[1] has no such luxury. Unable to entertain even the prospect of having options, he bitterly complains: "Don't talk to me of being free. A rich man may be free on an income of a million net. A poor man may be free because nobody cares what he does. But a fellow in my position has to sweat it out until he drops dead" (49). Whereas Joseph quarantines himself from the money-sick society, Leventhal takes refuge in his paranoiac distortions of reality, and Augie depends on love to avoid "the free-running terror and wild cold of chaos" (403), Wilhelm is out in the open, stripped of all protections, exposed to the world's sharkish materialism. Yet Wilhelm is by no means the immutable economically determined victim of the naturalistic novel. Bellow has made him out to be a changeable creature with far too many comic peculiarities to be convincing as the static, hapless brute. Moreover, he has instilled in Wilhelm a spark of nobility which in the end allows him to accept his ignominy and lights the way for him to redeem the present.

[1]. Citations from this novel are to *Seize the Day* (New York: Viking Press, 1956).

But until that redemption, what Bellow has said about modern comedy in general also pertains to Wilhelm's particular situation: "It is obvious that modern comedy has to do with the disintegrating outline of the worthy and humane Self. . . ."[2] During the greater part of the novella Bellow portrays the progressive disintegration of Wilhelm's "worthy and humane Self"—the collapse of his tenuous self-esteem and the shattering of his fragile equanimity.

Since the action of the story takes place during a twenty-four-hour period, Bellow has Wilhelm recall the crucial damage that has occurred to him in the past, along with dramatizing the accelerated stages of Wilhelm's breakdown in the present. His plight is harrowing enough to demand our compassion, yet it is odd and incongruous enough to elicit our mirth as well. Denied a well-earned promotion at the Rojax Corporation, Wilhelm has imprudently resigned, only to enact his own version of *Death of a Salesman.* But he is not permitted even to die in peace. His termagant wife, who sought to rob him of his identity during marriage, is now determined to rob him of his waning funds. Even though she will not grant him a divorce, he must send her the usual support payments, assume responsibility for his sons' life insurance policies, and subsidize her higher education. He must therefore give up his spacious apartment in the Massachusetts countryside to take a cramped room in the same New York hotel where his affluent elderly father resides. Here at the Hotel Gloriana, the inglorious retreat of a fading gerontocracy, Wilhelm, a man in his middle forties, is compelled to be a petulant child again to obtain affection and money from his niggardly parent. On Wilhelm's "day of reckoning" (96), the point at which he faces total financial ruin, his father not only refuses to help him, but heartlessly disowns him as well. Feeling "like a man about to drown" (104), Wilhelm has no recourse but to ride on the back of the unscrupulous Dr. Tamkin in a desperate attempt to keep his head above water. Thus on this day (in the season which precedes Yom Kippur, the most sacred of Jewish holidays during which a man's life is assessed and his fate decreed), Wilhelm, a latter-day Jonah, harkens to the voice of the false prophet Tamkin and invests his last seven hundred dollars in the most unkosher commodity of all—lard. Thereupon Wilhelm and his

2. Saul Bellow, "Some Notes on Recent American Fiction," *Encounter* 21 (November, 1963): 28.

profits are immediately swallowed up. Yet Wilhelm lands not in the stomach of the whale but in the interior of a Jewish funeral home, where he feels a "splash of heartsickness" (117) as he stands before an unknown corpse. Flooded with tears, Wilhelm's drowning is at last complete.

On the surface it appears that the plights of Wilhelm and Augie are identical. Each is plagued with a heavy concentration of unusual woes in a short period of time. Uniformity of action, however, is not present in *The Adventures of Augie March*. For every upset Augie experiences, there is a concomitant frolic. For every exploitation he suffers, there is a compensating good fortune. The same is not true for Wilhelm. The action of *Seize the Day* is exasperatingly uniform, with the absence of any marked differentiation among Wilhelm's upheavals, or interrupting spells of extended merriment. If any comic relief exists, it arises from the fall guy compounding of Wilhelm's difficulties. Given such opposite conditions, Augie fares much better; despite his many scrapes, he remains so intact that he scarcely seems human. Wilhelm, on the other hand, is so ravaged from his proliferation of troubles that he seems too human. According to Irving Howe, he is another suffering Dostoevskian buffoon who

> functions like an amusement-park mirror [in which] . . . you see your face and body horribly distorted; yet when you look more closely, you may find that the very process of distortion reveals something about you (that leer, that grin, that simper, that smirk) which you might not see in an ordinary mirror. In short, the buffoon causes us to see a part of ourselves that we do not like to acknowledge.[3]

Indeed, if we are individuals like Wilhelm's father, the fastidious Dr. Adler, and the inflexible society he represents, we do not like to "see a part of ourselves" in the "large, odd, excited, fleshy, blond, abrupt personality named Wilhelm" (39). Priding ourselves on our self-gained composure, we resent having the slightest resemblance to any weak-willed creature whose life is controlled by pills—"first stimulants and then depressants, anodynes followed by analeptics, until the poor organism doesn't know what's happened" (32–33). Pleased with our good breeding, we shudder to think that we might have anything in

3. Irving Howe, "Introduction to *Seize the Day*," *Classics of Modern Fiction*, ed. Irving Howe (New York: Harcourt Brace & World, 1968), p. 461.

common with such an uncouth fellow who uses the red tapes of cigarette packages as dental floss and greedily devours the remains of another person's breakfast. Above all, protecting our immaculate conception of ourselves, we try to keep at a distance a Tommy Wilhelm "who [doesn't] even wash his hands in the morning" (36), and whose room reeks of dirty clothes.

But Bellow's attitude toward Wilhelm is not that harsh. Unlike his aloof treatment of Leventhal and his uncharitably ironic exposure of his manufactured grievances, he appreciates what Wilhelm is up against and therefore sympathetically pardons his buffoonish deviations and improprieties. Rather, it is those who frown upon Wilhelm that meet with Bellow's censure.

Bellow also jocularly accepts Wilhelm's traits as a *schlemiel,* the character in the Yiddish folk mind who is both affectionately and contemptuously regarded as "an awkward, bungling fellow . . . [who] is forever getting in his own and everybody else's way and [who] spoils everything he attempts."[4] Undeniably Wilhelm is a mistake-making creature whose first wrong decision was quitting college to pursue a Hollywood career. Although he instinctively knew that such a move was foolhardy, like the grotesques of Nathanael West's *The Day of the Locust,* he could not be deterred from migrating to California. Such action "was typical of Wilhelm. After much thought and hesitation and debate he invariably took the course he had rejected innumerable times" (23). Even after the talent scout, Maurice Venice, saw him as "the type that loses the girl to the George Raft type or the William Powell type" (21), he still retained a glamorous image of himself. It took seven years of drifting in Hollywood with only one role to his credit—playing soundless bagpipes in the film *Annie Laurie*—to convince him that perhaps he really wasn't star material. By that time it was too late to take up any of the other professions. Wilhelm's marriage to Margaret had been another gross error. "He had made up his mind not to marry his wife, but ran off and got married" (23). When he no longer could force himself to conform to her image of a husband, he followed the advice of the Jewish proverb, "It is better to dwell in the wilderness, than with a contentious and angry woman."[5]

---

4. Nathan Ausubel, "Introduction: *Schlemihls and Schlimazls,*" *A Treasury of Jewish Folklore,* ed. Nathan Ausubel (New York: Crown Publishers), p. 343.

5. Quoted *ibid.,* p. 344.

But even in the wilderness of New York City, Wilhelm not only failed to escape his wife's cruel domination, but also committed another blunder. He foolishly worshipped "the golden calf of speculation." [6] He was determined not to invest his money with Tamkin, and then, "ripe for the mistake" (58), he "had given him the check" (23). Thus Wilhelm experiences no difficulty in becoming a "loser." As a *schlemiel,* it seems to be his "avocation and profession to miss out on things, to muff opportunities, to be persistently, organically, preposterously and ingeniously out of place." [7]

Even though Tommy Wilhelm is the *schlemiel* who proverbially "lands on his back and bruises his nose," [8] he is still likely to be vain about the appearance of his nose. He is one of those ridiculously affected little men who, according to Bellow, try to ape "the dignity and refinements of the leaders of society." [9] More specifically, Wilhelm is the "burlap hero" who strains to be the man in the gray flannel suit. As omniscient narrator who is both commentator on and spokesman for Wilhelm, Bellow captures both the humor and the pathos of his labored masquerade. He wryly informs us that Wilhelm is "shaved and in the lobby by eight o'clock" (4), deliberately wearing a hat and smoking a cigar to appear more purposeful. Although Wilhelm claims "he worried about his appearance . . . mainly for his old father's sake" (3), it is evident that he constantly glances in the mirror to satisfy his own vanity. Even though he is no longer the charming college freshman with "a raccoon coat and a beanie on his large blond head" (6), he clings to the belief that his good looks have not entirely vanished, especially when he is wearing his eighteen-dollar Jack Fagman shirt. Even when he is not outfitted in particularly flattering apparel, he still retains pride in his ability to "wrinkle his forehead in a pleasing way. Some of the slow, silent movements of his face were very attractive" (5). Wilhelm's vanity, however, is not long-lasting. He is one of those Bellow heroes who, according to Earl Rovit, "yearn after dignity, but as soon as they catch themselves groping to achieve

6. David D. Galloway, "The Absurd Man as Picaro: The Novels of Saul Bellow," *Texas Studies in Literature and Language* 6 (Summer, 1964): 243.

7. Maurice Samuel, *The World of Sholom Aleichem* (New York: Schocken Books, 1943), p. 187.

8. Quoted in Irving Howe, "Introduction to *Seize the Day*," p. 462.

9. Saul Bellow, "Literature," *The Great Ideas Today,* ed. Mortimer Adler and Robert M. Hutchins (Chicago: Encyclopedia Britannica, 1963), p. 163.

it, they are quick to mock their own attempts as comically futile."[10] As with Leventhal and Herzog, Wilhelm's subsequent self-deflation proves more risible than his initial self-inflation. Just after he assumes the airs of a businessman, he confesses that his "chief business" (4) is getting up in the morning, buying the paper, and drinking Coca-Cola before breakfast. Or right after he gazes admiringly at himself in his Jack Fagman shirt, he acknowledges his untidiness. "He liked to wear good clothes, but once he had put it on each article appeared to go its own way" (5–6).

Wilhelm's body behind the masquerade is also subject to ridicule. Unlike "the tragic poet" who Bergson claims "is so careful to avoid anything calculated to attract attention to the material side of his heroes" for fear of introducing "the comic element,"[11] Bellow stresses Wilhelm's physical characteristics, especially the unfavorable ones, to insure his being the object of laughter. Were he to avoid mentioning the corporeal and depict Wilhelm merely as an abstraction of the exploited man, his exploitation would lack any vital complexity. We would then be deprived of witnessing any of the antic shocks and mystifying bruises that only flesh is heir to. We would also be denied the possibility of identifying with him. But because Bellow makes Wilhelm out to be such an imperfect somatic specimen, with so many unflattering reminders that he is not a god, he qualifies as the limited representative of the human comedy; his clumsy defeat is at once familiar, yet inscrutably funny. Thus, contrasting Wilhelm's features with the unmarred "gold embossed portraits of famous men" (6) on cigar boxes, Bellow purposely focuses on the "wide wrinkle like a comprehensive bracket sign" written on Wilhelm's forehead, "the patches of brown on his dark blond skin," his "troubled desirous eyes," his "big round face," his "wide, flourishing red mouth" and "stump teeth" (6–7). Or describing Wilhelm at the commodities exchange, Bellow singles out "his Buddha's head, too large to suffer such uncertainties" (82). Also, whenever Wilhelm has a painful recollection of a past injury or is undergoing a disturbing experience in the present, Bellow undercuts its seriousness by giving an elaborate account of his physio-

10. Earl Rovit, *Saul Bellow,* University of Minnesota Pamphlets on American Writers, no. 65 (Minneapolis: University of Minnesota Press, 1967), p. 11.

11. Henri Bergson, "Laughter," in *Comedy,* ed. Wylie Sypher (New York: Doubleday & Co., 1956), p. 94.

logical state. While he briefly registers Leventhal's physical complaints, he heightens our amusement by sparing none of Wilhelm's symptoms as well as showing their effects in full force. Throughout the novella Bellow pictures Wilhelm as "horribly worked up, his neck and shoulders, his entire chest ach[ing] as though they had been tied with ropes" (55–56), his heart pushing upward, the air vanishing from his lungs, his tongue going soft and paining him in the cords and throat.

Not only does Bellow as omniscient narrator reveal Wilhelm's physical peculiarities; he also assigns the fault-finding task to Wilhelm's father, Dr. Adler. Since the defects of the sons are generally magnified by the fathers, this magnification provides an additional source of humor. In the old man's hypercritical eyes Wilhelm is "a regular mountain of tics" who is "either hoisting his pants up and down by the pockets or jittering with his feet" (28). Sorely disappointed in the son he has given to the world, he is repelled by the "weak strain of Wilhelm's voice . . . the droop of his face, the swell of his belly against the restraint of his belt" (45).

Dr. Adler's disgust is surpassed by Wilhelm's own contempt for the grossness of his body. Like Leventhal, he believes that his "big, indecently big, spoiled body" (29) impedes his ascendance to a higher level of being. If anything, it reduces him to the level of an animal. Indeed, Wilhelm often jests at his own expense by referring to himself as "a fair-haired hippopotamus" (6). There is more truth to the jest than he at first recognizes. Tamkin, with whom he has been dealing, is depicted in birdlike imagery: "What a rare peculiar bird he was, with those pointed shoulders, that bare head, his loose nails, almost claws, and those brown, soft, deadly, heavy eyes" (82). According to the folklore of natural history, birds ride on the backs of hippopotami to pull out insects from their hide and to guide them. Tamkin is clearly the bird on Wilhelm's back who is more of a parasite than a guide.[12] When it comes to his wife, Wilhelm immediately grasps the full import of his bitter hyperbole that he is a "Brahma bull" being devoured by piranha fish (76). Yet when he chastises himself for being an "Ass," a "Wild boar," and a "Dumb mule" (55), he does not know he has internalized his father's view of him as a despicable

12. For a fuller treatment of this idea, see Hugh Hartman, "Character, Theme and Tradition in the Novels of Saul Bellow" (Ph.D. diss., University of Washington, 1968), p. 96.

beast. Bellow, however, does not always employ such grim or unsympathetic animal designations. He poignantly intimates that Wilhelm, in his frantic bid to be a Hollywood celebrity, is much like "a
pigeon about to light on the great chain that supported the marquee
of the movie house . . . [his] wings beating strongly" (4). He playfully suggests that Wilhelm looks more like a bear than a hippo in
his screen test: "His walk was bearlike, quick and rather soft, toes
turned inward, as though his shoes were an impediment" (23). He
wryly associates Wilhelm with his Australian sheep dog, Scissors, since
he is such a gentle animal and has such "unusual delicacy about eating or talking" (47). Unlike Jack London or Frank Norris, Bellow
does not view Wilhelm in animal terms to repel us with his essential
rapacity or stolidity. For the most part, he endears Wilhelm to us by
pointing up his fleeting resemblances to those droll, less formidable
animals which are, by an inventive stretch of the imagination, like him
in size and behavior. For a moment he capitalizes on the comic incongruity of such ostensibly preposterous yet amazingly plausible affinities.

Bellow also casts an antic eye upon what most differentiates Wilhelm from animals—his hyperactive emotions. In particular, he judges
him guilty of the same crime he has accused the Jewish imagination
of committing: "over-humanizing everything . . . making too much
of a case for us, for mankind. . . ."[13] In this respect Wilhelm is like
Isaac Bashevis Singer's Gimpel the Fool, who always manages to find
some excuse for evildoers so he can exonerate them and live amicably
in their midst. If an excuse is not available, he readily blames himself. Similarly Wilhelm refuses "to believe anything very bad about
Venice" (24), the fraudulent talent scout, even after he has been in-
dicted for pandering. Although he suffered from his association with
him, he still thinks of writing to Venice in prison "to say how sorry
he was" (24). He musters up equal compassion for one of his dad's
despicable friends, Mr. Perls, simply because the old man had "grief
with his teeth" (31) and an uncommon number of wrinkles. Wilhelm
is still ridden with guilt for causing Olive, his Catholic girlfriend, to
be late for mass, even though she had agreed to spend the night with
him and had overslept. But above all Wilhelm's hyperactive emotions

13. Saul Bellow, "Introduction," *Great Jewish Short Stories,* ed. Saul Bellow (New
York: Dell Publishing Co., 1963), p. 10.

get him "in dutch" (56). Because his feelings have been hurt, he voluntarily gives up a respectable job in exchange for the humiliating position of a vagrant. Because he is so concerned about the welfare of his sons, he permits his wife to make him destitute when he knows that "no court would have awarded her the amounts he paid" (29). Because he genuinely loves his father, he tries to establish rapport with him, even though it means resorting to abnormal means to do so—choking himself in his presence and begging for pity. And when he fails to receive any paternal support, the emotionally dependent Wilhelm far too eagerly places himself in the hands of Dr. Tamkin, a father substitute whom, ironically enough, he ends up supporting.

Bellow does not regard Wilhelm's excessive emotionality as entirely without cause. He is clearly the individual under great stress, much like the character whom Bellow has found existing in many contemporary novels. "Labouring to maintain himself, or perhaps an idea of himself (not always a clear idea), he feels the pressure of a vast public life which may dwarf him as an individual while permitting him to be a giant in hatred or fantasy. In these circumstances he grieves, he complains, rages or laughs." [14] So, too, Wilhelm, lost in the technological maze of the city—"the end of the world, with its complexity and machinery, bricks and tubes, wires and stones, holes and heights" (83)—has been forced to be "a giant in fantasy." At the age of twenty he had sought to transform himself into the most glowing star of the Hollywood galaxy simply by changing his name from the restrictively Jewish "Wilhelm Adler" to the liberatingly Christian "Tommy Wilhelm." As Donald Markos has noted, "Wilhelm's change of name . . . was like Gatsby's 'platonic conception of himself,' an attempt to transcend the limitations of ordinary reality." [15] As it turns out, his fancy moniker makes him more limited than ever. Not only has he failed to become the screen luminary, but he has even suffered an eclipse as a toy salesman and has been devastated as a penny ante speculator. Thus the new name which Wilhelm thought would allow him to project a more winning self has not freed him of his old undesirable identity. If anything, this presentation self has been what Bellow terms

[14.] Bellow, "Some Notes on Recent American Fiction," p. 23.
[15.] Donald Markos, "The Humanism of Saul Bellow" (Ph.D. diss., University of Illinois, 1966), p. 80.

"a painted millstone," a "burden which [the civilized individual] . . . believes gives him distinction," [16] when in reality it imposes the added strain of keeping up appearances. Understandably, then, Tommy Wilhelm speaks of being oppressed by "the peculiar burden of his existence which lay upon him like an accretion, a load, a hump" (39). So he justifiably "grieves" and "complains." But like the foolishly "heart-flooded" Herzog, Wilhelm sometimes cries merely to hear the sound of his own tortured voice, or like the exhibitionist Henderson, he offers his lachrymose performances at the slightest encouragement. Until the present time he has not bothered to ascertain what this "mysterious weight, this growth or collection of nameless things" (39) is that he is carrying, or why it is his lot to carry it. Although he claims to be "a visionary sort of animal who has to believe that he can know why he exists . . . he has never seriously tried to find out why" (39). But on this crucial day when he is to lose his entire fortune, he is also to gain a more valuable fortune—the answer to why he exists. As he spends this twenty-four-hour period smarting from his father's rebuffs, wincing from his wife's tirades, and reeling from his beatings on the market, he has faint intuitions of the healing insights which will later revitalize him. In the past, for example, when Wilhelm talked about his problems, he only "made himself feel worse, he became congested with them and worked himself into a clutch" (43). Now, from a "deeper source" within himself, he knows that if he "didn't keep his troubles before him he risked losing them altogether, and he knew by experience that this was worse" (43). He is like Sammy, the caricature of the borscht belt Jew in Edward Wallant's *The Children at the Gate,* who claims, "I'd be afraid *not* to suffer. . . . Because, you know, it's the worst, worst feeling I ever have. It's so *lonely* not to suffer, so *lonely*." [17] Similarly, Wilhelm vaguely realizes that by not acknowledging his troubles, he would be deprived of what defines him as a human being, what makes him feel most alive, and what establishes a bond with other tormented men. Moreover, instead of berating himself for succumbing to grief,

16. "Saul Bellow on the Modern Novel," radio lecture, July, 1961, quoted in John J. Clayton, *Saul Bellow: In Defense of Man* (Bloomington: Indiana University Press, 1968), p. 95.

17. Edward Wallant, *The Children at the Gate* (New York: Popular Library, 1964), pp. 96–97.

. . . he received a suggestion from some remote element in his thoughts that the business of life, the real business—to carry his peculiar burden, to feel shame and impotence, to taste these quelled tears —the only important business, the highest business was being done. Maybe the making of mistakes expressed the very purpose of his life and the essence of his being here (56).

Wilhelm is beginning to grasp the view that genuine suffering is an achievement, since it cultivates understanding and compassion. It is therefore the mark of the chosen rather than of the rejected. Along with such promptings, Wilhelm recalls snatches of English poetry whose full significance he is yet to comprehend. In the morning "involuntary memory brought him this line" (12) from Shakespeare's seventy-third sonnet: ". . . love that well which thou must leave ere long" (12). This exhortation to appreciate his life because the end is imminent immediately suggests to Wilhelm Milton's "Lycidas" and the kind of end he might experience, "Sunk though he be beneath the wat'ry floor" (13). Throughout the day echoes of the elegy recur to him as he becomes more and more submerged by "the waters of the earth" (77) and his own mounting tears. Finally, while Tamkin is expatiating on the worth of living in the carefree present, Wilhelm is not listening to him but is remembering the lines from Keats's "Endymion" which intimate a more exalted kind of existence: "Come then, Sorrow!/ . . . I thought to leave thee,/ And deceive thee,/ But now of all the world I love thee best" (90).

Wilhelm's attention is rapidly diverted from such reflections by the mesmerizing operations of the exchange, whose machinery "hummed and whirred like mechanical birds" (105). But when he is closed out by an "electronic bookkeeping device" (104) and no more mechanical birds hum for him, Wilhelm comes to hear a different kind of music. Frantically searching for the culprit Dr. Tamkin, he thinks he sees him in a crowd entering a Jewish funeral parlor. Tamkin is not there, but Wilhelm is swept "forward by the pressure of the crowd" (116) and involuntarily becomes one of the mourners. When his turn comes to view the deceased, he cannot move on. He is struck by the appearance of the dead man "with his formal shirt and his tie and silk lapels and his powdered skin [which] looked so proper" (117). But he is soon overwhelmed with grief by what existed beneath the surface. On one level, Wilhelm is the object of laughter for sobbing uncontrollably before the corpse of a stranger. Yet there is a more subtle humor operative through which we come to know Wilhelm and discover his nobility. Bellow points up the comic incongruity of the disheveled, anguished Wilhelm stationed before the impeccable corpse beyond all anguish and surrounded by the other mourners, who with their staid bearing and vapid condolences are half-dead already. Only the quirky Wilhelm, whose body is convulsed, head bent, shoulders bowed, face twisted, and hands crippled, is truly alive and capable of change. Only for him can the "man's corpse [represent] the death of this false soul and the possibility of new life, liberated from this soul." [18] "The heavy sea-like music" (118) which inundates him sounds the death knell of the inauthentic "Tommy Wilhelm." But his authentic soul, "the one by which his old grandfather had called him—Velvel" (72), does not die. As Milton says of Lycidas, "Sunk though he be beneath the wat'ry floor," he still "mounted high"; so Bellow seems to imply that the Velvel who survives the flood can go on living. Although Velvel will not be "mounted high," but will remain an "imperfect and disfigured" (84) human being whom society will still judge an economic failure, he has learned he must "love that well which [he] must leave ere long" (12), including the "sweetest sorrow" (89), which is not only an ineluctable, but also a meaningful part of life.[19]

Wilhelm does not arrive at his anagnorisis through the employment of his intellect. His hidden depths unknown even to himself are responsible for effecting "the consummation of his heart's ultimate need" (118). This is not to say that Wilhelm never exercises his mental powers. He may not be as intelligent as the other Bellow protagonists; yet, as he says in his own defense, "You don't have to think I'm a dummy, though. I have ideas, too" (72). In his own simpleminded fashion Tommy Wilhelm is able to discern and express what is ludicrous in the human situation. For one thing, he is appalled by the renovated Tower of Babel, the absurd monstrosity which looms in every metropolis and especially in New York City. In the midst

---

18. Clayton, *Saul Bellow*, p. 133.

19. Keith Opdahl's discussion of the significance of the lines from Keats's "Endymion," Shakespeare's seventy-third sonnet, and Milton's "Lycidas" contributed to my understanding of the novel's conclusion. See *The Novels of Saul Bellow: An Introduction* (University Park: Pennsylvania State University Press, 1967), p. 117.

of this verbal chaos he sees all kinds of oddities; the crazy are indistinguishable from the sane, "the wise from the fools, the young from the old or the sick from the well. The fathers [are] no fathers and the sons no sons" (84). Above all, Wilhelm finds that men are so engrossed in their own affairs that they do not wish to communicate with their neighbors. To safeguard their privacy they purposely construct their own elaborate systems of abtruse thought and formulate their own esoteric language to express this thought. It is therefore almost impossible for an individual wishing to escape loneliness to make himself understood in the city where "every other man spoke a language entirely his own, which he had figured out by private thinking" (83). To prove his point Wilhelm humorously exaggerates the difficulties involved in communication in the modern city:

> If you wanted to talk about a glass of water, you had to start back with God creating the heavens and the earth; the apple; Abraham; Moses and Jesus; Rome; the Middle Ages; gunpowder; the Revolution; back to Newton, up to Einstein; then war and Lenin and Hitler. After reviewing this, and getting it all straight again you could proceed to talk about a glass of water. . . . And this happened over and over with everyone you met. You had to translate and translate, explain and explain, back and forth, and it was the punishment of hell itself not to understand or to be understood . . . (83–84).

Because of such insuperable language barriers, Wilhelm concludes, "You had to talk to yourself in the daytime and reason with yourself at night. Who else was there to talk to in a city like New York?" (84).

Along with commenting on the city-dwellers' unwillingness to communicate with one another, Wilhelm indicts these same people for their dissatisfaction and hence their cynicism. "Cynicism was bread and meat to everyone" (16). He also condemns them for their avarice: "Uch! How they love money. . . . They adore money! Holy money! Beautiful money! It was getting so that people were feeble-minded about everything else except money" (36). Wilhelm finds it even more absurd that society judges an individual's worth by his money-making capacities. If he has not accrued a fortune overnight, he is automatically considered "a dummy [who] had to excuse himself from the face of the earth" (36). If creditors are hounding him, he does not have even the refuge of debtor's prison. A subtler torture has been devised—he must work himself to death.

Admittedly, Wilhelm's findings are not very original, nor does he examine them in any depth. But because he is the one ensnared by the world's business and not a disentangled spectator, he does succeed in pinpointing some of the maddening aspects of twentieth-century life and getting at the source of his personal malaise. Other than that, perhaps the venting of anger and frustration, without benefit of much witty concealment, is all we can expect from such an encumbered and untrained comedian of ideas.

Bellow, not wishing to disappoint us, introduces a more or less trained comedian of ideas, Dr. Tamkin, who is so unencumbered that he flits from role to role before offering his assessment of contemporary humanity. He is, first of all, an accomplished portrayer of the stock Jewish character, the *schnorrer* or professional beggar. Rather than humbly soliciting alms like an ordinary beggar, Dr. Tamkin makes it appear that he is doing Wilhelm a favor by supervising his funds. Unlike the obsequious beggar who demeans himself, Dr. Tamkin, amply endowed with arrogance and vanity, represents himself as most qualified to invest Wilhelm's last seven hundred dollars. He assures his patron that other men foolishly gamble away their money, whereas he, "a keen mental scientist" (61), has made a careful study of the market and will surely make a profit from it. In addition to the *schnorrer*'s vanity, Tamkin has his *chutzpah,* his unmitigated gall. For once Tamkin has tentatively won Wilhelm's confidence, he has no compunction about asking him to contribute most of the money for what was supposed to be a joint venture. And most importunate of all, Tamkin insists that he be given power of attorney over all of Wilhelm's assets. It takes more than duplicity and *chutzpah* for the *schnorrer* to accomplish his devious aim, however. In the Eastern European ghetto it was necessary for the *schnorrer* to be very learned in the Torah, for Torah scholarship not only made the *schnorrer* more persuasive; it also served to divert the philanthropic sheep while it was being fleeced. Moreover, "it often required the superficial glitter and respectability of the *schnorrer's* Torah-learning to make a kind-hearted Jew, steeped in the bookish traditions of his people, feel that it was a privilege to be mulcted." [20] So Tamkin, the latter-day *schnorrer,* talks "about the deeper things of life" (69) not only to impress Wilhelm with his profundity, but also to distract him from the fact

[20] Ausubel, "Introduction: *Schnorrers* and Beggars," p. 268.

that he is being bilked of all his money. To be sure, Wilhelm is a "sucker" (69) for such profundity; yet, unlike the kind-hearted Jew of the ghetto, Wilhelm does not consider it a privilege to be defrauded by the *schnorrer*. But if he must be defrauded, Wilhelm certainly prefers that the fraud be a man who "spoke a kind of truth and did some people a sort of good" (63).

Whereas Tamkin authentically portrays the *schnorrer*, he presents a ludicrous imitation of the Jewish *zaddik* or saint-mystic. The original *zaddik* of the seventeenth-century Eastern European ghetto was considered the holy man and redeemer by the Hasidim, the popular sect of pious though illiterate Jews. According to Martin Buber, he was the man who they believed "would lift them onto [his] strong shoulders . . . give certainty to [their] bewildered soul[s], order and form to an existence which had become chaotic, and would, above all, enable them again both to believe and to live." [21] The *zaddik* strived to conform to the lofty opinion the Hasidim had of him. Divesting himself of conceit, he humbly went forth to heal and save the people even before they approached him for help. Regarding the "spoken word [as] one of the keys which could unlock the treasure-house of the human spirit," [22] the *zaddik* tried to alleviate the fears and suffering of his charges through the use of commonplace analogies, simple parables, and mild censure. In *Seize the Day* Tommy Wilhelm resembles the misery-laden, simple Hasid who placed all of his confidence in the miracle-working *zaddik*. Wilhelm actually believes he has left the ground and is riding on Tamkin's back. "It was for Tamkin to take the steps" (96). And Tamkin, if one believes what he says about himself, is a contemporary *zaddik*. Like the *zaddik* who had dedicated his life to helping anyone who needed his services, Tamkin professes to help any people in distress. Like the selfless *zaddik*, Tamkin claims to have subordinated all personal desires to pursue his divine calling as a healer: "I would like to escape from the sicknesses of others, but I can't. I am only on loan to myself, so to speak. I belong to humanity" (95). Moreover, like the *zaddik*, Tamkin often takes the initiative to seek out individuals with problems even before they gather the strength to contact him. And once he has ascertained the precise nature of their problems, like the *zaddik*, he attempts to cure them

[21.] Martin Buber, *Hasidism* (New York: Philosophical Library, 1948), p. 19.
[22.] Samuel H. Dresner, *The Zaddik* (New York: Abelard-Schuman, 1960), p. 189.

with his own peculiar kind of parables and analogies. Finally, like the *zaddik* for whom virtue is its own reward, Tamkin insists he is only interested in the "spiritual compensation" (66). He altruistically maintains, "I am at my most efficient when I don't need the fee. When I only love. Without a financial reward" (66).

Never let it be said that Tamkin's acting is confined to the parochial characterizations of the *schnorrer* and the *zaddik*. He is equally convincing in the secular role of the diabolic confidence man whose physical characteristics immediately suggest that he may be the devil in disguise: his shoulders have "two pagoda-like points"; he stands "pigeon-toed"; his eyes have "a hypnotic power" (62) and his smile is "wizardlike . . . secret, potent" (64). Tamkin also dresses the part of the flashy confidence man. Wearing his gray straw hat with its wide cocoa-colored band, his velvet shirt from Clydes and his painted necktie, he seeks to bedazzle Wilhelm with his affluence and good taste. Even more important, Tamkin, like any deft confidence man, makes a special effort to impress Wilhelm with his many achievements. He subtly advertises his ingenious inventions, his astronomical earnings on the stock market, his occupational versatility, and his cosmopolitan intrigues. Moreover, like any self-respecting confidence man who regards himself as the intellectual among thieves, he conspicuously displays his knowledge to convince Wilhelm that he has "read the best of literature, science and philosophy" (72). Yet Tamkin's parading of his worth is not alone effective in winning Wilhelm's complete trust. He must first flatter him if he is to succeed in duping him. He thus glowingly refers to Wilhelm as "a profound personality with very profound creative capacities" (72). Unable to resist such lavish praise, Wilhelm soon consents to being Tamkin's mark.

While Tamkin is a believable confidence man, he is, according to Daniel Weiss, a "representation of the psychoanalyst as a figure of fun, whom even the patient can think of as being part faker."[23] Indeed, Dr. Tamkin's professional competence is comically suspect, for he himself appears to be in dire need of treatment. Not only does "fear stare from his eyes" (96), but he also admits to feeling "so worked up and tormented and restless" (9) just because other men

---

23. Daniel Weiss, "Caliban on Prospero: A Psychoanalytic Study of the Novel *Seize the Day*, by Saul Bellow," in *Psychoanalysis and American Fiction*, ed. Irving Malin (New York: E. P. Dutton & Co., 1965), p. 307.

are making fortunes on the stock market. So disturbed is he that he cannot bathe regularly or write legibly when signing checks. All he can do is comment on the madness of everyone around him, especially the psychoses of successful businessmen. And even when Dr. Tamkin is supposedly in control of himself, his psychoanalytic procedures are still zany. He freely discusses his own past traumas with his patients. He readily violates medical ethics by divulging one patient's confidences to another, adding his own lurid details whenever the original version is not sensational enough. Claiming to be "a radical in the profession" (66), he has no reservations about treating his own friends just as long as he can be beneficial to them. He had even tried to heal his own suicidal wife, but unfortunately she drowned herself before his therapy could take effect. At the present time Dr. Tamkin conducts his sessions at the oddest times and in the oddest places. Before eight o'clock in the morning he consults with one patient on the phone. In the middle of the afternoon he provides an unsolicited analysis of Tommy Wilhelm in a Broadway cafeteria over "pot roast" and "purple cabbage." Later in the day he instructs him in " 'here-and-now' mental exercises" (89) at a stockbroker's office. In the middle of the night he teaches a young man Greek to prevent him from "howling from his window like a wolf" (67). With such carrying on, it is no wonder that Tommy Wilhelm regards Dr. Tamkin as "a puffed-up little bogus and humbug with smelly feet" (95–96).

Yet Wilhelm has to admit that Dr. Tamkin, for all his charlatanry, is a kind of sage who "understands so well what gives" (99) and thus "spoke of things that mattered" (82). This is not to say that Dr. Tamkin is beyond ridicule in such a capacity. He is anything but an original and systematic thinker. At best, he is, as Richard Chase describes him, "an adept in the wildly eclectic world of semi-enlightenment and semi-literacy which constitutes the modern mass mind when it expresses itself in ideas, the crazy world of half knowledge . . . popularized science, and occultism, the rags and tatters of the world's great intellectual and religious heritages." [24] Yet within these "rags and tatters" Dr. Tamkin's comedy of ideas is still worth salvaging. He provides, for instance, a very sound explanation for the existence of the "human tragedy-comedy" (72), which also serves to illuminate

24. Richard Chase, "The Adventures of Saul Bellow: Progress of a Novelist," *Commentary* 27 (April, 1959): 326.

Wilhelm's plight. According to his view, man possesses two principal souls, the real soul and the pretender soul, which are constantly at odds with one another. The pretender soul, whose aim is to please society, saps the true soul of its vital strength. The true soul, in turn, grows tired of playing the host and schemes to exterminate the parasitic pretender soul. Tamkin therefore concludes that man spends his time committing suicide in one way or another, or, when he is not destroying himself, is intent on killing others. Yet the good doctor insists that man does not have to engage in or be subject to such predatory activities. Nor does he have to "marry suffering," or if he goes "with joy" think he is committing "adultery" (98). All he has to do to transform his life from a tragedy to a comedy, according to Tamkin's facile instructions, is to forget the failure-ridden past, ignore the anxiety-filled future, and luxuriate in the "eternal present . . . — colossal, bright and beautiful . . ." (89). Clearly Tamkin's *carpe diem* philosophy is but a "cheapened version of Augie March's belief that one can be regenerated at any time by returning to the 'axial lines' of one's true being." [25] But this does not mean that Bellow rejects the worth of such regeneration or thinks that it is impossible to bring about through a heightened awareness of the present. Because Bellow does wholeheartedly subscribe to such a view and does not want to be accused of sentimentality, he relies on the comic irony of having Tamkin bastardize his legitimate thoughts. Yet the fact remains that Tamkin's advice is essentially correct. Wilhelm must seize the day. And although he must do so by plumbing greater depths than Tamkin can ever fathom, Wilhelm is still prodded in the right direction. Thus Tamkin, as the chief articulator of the novella's comedy of ideas, is more than just a "confuser of the imagination" (93); he is an expander of the imagination as well.

Although Dr. Tamkin disturbs and diverts Wilhelm the most, he is not the only vexingly funny character who crosses Wilhelm's path. In the past there had been Maurice Venice, the phony talent scout who had lured Wilhelm from college with the glittering bait of instant stardom. As it turned out, Venice was but a grotesque double of Wilhelm. More ludicrously cumbersome than Wilhelm, Venice was "huge and oxlike, so stout that his arms seemed caught from beneath in a grip of flesh and fat" (17). His body also frequently

25. Markos, "The Humanism of Saul Bellow," p. 86.

shattered his ridiculously affected conception of himself. He could not be a polished speaker because the "fat in his throat (17) made his voice difficult and husky. He could not be a suave dresser because "his trousers hugged his [fat] ankles" (17). Yet, like Wilhelm, Venice struggled to maintain his facade by either nervously bragging about his former success, or by apologizing profusely for his temporary lack of success. Despite his elaborate pretense, it was readily apparent that Venice, like Wilhelm, was an accomplished *schlemiel* who had bungled all opportunities until he had become "the obscure failure of an aggressive and powerful clan" (20).

Wilhelm encounters laughable characters in the present as well. There are such foolishly vain men as the near-blind newsstand attendant who, though hidden behind his counter, insists on wearing a "rich brown suit" and a "Countess Mara painted necktie" (5), and the stock office manager who, though unshaven, affectedly carries a pair of opera glasses for reading the board. Accustomed to the arbitrary and esoteric rules of the financial game, these two dandies, fancying they "knew and knew and knew" (60), look askance at anyone who is not equally informed. The older people are just as ridiculous. Perls and Rappaport are "money-driven crones, selfish and diseased, Dickensian caricatures who live for nothing but the latest stock quotations." [26]

Dr. Adler, Wilhelm's father, has many of the same comic flaws. Although he will soon be eighty years old, he is still as foppish as the best of them. Treating his body to massages, cultivating a pleasing low voice, and purchasing his clothes in a college shop, he tries "with all his might" (38) to be the dapper senior citizen. Formerly one of New York's finest diagnosticians, he still expects admiration from the hotel's less distinguished residents. To safeguard his position of eminence, he is quick to conceal any information which might discredit him. He mendaciously claims that his son is a sales executive whose income is "up in the five figures somewhere," even though he never had "the patience to finish school" (13). False boasting, however, is about all Dr. Adler will do for his son. It is a tragicomic truth that the old man is so absorbed with preserving his decrepit self that he cannot be appreciably bothered by Wilhelm's problems, except for treating him as if he were his patient—prescribing hydrotherapy and

26. Howe, "Introduction to *Seize the Day*," p. 464.

reduction in drug consumption. Dr. Adler is a confirmed sadist who incurs Bellow's unsympathetic laughter. Gleeful that he has reversed the Plautine comic situation "in which *juvenis* outwits and conquers *senex*," [27] Dr. Adler delights in injuring Wilhelm by contrasting his own spotlessly clean, orderly ways with his son's filthy, untidy habits. He dwells upon his own successes, knowing full well that such talk will exacerbate Wilhelm's feelings of inferiority. He relishes censuring Wilhelm for his economic and marital failures and even insinuates that Wilhelm lost his job because of a scandal with a man. Dr. Adler's treatment of Wilhelm forms "an ironic parallel to the story of the prodigal son." [28] In contrast to the biblical father who welcomed his son with joy and forgiveness, Dr. Adler greets Wilhelm with reproach and demands that he vanish.

Seize the Day not only contains an odd assortment of comic characters; it also has its own peculiar kind of comic language. Since Tommy Wilhelm hasn't read a book in over twenty years and associates with people whose only concern is the rise and fall of the dollar, there is not the wealth of learned references which enriches the verbal humor of *The Adventures of Augie March*. To be sure, Bellow employs certain grand allusions to accentuate how comically ignoble the world of *Seize the Day* is. The Hotel Gloriana, essentially a shabby old folks' home located in New York City's congested Upper West Side, could not, for example, be conceived of as an idyllic Spenserian fairyland. Tommy Wilhelm, the disabled survivor of life's assaults and his own self-inflicted wounds, would never be mentioned in the same breath with such triumphant men as Garcia, Edward VII, and Cyrus the Great. Mr. Rappaport, the miserly octogenarian who had once been a small-time chicken slaughterer, would never be compared to the greatest magnate and philanthropist of them all, John D. Rockefeller. Yet Bellow does make these outlandish comparisons for the sake of a rueful chuckle and a minor relief from the gloom.

Other aspects of Bellow's comic style are more prominent in *Seize the Day* than the use of mock-heroic allusions. There is the same comic profusion of language which exists in *The Adventures of Augie March*. But Wilhelm talks too much for different reasons. Because he is powerless to check the harassment of those around him, he, like

---

27. Weiss, "Caliban on Prospero," p. 280.
28. Markos, "The Humanism of Saul Bellow," p. 85.

his Eastern European ancestors, is compelled to become a man of
words rather than of actions. He punishes himself for his vulnerability
by confessing to strangers and intimates alike all the shameful particulars of his present condition. Such prolix confessionals are generally
followed by equally prolix reprimands for his lack of verbal restraint.
Especially after he tries to communicate his difficulties to his father
and ends up "trading insults" (55) with the old man, he indulges in
an orgy of self-recrimination.

Not only is Tommy Wilhelm a man of many words; he is a man of
different kinds of words as well. The combination of the many varieties of language also makes for the verbal comedy in Seize the Day.
When Wilhelm is particularly distraught, he, like Sholom Aleichem's
Tevyeh the dairyman, has a heart-to-heart talk with God. Only Wilhelm's address is not in the form of "an edifying rabbinic discourse"
which is comically "impudent and sophisticated." [29] Expressing himself
in slang, Wilhelm straightforwardly acknowledges his fallibility and
humbly appeals to God for help: "Let me out of this clutch and into a
different life. For I am all balled up" (26). When Wilhelm is walking
in an underground corridor and feels a sudden overpowering love
for humanity, he bursts out in a rhapsodic hymn of praise for all the
"imperfect and lurid-looking" (84) people. He is soon embarrassed
by his sentimental remarks and attempts to minimize his "onrush of
loving kindness" (85) by describing it in what Keith Opdahl calls the
pseudo-mystical language of "concert hall spiritualists." [30] Wilhelm
tells himself that the experience is "the right clue and may do me the
most good. Something very big. Truth, like" (85). Not content with
this debasement, Wilhelm further discredits his effusive statements by
crudely terming the experience "only another one of those subway
things. Like having a hard-on at random" (85). When commenting on
the corrupt economic system, Wilhelm becomes so outraged that he
utters a string of epithets: "Chicken! Unclean! Congestion! . . . Rat
race! Phony! Murder! Play the Game! Buggers!" (17).

Wilhelm is not the only creator of rhetorical fun. There are other
verbal pranksters as well. Maurice Venice delivers his ungrammatical,
Yiddish-accented sales pitch with its movie magazine clichés, its side-

29. Irving Kristol, "Is Jewish Humor Dead?" in Mid-Century, ed. Harold U. Ribalow
(New York: Beechhurst Press, 1955), p. 433.
30. Opdahl, The Novels of Saul Bellow, p. 114.

walk indecencies, and its mimicked dialogue of starlets he has known. Dr. Adler, parsimonious with his affections and his money, is equally stingy with words. Yet he, too, contributes his comically euphemistic language, his jejune health lectures, his wicked innuendoes, and his harsh curses. Mr. Rappaport, the only successful speculator around, gratuitously offers his verbose reminiscences of his brief encounter with Teddy Roosevelt, yet is humorously curt when answering questions about the stock market.

These characters are mere amateurs at verbal play compared to *Seize the Day*'s professional comedian of language, Dr. Tamkin. One of his routines is best described by Bellow himself in an address he delivered to the International P. E. N. Congress: "Americans take great pleasure in the comedy of terms. We pay psychologists to penetrate our characters and redescribe them to us scientifically, rationalizing consciousness on the verbal level at least. We are delighted to hear that we are introverted, fixated, repressed here or there, attached to our mothers thus and so." [31]

So, too, Dr. Tamkin has an ample supply of risibly well-worn psychological terms which he freely dispenses. Just as Nabokov includes headmistress Pratt's fatuous analysis of Lolita's emotional development to belittle psychiatrists and their dim-witted view of the world, Bellow has Tamkin "redescribe" Wilhelm to disparage the inane, mechanical phrases of the trade. For example, Dr. Tamkin tells Wilhelm that he has an "obsessional look on [his] face" (57) and "lots of guilt" (73) in him because of the "elemental conflict of parent and child" (61). If Wilhelm would only free himself of "morbid guilt feelings and follow [his] instincts" (97), Dr. Tamkin is confident he would enjoy "spontaneous emotions, open receptors and free impulses" (96). Whereas Miss Pratt's understanding of Lolita is flagrantly inaccurate, there is some truth to Dr. Tamkin's diagnosis of Wilhelm, but his ossified expressions humorously obstruct this truth. Perhaps even more ridiculous is Dr. Tamkin's use of psychological jargon in his discussion of the stock market. He speaks about the investor taking "a specimen risk so that [he can] feel the process, the money-flow, the whole complex" (61). Or he claims that "lard will

[31.] Saul Bellow, Keynote Address before the Inaugural Session of the XXXIV International Congress of Poets, Playwrights, Essayists, Editors, and Novelists, June 13, 1966, at New York University.

go up" because he has "made a study of the guilt-aggression cycle which is behind it" (64). The incongruous application of such inappropriate terminology serves to mock both business and psychology.

Dr. Tamkin is also skilled in creating ludicrous imitations of thought-provoking works. His theory of why men play the stock market is, according to Ihab Hassan, "once again the Freudian equation of money and death, success and aggression."[32] Tamkin glibly yet correctly asserts, "*M*oney and *M*urder both begin with *M*. . . . Money-making is aggression. . . . People come to the market to kill. They say, 'I'm going to make a killing.' . . . Only they haven't got the genuine courage to kill and they erect a symbol of it. The money. They make a killing by a fantasy" (69).

Similarly, Tamkin's "here-and-now" exercises stressing deliberate concentration on present physical objects seem to be a parody of exercises in gestalt perception which Frederick Perls, Ralph Hefferline, and Paul Goodman have described in their book *Gestalt Therapy*. Claiming that such exercises are "directed at helping you to heighten your feeling of what is actual," the authors recommend: "Try for a few minutes to make up sentences stating what you are at this moment aware of. Begin each sentence with the words 'now' or 'at this moment' or 'here and now.' "[33]

Tamkin fancies himself a poet as well, but his opus "Mechanism vs Functionalism, Ism vs Hism" is a travesty of a transcendental poem. Tamkin has taken a fairly obvious transcendental idea—the necessity for man to realize his worth—and made it seem more profound by dressing it up in clumsy poetic trappings. As one would expect from such a semi-literate, he uses incorrect archaic pronouns and verb forms, awkward syntax, strained rhyme schemes, stilted personified abstractions, facile poetic catalogues, and pompous biblical diction. These poetic violations evoke laughter in their own right; yet they appear even more absurd when compared to the flawless lines from Shakespeare, Milton, and Keats which Bellow has artfully interspersed

[32]. Ihab H. Hassan, *Radical Innocence: Studies in the Contemporary American Novel* (Princeton: Princeton University Press, 1961), p. 315.

[33]. Frederick Perls, Ralph Hefferline, and Paul Goodman, *Gestalt Therapy* (New York: Dell Publishing Co., 1951), pp. 30–31. I am indebted to Donald Markos for suggesting the similarities between Tamkin's "here and now" exercises and the exercises in Gestalt perception. See "The Humanism of Saul Bellow," p. 87.

throughout the novella, lines which are a true guide to the perplexed, unlike Tamkin's spurious source of inspiration.

In addition to the comic juxtaposition of many kinds of discourse, *Seize the Day* contains the humor of verbal retrieval which appears in *The Adventures of Augie March*. There is a difference in expression, due partly to the different life experiences of the two protagonists. As Tony Tanner observes, "Augie saw his life as a series of mistakes, but his mistakes did not catch up with him. Wilhelm's life is also a sequence of errors: but every one serves to limit his freedom, curtail his choices, corner him. . . ." [34] Wilhelm is accordingly driven to employ a more extreme form of verbal exaggeration to rout his melancholy. To endure his victimization by a predatory society, he makes such mordantly comic accusations as, "The money! When I had it, I flowed money. They bled it away from me. I hemorrhaged money" (40). Like Herzog, who claims to have writhed under Madeleine's "sharp elegant heel," Wilhelm histrionically demonstrates a similar persecution. "Like this they ride on me with hoofs and claws. Tear me to pieces, stamp on me and break my bones" (105). He makes light of the difficulty he has in obtaining compassion from his father by hyperbolically claiming that "he had to undergo an inquisition to prove himself worthy of a sympathetic word" (52). He caustically jests about his unenviable position as a badgered husband by overstating his hardship: "The Emancipation Proclamation was only for colored people. A husband like me is a slave, with an iron collar" (49). Admittedly, Wilhelm's verbal retrieval is not especially hilarious. Yet it does serve to drain off his venom and thus make his adversity less painful.

In *The Marriage of Heaven and Hell* Blake said: "Excess of sorrow laughs. Excess of joy weeps." For the greater part of his life Tommy Wilhelm has had an excess of sorrows. He has therefore devised the funny and unfunny lines to keep himself laughing. He has also made himself the butt of inordinately practical jokers. But by the end of the novella, when he sinks "deeper than sorrow" (118), he no longer has to amuse himself with his own forced humor or bear the cruel humor of others. Having confronted the death of a stranger and in the process accepted his eventual mortality and present fallibility, he experiences a great sense of release amounting to joy. This joy does

---

[34.] Tony Tanner, *Saul Bellow* (Edinburgh: Oliver & Boyd, 1965), pp. 58–59.

not approach the euphoria of *Augie March,* since Wilhelm does not have hopes of discovering a new uncorrupted world and being the trailblazer in it. Yet it is far removed from the despair of *Dangling Man* and *The Victim,* since Wilhelm does not think the world is utterly uninhabitable and attempt to retreat from its noxious presence. Even though he is the "part of humanity . . . that did not get away with it,"[35] he does not renounce himself or humanity. He is able to embrace both in "the great and happy oblivion of tears" (118) and even envision being part of a "larger body" from which he cannot be separated. And this, Bellow implies, is a sizable affirmation for one of life's vanquished.

[35.] Saul Bellow, *The Victim* (New York: Vanguard, 1947), p. 20.

The Narcissus Intoxicated Mad Laugher

6

Henderson the Rain King[1] is Bellow's tale of an Oblomov[2] who gets up from bed and comes crashing through the world to try "to burst [his] spirit's sleep" (76). Not content to remain buried in himself, Henderson is eager to awaken to a nonsolipsistic reality. But he first wants to make sure that such a reality is habitable. Just as Augie is on a pilgrimage to relocate the axial lines of "truth, love, peace, bounty, usefulness [and] harmony" whose embrace will remove man's "dread of fast change and short life" (454–455), Henderson embarks upon a safari to hunt for life's noble ideals and incorporate them into his own being before death denies him the opportunity to do so. Just as Augie attempts to affirm that there are meaningful stays against dissolution, Henderson endeavors to prove that "chaos doesn't run the whole show, that this is not a sick and hasty ride, helpless, through a dream into oblivion, [that] it can be arrested by a thing or two" (175). While the intent of Augie's and Henderson's quest is the same, the outward form differs. In *The Adventures of Augie March* the gravity of the under-

[1]. Citations from this novel are to *Henderson the Rain King* (New York: Viking Press, 1959).

[2]. In one of the early drafts of *Henderson the Rain King* among the Bellow manuscripts located at Harper Library, University of Chicago, Henderson likens himself to Oblomov. Although Oblomov is never mentioned *per se* in the published version of the novel, Henderson does say, "If I hadn't come to Africa, my only other choice would have been to stay in bed" (188).

taking is seldom minimized, its speculative definition seldom under-mined, and the earnestness of the seeker seldom wavering. To avoid the monotony of an identical search for essentials and to dispel any exces-sive solemnity or sentimentality which might vitiate the search, Bellow places Henderson's mission in the context of a whimsical fantasy. Here it is often treated with sportive irreverence where tipsy ideas in-trude to unbalance sober ones, established truths from previous novels vie with recent travesties, and Henderson himself vacillates between commitment and clowning.

At the start of the novel Henderson shares the attitude which Bellow expressed in the following Alfred Kazin anecdote. "Some time ago, when a Fuller Brush man at his door who had got nowhere with him finally demanded, 'Won't you even take it as a gift?' Bellow is sup-posed to have replied, 'I've been given the gift of life, and it's more than I know what to do with.' " [3] Similarly, Henderson has been given the gift of life, and an exceedingly generous gift it is. Well-born as his first name, Eugene, suggests, he has inherited a sprawling country estate and "three million dollars after taxes" (3), a fortune be-yond Tommy Wilhelm's wildest imaginings. He is the scion of eminent statesmen and scholars, ancestors more illustrious than the orphan Augie March could invent for himself. He is the Gentile who frequents all the exclusive social circles and restricted clubs which Leventhal could never hope to join. He is the celebrated war hero whom Joseph secretly desired to be. Yet with all these endowments, Henderson, like Bellow in the anecdote, admits that he "never knew what to do with life . . ." (312). In over half a century he still has not found any proper function, any satisfying employment of his energies. Judging himself unworthy of his vast legacy and guilt-ridden by his inability to put it to good use, he is one of those "people who feel that they occupy the place that belongs to another by rights" (34). As the self-proclaimed unentitled heir and trespasser, Henderson ini-tially spends most of his time disturbing the peace in his own zany fashion.

The most obvious comic trait of the typical Bellow hero is his affectation, his pretending to be better than he really is. Tommy Wil-helm, for example, is very much the outcast shabby fellow who strains to be the affluent gentleman but cannot achieve his aim. Even though he cultivates the dress and mannerisms of a polished business man, beneath his guise he is still an unkempt ne'er-do-well. Henderson is just the opposite. He already is the affluent gentleman. But since he feels oppressed by his wealth and prestige, he strains to be the outcast shabby fellow, to be worse than he really is. He therefore exhibits an equally comic inverse affectation. Instead of being the tastefully attired man of means, he purposely wears outlandish apparel to be the laughing-stock of a distinguished line. He deliberately seems to apply what Arthur Koestler has observed about the humor of peculiar dress. "Eccentric clothes, including foreign or the fashions of past periods are comic because we regard normal, conventional articles of apparel as functional parts of their wearer, whereas an unusual hat, umbrella or boot disrupts the functional unity, focuses attention on its nonfunctional aspects and thus automatically becomes incongruous, absurd, preposterous." [4] At a casual gathering Henderson appears in a midnight blue tuxedo; at a ladies' tea he parades about in a red velvet dressing gown, sweat socks, and a red hunting cap à la Holden Caulfield; in Africa he cavorts about in his enormous pith helmet, travel-stained jockey shorts and green transparent flowing trousers; and on his return home he is conspicuously arrayed in his "corduroy outfit, burgundy colored and an alpine hat with Bersagliere feathers" (332). A sartorial freak, Henderson thus succeeds in being laughably devoid of "functional unity."

Along with being the worst dressed, he is the worst behaved. Unlike Augie, who fights his malice too much, or Wilhelm, who is too gentle and self-loathing to express his anger fully, Henderson is the violent, sottish Gentile of Leventhal's nightmares. Yet, on closer scrutiny, violence is not an indelible part of his character; instead, it springs from a temporary perverse desire to create a tempest in his aristocratic teapot. Rather than remaining the sedate and refined member of the privileged class, his view of himself as an imposter compels him to act the rowdy commoner. Though he gives full vent to his hooliganism— getting drunk before noon, brawling in country saloons, tongue-lashing his neighbors, and swearing at his wife in public—he so fully and gleefully advertises his outrageous conduct that it appears more mirth-

4. Arthur Koestler, *Insight and Outlook* (New York: The Macmillan Company, 1949), pp. 85–86.

ful than malevolent. Especially when he is forced to be part of a social group, he, like Joseph and Leventhal, becomes inimical and strikes out. The only difference is that Henderson's hostile acts are so impious that they resemble the pranks of a bad boy. As he admits about himself, "Society is what beats me. Alone I can be pretty good, but let me go among people and there's the devil to pay" (49). "There's the devil to pay" when Henderson plays Goliath at a posh southern resort (using his children's slingshot to smash bottles on the beach to infuriate the other guests), or when he persists in alienating his wife's snobbish friends with his highly calculated boorishness. Not even his own Hemingwayesque buddy, Charley Albert, is spared his uncouth ways. As best man at Charley's wedding, he not only neglects to kiss the bride, but at the dinner insists that the Parmesan cheese tastes like Rinso, spits it out on the tablecloth, and even blows his nose in his foulard.

But these are minor breaches of etiquette compared to Henderson's major transgression—the defilement of the family's cultural values. A comic inversion of the economically unencumbered Jamesian hero who develops intellectually and aesthetically, Henderson wears "gold ear-rings to provoke fights" (23) at a renowned Ivy League university and gets drunk in "every one of the great cathedrals" (16) of Europe. The greatest insult to the memory of his venerable forebears is his conver-son of the noble ancestral estate to an ignoble pig haven. The only explanation Henderson offers for such a desecration is his fiendish whim to vex Nicky Goldstein, a Jewish army cohort, who after the war said he was going to raise minks in the Catskills. Another explana-tion might be Bellow's irresistible desire to include a self-ridiculing Jewish joke—to spoof the popular ethnic taboo and status symbol in his only novel that is conspicuously a-Semitic. In any case, no matter how ridiculous Henderson's motivation may have been, the conse-quences of his actions are even more ridiculous. Overnight he creates his own Orwellian *Animal Farm,* with pigs taking rude possession of the "handsome old farm buildings" (20), trampling the rare flowers, and toppling "statues from Florence and Salzburg" (20–21). Although the two-hundred-year-old property reeks of swill and dung, for the time being Henderson is convinced that the only kind of worthwhile breeding is pig breeding.

Henderson is not content to play the ludicrous scapegrace for long.

He is, as Bellow claims, "the absurd seeker after high qualities." [5] Beneath his Yahoo facade he is essentially a Don Quixote figure—only his chivalric romances are mental logs; his Amadis de Gaul is Sir Wilfred Grenfell. His knight errant is the physician errant, armed with scalpel and stethoscope, setting out to rescue humanity in distress. Only by adopting such an estimable profession does Henderson feel he can "carry his life to a certain depth" (191). Up to this point, carrying "his life to a certain depth" has meant reading everything written by and about Sir Wilfred Grenfell, urging his son to become a medical missionary, daydreaming about performing "errands of mercy" with a dog team (189), and braving the winter in a homemade igloo. Clearly, such measures have not placated his nagging service motivation. If he is to make a significant contribution, he realizes he cannot do so by dreaming about it in stultifying Connecticut. He must leave the distractions of effete civilization to discover revitalizing fundamentals in some pristine wilderness. In contrast to Augie, who is a young "Columbus of those near-at-hand" (536), Henderson embarks for the Dark Continent to become the fifty-five-year-old explorer of those far removed. Instead of being the Connecticut Yankee in Kenyatta's Court, Henderson sets foot in a make-believe, prodigious Africa, entirely removed from the twentieth century, with "no history or junk like that" (46).

Just as we laugh at the spare-bodied, weak-visaged Don Quixote sallying forth to accomplish feats of valor, we laugh at the mammoth Henderson, "whose face is half the length of another person's body" (315), heaving his way through the hinterland to aid the unfortunate. Since Bellow has created such an extraordinary Africa, exceeding the wildest expectations of Tarzan movie-viewers, he has made Henderson a larger-than-life character to be able to survive in it. And since Henderson is a creature of such unlimited desires and such immense frustrations—"an exceptional amalgam of vehement forces" (271)—Bellow had endowed him with an exceptional and immense body to correspond to his titanic emotions. But most of all, Bellow has made Henderson's exterior so oversized and grotesque in order to provide us with a caricature of the questor, should he get too carried away with his role. By dwelling on Henderson's strapping 230 pounds, his "enormous head, rugged with hair like Persian lamb's fur . . . [his]

5. Nina A. Steers, "Successor to Faulkner?" *Show* 4 (September, 1964): 38.

great nose" (4), his face "like an unfinished church" (76), and his 22 collar size, Bellow humorously distracts us from the higher faculties of Henderson's nature and thus playfully undercuts his image as a high-minded pursuer of meaning and performer of good works. Like the literary jesters through the ages, Bellow utilizes the ploy of having his hero utter the grand speech while simultaneously trivializing it by having him wiggle his nose and scratch his backside. Thus in the same breath that Henderson expresses his appreciation of the exquisite color of an African evening, he also mentions his "old knees, lined and grieved looking; like carrots" (102). At the same time that he describes himself as "thinking" and "moody," he hastens to add that "[his] belly is hanging forth" (76), or right after he is stirred by the lofty words of King Dahfu, he informs us that his face stretched "until it must have been as long as a city block" (215). With the inclusion of such diverting physical details, it is impossible to take Henderson altogether seriously in his aesthetic, reflective, and inspired moments.

Unlike Bellow's other corpulent heroes, Henderson does not shame-facedly try to conceal his hulking self from the public eye. Since he has not, like Tommy Wilhelm, neglected his body and given up the battle to keep physically fit, he is rather proud of his gargantuan proportions. As Bellow's Gentile muscle-man, he is formidable enough to overwhelm the "barbaric fellahin" which terrify the flabby Leventhal and has the stamina to exist in the "Mongolia or clear light desert minus trees" (480) which Augie is too frail to withstand. Thus Henderson can afford to mock his own grossness. When ascending the stairs of his mistress' tenement, he can jocularly refer to himself as a "great weight, a huge shadow" (12); when traveling in a small French convertible, he can playfully comment on his "grand size" towering out of the seat; and even when confronting a presumed African adversary, he can facetiously describe himself as "some kind of mushroom, imposing in size but not hard to knock over" (52).

Henderson's body is not always a source of pride or painless amusement to him, especially when it vexes or obstructs what Bergson terms "the moral personality." [6] While Bellow's rotund characters are impeded by their bodies, they do not all suffer the same degree of vexation. Since Leventhal and Wilhelm are for the most part intellectually

---

[6] Henri Bergson, "Laughter," in *Comedy,* ed. Wylie Sypher (New York: Doubleday & Co., 1956), p. 93.

and spiritually phlegmatic, they are not nearly as upset as Henderson is at having their souls weighted down by their bodies. Henderson, by contrast, is literally a *luftmensch,* a man of the air, borne aloft by his own flights of fancy and high-flown idealism. He resents being forced down to earth by corporeal demands. When, for example, he is about to be the sagacious philosopher, speaking of ultimates with Queen Willatale, he is at once stopped short by his "bargain basement of deformities" (83). Or when he considers becoming the valiant prime mover of Mummah, the ponderous Wariri idol, he is momentarily disgusted by his "portly front and the other strange distortions that attend all the larger individuals of a species" (182). By having Henderson repeatedly grounded by the irksome claims of the physical, Bellow exploits the Bergsonian humor of the soul being *"tantalized* by the . . . body." [7] Moreover, like the little slave assigned to whisper in the ear of returning Roman conquerors that they are only men and not gods, Bellow, with his incessant reminders of Henderson's "enormities and deformities" (334), tries to puncture his superman illusions and establish his mortal state.

Despite such attempts to convince us of Henderson's flesh and blood reality, he often resembles a cartoon character who is battered and worsted at every turn. Perhaps externalizing both the self-destructive and rallying powers of his fictional brethren, he stars in the richest offering of slapstick comedy yet produced by Bellow. Although Augie has weathered his share of innocent and not so innocent knocks, he is still a novice compared to Henderson, a veteran sustainer of nearly incapacitating blows. Nor is Augie as gruesome and riotous in his descriptions of his upsets as Henderson is in his. Especially in his account of the wrestling match with Prince Itelo we are spared none of the "physical mishaps, pratfalls and loud collisions . . . the crudest products of . . . comic 'automatism' ": [8]

> . . . I fell on my front and very painfully, too, so that I thought I had split myself upward from the navel. Also I got a bad blow on the nose and was afraid the root of it had parted. I could almost feel the air enter between the separated bones. . . . Prince Itelo now took a grip high on my chest with his legs; owing to my girth he could never have

7. *Ibid.*

8. Wylie Sypher, "Our New Sense of the Comic," in *Comedy,* ed. Wylie Sypher (New York: Doubleday & Co., 1956), p. 209.

closed them about me lower down. As he tightened them, I felt my blood stop and my lips puffed out while my tongue panted and my eyes began to run (67–68).

Although we know that Henderson, the "fighting Lazarus" (217), will ultimately rise again, we are, for the time being, still convulsed with Hobbesian laughter arising from the "sudden glory" we feel at the sight of someone more wretched than ourselves.

Indeed, Henderson himself is all too aware of how wretched he is, even when he is not being thrown in wrestling. While we find his cartoon fragility and indestructibility preposterously funny, we find his all too human emotional vulnerability more familiar and thus even more laughable. Like Don Quixote, he is a "Knight of the Woeful Countenance." As he describes himself, "Whole crowds of feelings, especially the bad ones, wave to the world from the galleries of my face" (53). But because we are not shown adequate grounds for his misery and receive only his rapid-fire volley of complaints, we are hard pressed to believe in him as a genuine sufferer. He is instead more credible as a ludicrous Pagliacci impersonator who "rehearses his agonies at operatic volume for all to hear." [9] Before the uncomprehending Arnewi he not only sings from Handel's Messiah, "He was despised and rejected, a man of sorrows and acquainted with grief," but also keens, "Oh it's miserable to be human. You get such queer diseases. Just because you're human and for no other reason" (83). Before his trusty guide Romilayu he expresses his "anguish of spirit" (120) at having broken one of his bridges "in the wilds of Africa" (120). So distraught is he that with the earnestness of a Proust he recites his own remembrance of teeth past, including a painful experience with a large-busted French dentist, Mlle Montecuccoli. Before King Dahfu he recounts his dental woes, as well as the history of his hemorrhoids and fainting spells. And even when he has no audience he entertains himself with his fretful refrain: "Oh, my body, my body! . . . I have loaded it with my vices, like a raft, like a barge" (182) and then concludes with his own desperate Pauline entreaty: "Oh, who shall deliver me from the body of this death?" (182). Henderson is prevented from becoming one of the exasperating chronic

9. Earl Rovit, *Saul Bellow,* University of Minnesota Pamphlets on American Writers, no. 65 (Minneapolis: University of Minnesota Press, 1967), p. 12.

complainers of Bellow's earlier novels by his awareness of how un-justified and excessive his bids for sympathy are. He is thus in a posi-tion to ridicule his own querulousness. By employing such a hyperbolic analogy as "I am to suffering what Gary is to smoke. One of the world's biggest operations" (260), he is the originator of the jest rather than its object.

While Henderson recognizes he is a self-styled "monster of grief" (313), he is unmindful of the fact that he is comically preoccupied with his own self-realization. As John Clayton has noted, *Henderson the Rain King* "is a parody of the questing bourgeois self speaking of love but more concerned with its own improvement and fulfillment." [10] Such self-interest appears in the comic fiction Bellow has described elsewhere: "The private and inner life which was the subject of serious books until very recently now begins to have an antique and funny look. . . . *My* welfare, *my* development, *my* advancement, *my* earnest-ness, *my* adjustment, *my* marriage, *my* family—all that will make the modern reader laugh heartily." [11] Henderson begins his tale with a similar catalogue of selfish concerns: "A disorderly rush begins—my parents, my wives, my girls, my children, my farm, my animals, my habits, my money, my music lessons, my drunkenness, my prejudices, my brutality, my teeth, my face, my soul!" (3) Through most of the novel we hear his comically persistent "I-I-I" blocking the existence of all other pronouns. Fully aware, for example, that his landlord in France is cursed with sick children, a vicious wife, and financial ruin, he cannot be bothered to help him. Like Augie March, his search for a worthwhile fate requires all his energies. Or playing checkers with his children, he has to be the winner of the game even though he knows they will be shattered by their defeat. Even when he penetrates the awesome African wilderness, Henderson does not, like Faulkner's Isaac McCaslin, lose the sense of his own significance or the over-whelming need to assert his own identity. As soon as he encounters the Arnewi, he voices his characteristic egoism: "I have a hunch this spot is going to be very good for me" (47). Rather than discarding the accouterments of civilization, he utilizes his cigarette lighter to enact

[10.] John J. Clayton, *Saul Bellow: In Defense of Man* (Bloomington: Indiana University Press, 1968), p. 169.

[11.] Saul Bellow, "Some Notes on Recent American Fiction," *Encounter* 21 (Novem-ber, 1963): 28.

his own version of Moses and the burning bush so that he can appear to be the leader of the chosen people. Moreover, the prevailing reason why he agrees to help the drought-striken Arnewi is for the opportunity of accomplishing something that only *he* can do. Anticipating successful results from *his* ingenious contribution, he gloats, "This is going to be one of my greatest days" (100). And when his greatest day turns out to be his doomsday, he petulantly exclaims, "Why for once, just once!, couldn't I get my heart's desire?" (111). Again Henderson gives greater priority to his little boy wishes than to the wretched Arnewi and their parched cattle. But this momentous setback does not cure him of his overweening egocentricity, for even among the treacherous Wariri he is compelled to lift the immovable goddess to surpass the local Hercules. Pursued by Joseph's "fear of lagging," and fired by the American spirit of competitiveness, he admits, "I still couldn't pass up this opportunity to *do* and to distinguish myself" (186). It is only after receiving instruction in ego-shattering and confronting the "not me" from King Dahfu, who himself has been able to subordinate his will to a higher authority, that Henderson learns to be less self-centered, to replace his "I want! I want!" with *"she* wants, *he* wants, *they* want" (286). Yet it remains to be seen whether Henderson will be able to apply the new grammar upon his return to the United States.

Personal fulfillment is not Henderson's most pressing goal, however. In an interview in *Show* Bellow states:

> What Henderson is really seeking is a remedy to the anxiety over death. What he can't endure is this continuing anxiety: the indeterminate and indefinite anxiety, which most of us accept as the condition of life which he is foolhardy enough to resist.
>
> He tells the King that he is a 'Becomer' and that the King is a 'Be-er.' I believe I meant him to say that human life is intolerable if we must endure endless doubt. That is really what I feel is motivating Henderson. All his efforts are a satire on the attempts people make to answer the enigma by movement and random action or even by conscious effort.[12]

As Henderson's soul is tantalized by the needs of his body, so his body is tantalized by the obsession of his soul—the desire to transcend human limitation. The result, as Bergson would claim, is again comic rigid-

12. Steers, "Successor to Faulkner?" p. 38.

ity.[13] Like the ideal constructionists of *Dangling Man* and the Machiavellians of *The Adventures of Augie March,* Henderson has a machine-
like preoccupation with a fixed idea which prevents him from having
the flexibility of a variable, fully alive human being. A ludicrous victim
of his psychic inelasticity, he spends the greatest portion of his time
trying to flee from death. One of the oldest military survivors of the
bloodiest campaigns of World War II, Henderson is initially convinced
that he is "unkillable" (6). But when he confronts an octopus in a
French aquarium, he quickly changes his mind: "The eyes spoke to
me coldly. But even more speaking, even more cold, was the soft head
with its speckles . . . a cosmic coldness in which I felt I was dying.
The tentacles throbbed and motioned through the glass, the bubbles
sped upward and I thought, 'This is my last day. Death is giving me
notice!' " (19).

Not only does Henderson try to ignore the notice; he also struggles
to disprove the finality of death. Racing back to the United States,
he starts playing the violin to communicate with his dead mother and
father, "for it so happens that [he] has never been able to convince
[himself] the dead are utterly dead" (30). Whispering "Ma, this is
'Humoresque' for you," or "Pa, listen—'Meditation' from *Thaïs,*" he
plays "to the point of emotional collapse" (30). His attempts to reach
the deceased are interrupted by a fresh encounter with death. Miss
Lennox the cook, overcome by his ranting, expires in the kitchen. Henderson, discovering in her cottage the debris of a lifetime with which
she thought to insulate herself from death, is reminded of the grave:
"The last little room of dirt is waiting. Without windows. You, too,
will die of this pestilence. Death will annihilate you and nothing will
remain, and there will be nothing left but junk" (40).

Henderson is thus prompted to make a move again—only this time
he seeks to outdistance death by buying a one-way ticket to the ends
of the earth. In coming to Africa he hopes to be distracted from his
black thoughts. Among the Arnewi he seeks to avert the severe decree
by appointing himself the administrator of death. By letting "fall the
ultimate violence" (89) upon the detested frogs, he deludes himself

[13.] Keith Opdahl, also taking his cue from Bergson, makes the same point about Henderson's body being comically *"tantalized"* by a "dominant idea." See *The Novels of
Saul Bellow: An Introduction* (University Park: Pennsylvania State University Press,
1967), p. 121.

into thinking he is immune to such violence and can therefore relish what he is doing. "Poor little bastards was what I said, but in actual fact I was gloating-yuck-yuck-yuck! My heart was already fattening in anticipation of their death. We hate death, we fear death, but when you get right down to cases, there's nothing like it" (89). Among the Wariri, however, he is not allowed to play the lord high executioner. He can only cart away a dead body. Yet the tremendous physical exertion he employs to remove the corpse from his hut is a reflection of the tremendous mental exertion he employs to stave off death. Even his extraordinary feat of lifting Mummah can be viewed not only as a means of distinguishing himself, but also as a bid for immortality. Of course, Henderson's death-defying tactics do not ultimately succeed. All they accomplish is to convince us that Henderson is not a pliable human being, but a comic puppet vigorously pulled hither and yon by the strings of his obsession. In turn, we laugh at his mechanical bearing, his excessive movement, and his "random action."

Because Henderson is caught up in his energetic performances as a puppet, he does not perceive himself or his world accurately. Priding himself on being on "damned good terms with reality" (36), he thinks that he, like Hemingway's professional hunter in "The Short Happy Life of Francis Macomber," knows Africa and can accept her savagery. Differentiating himself from those Ivy League intellectual acquaintances who experience cruelty only by reading about it in books, Henderson boasts that he is prepared for the "very worst" the "old bitch" reality (150) has to show him. Unlike Leventhal, he thinks he's not afraid of acknowledging "the yellow revealed in the slit of the eye of a wild animal, say a lion, something inhuman that didn't care about anything human"(51). But when Henderson does confront the incarnation of evil, the actual ferocious lion who kills Dahfu, he finds he is not at all prepared to deal with such a tangible horror. Shrinking from it in dread, he is forced to admit that the only kind of horror he has been able to cope with has been his imaginary conception of it, his braggart tough guy's distortion of it. Instead of being an embracer of reality, he realizes that he has been a fabricator of "unreality." Yet such an anagnorisis does not free Henderson from all his comic fabrications; at the end of the novel he plans to enroll in medical school as *Leo* Henderson and, in his sixties, to cure the world of all its diseases.

Augie March tells us more about the secondary characters than he does about himself, and the Machiavellians are represented as being far more antic than Augie. Henderson, on the other hand, always gives himself top billing, and there is no doubt that he is the main comic attraction. Yet other members of the cast occasionally receive their share of laughs. Aside from briefly mentioning an imbecilic relative who "got himself mixed up in the Boxer Rebellion, believing he was an oriental" or another who "was carried away in a balloon publicizing the suffrage movement" (86), Henderson more fully reveals the comic aspects of his wife Lily. Among the eccentricities of Bellow's fictional spouses, Lily's are the least harmful and the most amiably ridiculed. Like Henderson, she has a large body that humorously calls attention to itself and wears clothes that are absurdly inappropriate to her size. But, unlike Henderson, she does not pretend to be worse than she is. Having married into wealth and prestige, she displays all the silly airs of the nouveau riche. She talks in a soft, lady-like fashion, entertains only the most prominent people, patronizes the most elegant establishments, and, above all, has her portrait painted like all the Henderson nobility. Yet Lily does not succeed in being the flawless gentlewoman. Like most of Bellow's fictional women, she is slovenly. Not only does she keep an untidy household; she also wears dirty "underthings" (16). Even Henderson, the caretaker of pigs, is offended by her unclean habits and has serious doubts about whether she will qualify as a doctor's wife. But, according to Lily's values, having a clean interior is more important than maintaining a clean exterior. In addition to playing the *grande dame*, she tries to be the great moralist. She constantly beleaguers Henderson with her elaborate ethical theories, yet she violates her own preachings. Comically hypocritical, she tells lies without the slightest hesitation and uses blackmail whenever the need arises. Nevertheless, she does have her virtues, the principal one being that she genuinely loves Henderson and accepts his unconventional ways. Perhaps this is what makes her so foolish, yet so endearing.

Another companion who is equally faithful to Henderson is his guide Romilayu. With tribal scars on his cheeks and a "dwarf-pine" head which has been baptized, he is a caricature of the converted heathen. Although he doesn't comprehend the intellectual concepts of his new faith, he is a zealous believer who is forever praying. Even in the midst of danger he does not slight his elaborate devotions. Romilayu is also an African Amy Vanderbilt, well-versed in all the intricacies of tribal etiquette. Especially as Henderson's interpreter he is a paragon of correctness. Even when he is awakened in the middle of the night by the Arnewi nobility, he immediately displays his "court manners" (96). Bellow thus exploits the comic incongruity of having a savage in darkest Africa act more "civilized" than a New England aristocrat. Romilayu is also Henderson's Sancho Panza; having been promised a jeep rather than an island, he accompanies his daft master on all his misadventures. Able to appraise situations realistically, he sees in an instant how foolhardy Henderson's schemes are. Yet he is powerless to restrain him and must suffer the painful consequences. Even though he has his prayers to console him, he is just as comically woeful as his superior.

The humor of *Henderson the Rain King* does not consist entirely of comedy of character. It contains a more pervasive comedy of situation than any Bellow novel except *The Adventures of Augie March*. Moreover, its comedy of situation has its own distinctive quality. Since Henderson is such a highly comic character in his own right, the incongruous situations in which he finds himself are rendered doubly funny because of his inimitable presence in them. There is, consequently, more amusement than agony in his predicaments.

In *Seize the Day* Tommy Wilhelm continually seeks money as an answer to his problems; instead of money, he finds the spurious wisdom of Dr. Tamkin. In the opening situation of *Henderson the Rain King* Henderson has just the opposite experience. In the library seeking wisdom—the source of the quotation, "The forgiveness of sins is perpetual and righteousness first is not required"—he finds only money. Whereas we ruefully chuckle at Tommy Wilhelm's unfortunate acquisition, we heartily laugh at the sight of Henderson, "the ironic hero in an age of affluence,"[14] spending the afternoon on a ladder shaking money out of books—the fives, tens, and twenties which his millionaire father used as book marks—and never finding "that statement about forgiveness" (4).

Similarly, there is far more whimsy than woe in Henderson's African romantic situations. Unlike Augie, who becomes involved in one erotic entanglement after another, or Herzog, who continually looks

14. Allen Guttmann, "Bellow's Henderson," *Critique* 7 (Spring–Summer, 1965): 34.

to women for fulfillment, Henderson is too caught up with his quest
to be amorously detoured. As a poor man's John Smith, he unintentionally wins the heart of the native princess; only the native princess
is not a svelte, comely Pocahontas, but Mtalba, the mountainous,
henna-colored darling of the Arnewi, who could easily qualify as the
fat lady of any circus. The contrast between her impassioned seduction of Henderson and his absolute unresponsiveness to her provides
the greatest hilarity. Not only does she place his hand on her expansive
breast, saying, "Mtalba admires you" (74), but she also effusively licks
his hand. He, in turn, quickly withdraws it and wipes her affectionate
saliva on his shorts. So smitten with love is she that during the night
she offers to be his bride, serenades him with her own *Song of Songs,*
and presents him with a huge dowry to convince him of her earnestness. Henderson, however, refuses to allow frivolous love to deter
him from his higher purpose of lifting the plague. Preoccupied with
devising an engine of destruction, he sends the love-sick Mtalba away.
Yet the next morning she publicly announces her betrothal to the
mighty warrior. The mighty warrior ignores the announcement and
Mtalba as he intently constructs his homemade bomb.

Amusingly enough, the only consummated love affair Henderson
permits himself in Africa occurs with an inanimate woman, Mummah, the Wariri idol. The humor of the situation turns on the fact
that he views her as an animate woman. Indeed, he is enamoured of
certain of her features—her wooden tresses, her ponderous breasts, and
her "elegant, graceful hands" (184). The fact that she is a *femme
fatale* attracts him to her. If any man makes the wrong move, she will
most certainly "crush him beneath her weight" (186). Equally appeal-
ing is the fact that she is not an easy conquest. She will not succumb
to the advances of any suitor. The lover that ultimately moves her
must be a physical giant. Faced with such a challenging woman, Henderson is bent on winning her—and win her he does, before a stadium
full of wanton onlookers. Like any jaunty male who has proven his
virility, Henderson exultantly describes all the sensual particulars of
his victory:

> Never hesitating, I encircled Mummah with my arms. I wasn't going
> to take no for an answer. I pressed my belly upon her and sank my
> knees somewhat. . . . We met as challenged and challenger, but also as
> intimates. And with the close pleasure you experience in a dream or on

one of those warm beneficial floating idle days when every desire is satisfied, I laid my cheek against her wooden bosom. I cranked down my knees and said to her, "Up you go, dearest. No use trying to make yourself heavier; if you weighed twice as much I'd lift you anyway." The wood gave to my pressure and benevolent Mummah with her fixed smile yielded to me. . . (192).

But such a pleasant experience brings about unpleasant consequences. Having lifted the rain goddess, Mummah, Henderson automatically becomes the rain king who, in turn, must endure his own reign of terror. His installation into office is a burlesque of all rites of investiture. Stripped of his great white father's costume and dressed only in vines and leaves, he is compelled to run about the village, cleansing ponds and whipping idols. The incongruity of his situation does not escape him. He is all too aware of how absurd it is that he, "Henderson of the USA, Captain Henderson, Purple Heart, veteran of North Africa, Sicily, Monte Cassino, etc., a giant shadow, a man of flesh and blood, a restless seeker, pitiful and rude, a stubborn old lush with broken bridgework, threatening death and suicide" (199), should be the rain king in remote Africa, nakedly chasing about with fiendish natives at his side. Recognition of absurdity does not eliminate the actual pain he experiences; Henderson still feels his feet lacerated and burned by the jagged, sulphurous rocks, his body scalded by the "super-heated sour water" of a cattle pond (198), and his face and head stung by the sharp cracks of frenzied whips. Yet the more intensely he reacts to his torture, the more it seems as if he is "mugging for the cameras and groaning for the microphones."[15] Except for a slight twinge of empathy, we the audience are prompted to laugh freely at the outlandish ceremonies Bellow has devised and at Henderson's incongruous distress within them.

Henderson also experiences incongruous distress in his encounters with various animals, with the degree of his distress in exact proportion to the size of the animal. Stationed in Italy during the war, he is the butt of the "humor of discomfiture."[16] Not only does he suffer the "mad itch" (22) of pertinacious crab-lice all over his body, but he also endures the greater agony of being denuded and shaved by

[15.] Clayton, *Saul Bellow*, p. 184.

[16.] Stephen Leacock, *Humour and Humanity* (New York: Henry Holt & Co., 1938), p. 91.

army medics in full view of passing troops and local residents. Fully aware of how ridiculous he must appear—bald, shivering, and naked —he does not hang his head in shame or bemoan his wretched state. With Augie March's *animal ridens* in him, he joins the spectators in their unsympathetic laughter at his plight.

Henderson is not always able to take such a light-hearted view of an unhappy state of affairs. His skirmish with the Arnewi frogs is one comic situation the jollity of which escapes him. It is readily apparent to the reader, however. Whereas undeserved misfortune is not always funny, misfortune that is brought about by the victim's misdirected efforts is irresistibly comical. Similarly, a simple fall is not nearly as humorous as the fall which follows pride. So it is with Henderson's frog fiasco. Playing the role of the bumptious Connecticut Yankee to the hilt, he seeks to bedazzle the underdeveloped savages with the highly developed magic of technology. Priding himself on his superior practicality and his innate mechanical ingenuity, he rigs his own makeshift bomb out of a flashlight case, a dozen .375 shells, a shoelace, and a Band-Aid. Supremely confident of the finished product's miraculous powers, he holds it aloft "like the torch of liberty in New York harbor" (107) and with due pomp and circumstance hurls it at the target. At the first sign of success, Henderson profusely congratulates himself. His self-praise is premature, for, unlike Hank Morgan, he does not resuscitate the well. Miscalculating the bomb's potency, he not only annihilates the frogs, but also demolishes the wall of the cistern retaining the water supply. Sickened by the havoc he has created, Henderson, the overactive, unquiet American, cannot stand idly by. His efforts to stem the catastrophe, however, prove just as foolish as his former technological horseplay. Throwing himself down against the escaping water, he tries to "breast it back" (109). But the water slips through his fingers. Only the dead frogs are very much with him, tumbling into his pants and open shoe. In a matter of minutes Henderson the hero becomes Henderson the pariah. His peripety is not tragic, however, for when a man is not only afflicted with ridiculous hubris, but also perfects the mechanism which undoes him, his downfall evokes laughter instead of tears.

While Henderson's rendezvous with the frogs tickles the funny bone, his tryst with the lioness convulses the entire body. In both situations Bellow underscores the comic discrepancies between man and animal. Among the Arnewi Henderson is the mighty oppressor, the six foot four, 230 pound ex-combat officer gleefully terrorizing "the fundamentally harmless semi-fishes" (89). Conversely, in the Wariri lion den Henderson is the physical and psychological misfit frantically groveling before Atti, the menacing queen of the beasts. His frantic groveling turns out to be more hilarious than his gleeful terrorizing. Possessing the same overactive imagination as Augie March, Henderson's zany fancy goes ahead of him and prepares the way. Before he ever sees the lioness, he has visions of the "animal washing its face in [his] blood" (221), greedily devouring his liver. Also, since he nearly killed a member of the cat family in the past, he assumes he will now receive an especially inhospitable welcome from one of the more powerful relatives. When he first meets Atti, he therefore thinks she has a murderous face with eyes like "circles of wrath" (223). Yet what he interprets as burning hostility is actually cool indifference. Aside from investigating his armpits and crotch, merely a sign of idle female curiosity, Atti, who is more than satisfied with her boyfriend King Dahfu, is mostly oblivious to Henderson's presence. Henderson, on the other hand, cannot for an instant forget that he is in the company of a formidable beast of prey. While Atti is all grace and ease, Henderson, the comic inversion of the self-possessed Daniel in the lion's den, is all awkwardness and fear and complains of the most unusual physical distress: "My nether half turned very cold. My knees felt like two rocks in a cold Alpine torrent. My mustache stabbed and stung into my lips, which made me realize that I was frowning and grimacing with terror, and I knew that my eyes must be filling with fatal blackness" (261).

Unlike Tommy Wilhelm, Henderson is given an opportunity to overcome his physiological distress by trying to imitate the lioness. He is urged to slough off the burden of consciousness and self-concern and become one of those creatures released on the ground who Augie claims "look with their original eyes" (330). Indeed, Henderson is not a novice at descending the evolutionary ladder, at incorporating the animal within himself. Much to his regret, his pigs have already become a part of him. With such a base animal conversion in his background, he is therefore not too reluctant to try for another more exalted metamorphosis with King Dahfu as the latter-day Ovid and Ringling Brothers circus trainer combined. Only Henderson does not succeed in becoming lionized. His uncoordinating jogging in no way resembles Atti's rhythmical trotting. When he gets on his hands and knees, his huge paunch, his ruddy alcoholic face, and his bulbous nose detract from his leonine pose. Much as he would like to deny it, his long association with pigs has made his cheeks white as lard, his supposed muzzle like a snout, and his haunches like hams. The only aspect of Henderson's lion act which is at all convincing is his roar, the "hot noise" bursting from him. Yet, upon careful listening, certain human words like "God," "Help," and "Lord have mercy" inevitably creep in. Bellow seems to be saying that man cannot lapse entirely into the beast, no matter how desirable it would be to absorb its litheness, spontaneity, and untamed ferocity. He must make do with his own awkwardness, his unavoidable constraints, and his inherent anxiety.

Although King Dahfu is delighted with Henderson's attempts to revert to the animal, Henderson is not at all delighted. As he crouches "in the dust and the lion's offal" (268), his arms and legs are racked with pain, his face is boiling, and he feels "dim and dark within the brain" (274). But because he has attempted the impossible, because his set of circumstances is so farfetched and his discomfort so excessive, we cannot sympathize with him. Possessing Bergson's "anesthesia of the heart," [17] we can only be overcome with mirth at Henderson's sorry state.

As we are amused by Henderson's comic situations, so we are amused by the "growling of his mind" (162) or his comedy of ideas. As far as reflection is concerned, Henderson likens himself to the "third man in a relay race . . . who rarely take[s] off in the necessary direction" (84). Indeed, his intellectual departures provide a measure of the cerebral fun as well as advance the serious concerns of the novel. When, for instance, he is in the midst of experimenting with every conceivable remedy to cure his chronic dissatisfaction, he suddenly realizes: "Of course, in an age of madness, to be untouched by madness is a form of madness. But the pursuit of sanity can be a form of madness too" (25). Or when he ruminates upon Queen Willatale's cryptic remarks, he is able to discern the ridiculous self-deception which man employs to obtain a release from mortality:

17. Bergson, "Laughter," p. 64.

The world may be strange to a child, but he does not fear it the way a man fears. He marvels at it. But the grown man mainly dreads it. And why? Because of death. So he arranges to have himself abducted like a child. So what happens will not be his fault. And who is this kidnapper—this gipsy? It is the strangeness of life—a thing that makes death more remote, as in childhood (84).

Or when he reads some lines of Whitman's poetry—"Enough to merely be! Enough to breathe! Joy! Joy! All over joy!" (160)—Henderson is struck with the idea that there are essentially two kinds of individuals: those who have realized their potential, and those who are still struggling to realize it. Of the two, the strugglers or "becomers" are the laughable neurotics, "always in a tizzy . . . always having to make explanations or offer justification to the Being people" (160).

Henderson, however, is not the novel's leading comedian of ideas. Aside from such a smattering of independent reflections, he is, according to Ihab Hassan, "the straight man in a Socratic dialogue with African Sages." [18] Like the "heavy-water brains" in *The Adventures of Augie March* and the intellectually lopsided Dr. Tamkin, King Dahfu, sage *par excellence,* is another "guy with a program . . . whose enthusiasms and visions swept him far out" (235). As Bellow's daffy version of Wilhelm Reich,[19] he is "triumphantly sure" (236) of the interrelatedness of flesh and mind. He not only believes that ailments of the body have their origins in the mind, but he is also convinced that all external physical features are a product more of the mind than of heredity. According to his extreme view, even "the pimple on a lady's nose may be her own idea" (237). Considering the "spirit of the person" to be "the author of his body" (238), he maintains that we have "whole faces of hope, feet of respect, hands of justice, brows of serenity . . ." (238). But even more incredible, in his estimation, are the varied personality distortions which the imagination produces. Enlarging upon Wilhelm Reich's character designations —the hysterical character, the compulsive character, the phallic-narcissis-

18. Ihab H. Hassan, *Radical Innocence: Studies in the Contemporary American Novel* (Princeton University Press, 1961), p. 321.

19. From conversations with Bellow during the writing of *Henderson,* Richard G. Stern learned of Bellow's interest in the somatic psychology of Wilhelm Reich. See "Henderson's Bellow," *Kenyon Review* 21 (Autumn, 1959): 661.

tic character, and the masochistic character [20]—Dahfu comes up with his own farfetched categories: "The agony, The appetite, The obstinate, The immune elephant, The shrewd pig. The fateful hysterical. The death-accepting. The phallic-proud or hollow genital. The fast asleep. The narcissus intoxicated. The mad laughers. The pedantics. The fighting Lazaruses" (217). Yet Dahfu claims that man does not have to settle for such a limited personality. An Emersonian transcendentalist as well as a Reichian, he is confident that "what Homo sapiens imagines, he may slowly convert himself to" (271). "It is all a matter of having a desirable model in the brain" (268). In particular, he believes that if Henderson patterns himself after a superior animal, he will become a superior person. Instead of being the "contracted and self recoiled" (264) resister, he will become Reich's free-flowing "genital man," the embodiment of ease and energy. Instead of being the fearful avoider, he will run toward rather than away from beauty. Above all, if he submits to the influence of the lioness Atti, Dahfu swears that "she will make consciousness to shine. She will burnish you. She will force the present moment upon you" (260). Instead of anxiously looking to the future to right the wrongs of the past, Henderson will be able to obey Dr. Tamkin's advice—to take pleasure in the here and now, to "seize the day."

Henderson, like Wilhelm, is not entirely convinced by his mentor's theories. Very frequently he considers Dahfu's brilliance to be an insecure gift, resting "on doubtful underpinnings" (269). For instance, he has his doubts about Dahfu's lion-transfer theory; although he admits that Dahfu resembled a lion in many ways, he cannot concede that "lions had made him so" (288). Such a notion strikes him as mere Lamarckian nonsense. He also has reservations about Dahfu's view that "inanimate objects might have a mental existence" (269), or his view concerning the distortion of sensations whereby a man "with a normal leg might be convinced that he had the leg of an elephant" (246).

Although Dahfu's "ideas often threaten to topple over into absurdity, or vanish into incomprehensibility," [21] what he says occasionally has merit. His view that the good cannot be achieved through "labor or

[20] Wilhelm Reich, *Character-Analysis,* trans. Theodore P. Wolfe (New York: Orgone Institute Press, 1949), pp. vi–vii.

[21.] Tony Tanner, *Saul Bellow* (Edinburgh: Oliver & Boyd, 1965), p. 78.

conflict" (169), his definition of the brave man as he who accepts blows but does not pass them on, and his faith in mankind's "noble possibilities," especially the wondrous potential of the human mind, genuinely inspire Henderson. The greatest wisdom Dahfu imparts, however, is not through precept but through example. He has solved what Henderson considers the "greatest problem of all"—how "to encounter death" (276). Dahfu is able to live with joy despite the fact that he might be strangled should he fail to gratify his sixty-seven wives. Moreover, just before his fatal confrontation with the death-dealing lion, he is still the complacent Be-er, eager to meet his ancestors. And even as he is dying, he displays the same equanimity that characterized his living. Dahfu's calm acceptance of his end compels Henderson to realize how frantic have been his own efforts to avoid death and, by extension, life. Having previously strived "to raise [himself] into another world" (284), he knows now that he can never "leave the body of this death" (182). Even though Dahfu may be a suspect philosopher-king, or what one critic termed a ludicrous "cross between a psycho-somaticist and psyche-semanticist,"[22] he, like Dr. Tamkin, is a man who "spoke a kind of truth and did some people a sort of good" (63).

While the comedy of ideas in *Henderson the Rain King* contains some weighty revelations, there is nothing weighty about the novel's style. It is a riotous linguistic carnival with all kinds of verbal spectacles. As in *The Adventures of Augie March,* there are improbable allusions aplenty. Henderson constantly likens himself to prominent figures of history, Bible, and myth, and in so doing makes his own clownish traits more prominent. Thus when he places himself in the same league as Sir Richard Burton, Mungo Park, and Dr. Livingstone, he appears by contrast the caricature of the African explorer. When he prides himself on his Pancho Villa marksmanship in shooting a defenseless cat, he underscores the foolishness of his villainy. When he compares himself to St. John the Baptist, eating locusts in the wilderness, he makes a mockery of his penance for his sins against the Arnewi.

Henderson does not employ allusions only to jest about himself; he also takes advantage of them to make sport of others. By likening his first wife Frances to "Shelley's moon, wandering companionless" (5), he accentuates the absurdity of her aloofness. By comparing Clara

22. "Dun Quixote-Henderson the Rain King," *Time* 73 (February 23, 1959): 102.

Spohr, a wildly flirtatious has-been beauty, to the Sicilian bandit Giuliano, he emphasizes how ridiculously unbecoming her conduct is. By viewing Dahfu as another Pascal, he makes Dahfu's lion studies appear more preposterous than ever.

Along with drawing unlikely parallels between Henderson and famous individuals, Bellow compares him to all kinds of animals. Like Swift, he produces a comically incongruous effect by viewing a higher order of being in terms of a lower one. In addition to creating comic situations in which Henderson has prolonged associations with pigs and lions, Bellow takes every opportunity to employ animal imagery in his depiction of Henderson, especially when he is in the grip of excessively powerful emotions. Then Bellow cannot resist the temptation of making Henderson appear much lower than the angels. When Henderson is filled with grief, for example, his heart is described as barking "with all three heads, like Cerberus" (82). When he is overcome with rage and wishes to sink his teeth into an entire building, he is likened to Moby-Dick devouring all boats in sight. When he passionately kisses a woman in her sixties, he is said to be "mad as a horsefly on the window pane" (128). When he is obsessed with being the center of attention in the Wariri stadium, he is represented as roaring "like the great Assyrian bull" (171).

Bellow also evokes laughter by investing animals with both exasperating and admirable human traits. Henderson insists that the pig is "basically a career animal" (56) with all kinds of ambitions and drives. He imagines that the Arnewi frogs with their "congested, emotional throats" (60) are singing Mozart's *Agnus Dei* as well as fulfilling their ideal in their watery sanctuary. Perhaps most humorous is his description of Atti as she listens to him roar: looking "very formal in attire," it seemed as though she "were attending an opera performance" (274).

Mocking allusions and farfetched animal-human imagery are not the only humorous features of the novel's prose. The incessant flow of Henderson's language is also comic. His tale, or more appropriately his "rush" of personal facts, appears entirely unedited. Just as there is no restraint in Henderson himself, or in his way of doing things, there is no restraint in the way he talks with the reader. He resembles, in this respect, the Jewish comic "type generally known in the old Catskill Borscht Belt as the *meshuggah*—the wild, irresponsible, disconnected buffoon who oscillates between the frenetic edges of obscenity and tearful sentimentality." [23] So, too, Henderson's life story is one prolonged "litany of blundering and inner anguish," [24] interspersed with endless indecent disclosures. Along with continually announcing his errors and needs, he forever mentions such unmentionables as his fully exposed "behind," his contracted sphincters, his "travel-stained" jockey shorts, the nature of his body odor, and the reaction of his "parts" to the lioness's sniffing of his crotch. With such a surplus of lamentations and earthy revelations, Henderson can never be accused of being reticent.

Henderson's language has great variety, along with its uninhibited nature. It is, for the most part, unreservedly colloquial. We especially laugh at the comic incongruity of a New England aristocrat with a master's degree speaking like an uneducated hobo. We also find Henderson's flippant speech comically incongruous with the serious import of the subject matter it expresses. There is the added incongruity of hearing Henderson's breezy colloquialisms not on the neon-lighted city streets of America, but in the middle of darkest Africa. Especially in his exchanges with King Dahfu all three incongruities operate. Not wishing to overstay his welcome, Henderson tells the King that he "had better blow" (164). Revealing the intimate details of his life, he states, "King, I'm going to give you the straight poop about myself, as straight as I can make it" (191). When he thinks that the Wariri are going to exploit him, he pleads, "Now listen, Your Highness, don't sell me down the river" (196). Minimizing his past achievements, he says with all due candor, "I've done a hell of a lot of things, too, both as a soldier and a civilian. I'll say it straight out, I don't even deserve to be chronicled on toilet paper" (211).

Not only does Henderson use glib vernacular when talking about himself, but "he thinks, in Africa, in city metaphors and of city events." [25] Such a practice exemplifies the kind of comic incongruity which D. H. Monro calls "universe-changing"—the importing into one sphere an entire "universe of discourse with all sorts of rich associations [and] all sorts of stock responses" which is appropriate only to an

23. Earl Rovit, "Jewish Humor and American Life," *The American Scholar* 36 (Spring, 1967): 242.

24. Robert Gorham Davis, "The American Individualist Tradition: Bellow and Styron," *The Creative Present*, ed. Nona Balakian and Charles Simmons (New York: Doubleday & Co., 1963), p. 127.

25. Marcus Klein, *After Alienation* (Cleveland: World Publishing Co., 1962), p. 49.

utterly different sphere.[26] Some of the novel's comedy of language comes from Henderson's continent-changing. When he is given the honorary title of Rain King, he likens it to "getting the key to the city from Jimmy Walker" (283). He accuses the bloodthirsty Wariri of dealing in corpses "wholesale" (149). He calls Dahfu's arch-enemy "the leader of the anti-lion forces" (251) and his henchman the "Phantom of the Opera" (250). He advises King Dahfu, unwilling to part with his beloved lioness, to "abdicate, like the Duke of Windsor" (231). Through Henderson's rare verbal imports, we experience the "sensation of being suddenly hurled from one universe into another," [27] and we are titillated in the process.

Henderson is not exclusively an importer of colloquialisms. He is also a rhetorical quick-change artist. In no time at all he shifts from unassuming idiomatic phrases to such inflated melodramatic expressions as, "It turns into chaos" (3), "I . . . couldn't bear the December ruins of my frozen estate and one-time pig kingdom" (33). When he is terrified by the withered head of a strangled sorceress, he comes up with an original prayer containing an odd mixture of philosophical circumlocutions, straightforward concrete diction, colorful expletives, and religious discourse. When verbally castigating himself, he uses such a Jewish-sounding epithet as "shmohawk" (187). When reminiscing about the battle wounds and Purple Heart he received in the Italian campaign, he talks like the tight-lipped Gentile Hemingway code hero: "The war meant much to me. . . . The whole experience gave my heart a large and real emotion. Which I continually require" (22). When overcome with the beauty of nature, he employs such rhapsodic Whitmanesque language as, "I am out in the grass. The sun flames and swells; the heat it emits is its love, too. . . . There are dandelions. I try to gather up this green. I put my love-swollen cheek to the yellow of the dandelions. I try to enter into the green" (283). On another occasion he expresses his appreciation of life in more Rabelaisian terms: "I am a true adorer of life, and if I can't reach as high as the face of it, I plant my kiss somewhere lower down" (150). When pitting his strength against Turombo, the Wariri strongman, he boasts like any cocky ring-tailed roarer: "Good man. . . . You are strong but it so

26. D. H. Monro, *Argument of Laughter* (Notre Dame: University of Notre Dame Press, 1963), pp. 45–46.
27. *Ibid.*, p. 46.

happens I am stronger. . . . This is a job for me. Yield, yield! Cede! Because here comes Henderson!" (186). When exasperated with practicing his violin exercises, he imitates the broken English of his Hungarian teacher: "Dear, take de bow like dis vun, not like dis vun, so. Und so, so so. Not to kill vid de bow" (30). At other times he sounds like a New York literary intellectual, effortlessly incorporating in his speech quotations from Whitman, Tennyson, T. S. Eliot, Shakespeare, and Blake. And at still other times he talks like a sententious minister citing any biblical passages which will serve as a fitting commentary on his life. The passage he apparently finds most appropriate (for he repeats it three times) is Daniel's prophecy to King Nebuchadnezzar: "They shall drive thee from among men and thy dwelling shall be with the beasts of the field." [28]

Although Henderson is a versatile man of words, it can be argued that each of his verbal routines is not comic in its own right. Nevertheless, the combination of them is indisputably funny. Similarly, the juxtaposition of Dahfu's clipped "Bellafrikanisch" [29] and his turgid philosophizing, or what Marvin Mudrick calls his "quasi-Oxonian ontological ditherings," [30] provokes mirth. Nor can we fail to be amused by the bizarre medley of the ennobling strains of Handel's *Messiah,* the cacophonous tribal rituals, Henderson's dulcet children's songs, and the jarring roars of lions and lion-imitators.

Another kind of comedy of language which is especially conspicuous in the novel and which many critics have commented on is parody. Indeed, Robert Alter finds *Henderson* to be a "composite parody of all the memorable twentieth century novels of personal or mythic quest into dark regions." [31] There are such clichés as "Grun-tu-molani. Man want to live" (85), which Allen Guttman claims to be straight from "the days of E. M. Forster and D. H. Lawrence." [32] There are also symbols galore: a reddening sun, a rosy dawn, white rocks, craggy mountains, teeming jungles, barren deserts, a drought, a deluge, a plague, emblematic beasts, noble savages, and savage nobles. Yet if we

[28.] Daniel 5:25 (King James Version).
[29.] Stern, "Henderson's Bellow," p. 659.
[30.] Marvin Mudrick, "Who Killed Herzog? Or, Three American Novelists," *University of Denver Quarterly* 1 (Spring, 1966): 77.
[31.] Robert Alter, "The Stature of Saul Bellow," *Midstream* 10 (December, 1964): 10.
[32.] Gutman, "Bellow's Henderson," p. 37.

heed Bellow's warning, "Deep Readers of the World, Beware," [33]
which appeared in the *New York Times* just one week before
Henderson the Rain King was published, we will realize he did not
wish us to take all of his symbols seriously. It is as if he purposely
included a superabundance of concrete particulars as bait for meaning
hunters and then sat back and laughed at the interpretive traps into
which they fell. There are also patterns out of Freud's *Totem and
Taboo,* Jung's *Archetypes and the Collective Unconscious,* and Frazer's
The Golden Bough; yet these, too, are ludicrous imitations. Finally,
there is Henderson himself, one of the "fabulous voyagers" [34] with
even more fabulous adventures. Instead of losing himself in the heart
of darkness and "feeling the 'horror, the horror,'" [35] he has the pleasant experience of kissing the ample belly of a clairvoyant grandmother
figure, trading philosophical gems with a connoisseur, and dancing
with an orphan child in the Newfoundland cold.

Since Henderson is such a "fabulous voyager," many of the predicaments he faces are so farfetched that they are far more rollicking than
roiling. The humor of verbal retrieval he employs is therefore not
particularly bitter or desperate. If anything, it consists of highly droll
comments about an essentially droll set of circumstances. When
Henderson contemplates the navel of Queen Willatale, for example, he
makes the experience even more humorous by his riotously inventive
description of it: "I felt as though I were riding in a balloon above
the Spice Islands, soaring in hot clouds while exotic odors rose from
below" (74). When the Wariri ignominiously baptize him with mud,
he transforms mortification into mirth by jocularly remarking, "I was
left standing in my coat of earth, like a giant turnip" (202). When confronting the tame lioness Atti, he makes his excessive fear appear
ridiculous by grossly exaggerating his physiological complications: "My
vocal cords . . . seemed stuck together like strands of overcooked
spaghetti" (266). And even when he goes out to hunt the truly vicious
lion, he jests about his vulnerability: ". . . it occurred to me that the
grass was high enough to conceal almost any animal except an elephant

33. Saul Bellow, "Deep Readers of the World, Beware!" *New York Times Book Review* 64 (February 15, 1959): 1.

34. Alter, "The Stature of Saul Bellow," p. 10.

35. Clayton, *Saul Bellow,* p. 168.

and that I didn't have so much as a diaper pin to defend myself with" (293–294). Through his uproarious verbal ingenuity Henderson is able to make the zany appear more zany.

Henderson the Rain King is clearly Bellow's most full-blown comic novel. The dreaded nightmare experiences of the earlier realistic novels are transformed into the playful and dreamlike episodes of romance. The comic flaws which the early heroes were often too obtuse to notice and ill equipped to eliminate through self-ridicule are magnified in Henderson, who both flamboyantly exhibits them and exorcises them through his own jocose language. But it would be a great injustice to dismiss the novel merely as a tall tale told by an idiot, full of sounds and frenzy, signifying nonsense. Beneath his bluster and buffoonery, Henderson is also a serious explorer who has hacked his way through the tangled underbrush and has learned from his mental travels. Despite Dahfu's directive lion therapy, he has come to know that he cannot escape from the endless cycle of "fear and desire" (297), the ineluctable condition of every living human being. Nor can he escape from his inevitable end, no matter how wily his stratagems or defiant his will. This recognition does not prevent Henderson from affirming, like Bellow's other yea-saying heroes, that "there is justice, and . . . much is promised" (328), and that "whatever gains . . . [were] made were always due to love" (339). However, Bellow's comic realism does not permit him to end the novel on such an unqualified euphoric note. Henderson, to be sure, is differentiated from the uncontaminated orphan child he holds on his lap. As the aging man unavoidably sullied by life, his Wordsworthian cloud of glory is described with rueful humor as being "dingy, mere tatters of gray fog" (339). Nor is Henderson finally imaged in regal, leonine terms. He is instead associated with the "wretched time-abused" trained bear, Smolak, with whom he used to ride a roller coaster in his youth. Like Augie, who concludes at the end of his quest that "imperfection is always the condition as found" (260), Henderson realizes now what Smolak instinctively knew then: "that for creatures there is nothing that ever runs unmingled" (339). Even so, Henderson can still be the "mad laugher" (217) and irrepressible *luftmensch*, coming home to raise mirth and soar again.

That Suffering Joker

7

"Look at us, deafened, hampered, impeded, impaired and bowel-glutted with wise counsel and good precept, and the more plentiful our ideas the worse our headaches. So we ask, will some good creature pull out the plug and ease our disgusted hearts a little?"[1] So Gooley MacDowell, Bellow's amateur Socrates and quirky monologist, addressing "the Hasbeens Club of Chicago," could very well be describing the plight of Moses Elkanah Herzog.[2] Like Joseph, Leventhal, and Wilhelm, those lachrymose obstructed heroes of Bellow's victim literature, his vulnerable psyche is assailed with specious "wise counsel and good precept." His head is throbbing with painful recollections and warring insights. But like Augie and Henderson, those plucky challengers of Bellow's rebel literature, Herzog can "ease his disgusted heart" by calling into play his resilient sense of humor. He can eventually unload his weighty egotism and affirm the value of community. Herzog's affirmation, however, is not so effortlessly achieved. Whereas Augie and Henderson are part-time cogitators who only flirt with ideas, they can more readily break free of them to mingle with all kinds of people and extol their worth. Herzog, on the other hand, is the professional egghead whose ideas are his all-absorbing companions. He initially thinks

1. Saul Bellow, "Address by Gooley MacDowell to the Hasbeens Club of Chicago," *Hudson Review* 4 (Summer, 1951): 226.
2. Citations to this novel are to *Herzog* (New York: Viking Press, 1964).

he can understand and improve humanity through his sage speculations about it, even though he is removed from humanity. As it turns out, his mind becomes so "jammed with thoughts" (319) and he grows so "sick with abstractions" (123) that he is blinded to ordinary reality and the existence of other human beings. Before he emerges from his cerebral retreat, we witness the comedy of his tilting at intellectual windmills and being deterred from encountering the concrete texture of life. But we also observe the agony caused by his hyperactive intro-spection. "A prisoner of perception" (72), he desperately wishes a reprieve from his sentence of hard mental labor to rejoin his fellow man. But just as no good creature pulls out Gooley's plug, no *deus ex machina* frees Herzog. He must struggle to extricate himself. The novel is a record of that struggle.

From Herzog's assessment of his experiences during the previous five days and from the memories of his recent and not-so-recent past precipitated by them, we learn how he has misconducted his life. Un-like his biblical namesake, he has spent his $20,000 patrimony, not on promised land, but on dilapidated property in the Massachusetts wilderness. He has strayed from the tribe of the Israelites to gain "a solid footing in white Anglo-Saxon Protestant America" (309), yet he has not escaped from being the "Jew-man of Ludeyville" (49). He has forsaken his orderly, benevolent first wife, only to have been forsaken by his disorderly, malevolent second wife. He has deteriorated from a productive, lucid scholar into a fallow, confused thinker. But because Herzog's misconduct is so extreme and extends to all spheres of his life, it is difficult to take it altogether seriously. His woes are so in-numerable and seemingly insoluble that his excessively dire circum-stances make for a burlesque of the trials of Job.

Herzog is, however, more a self-ridiculing than a self-righteous Job. In the process of explaining, having it out, justifying, putting into perspective, clarifying, and making amends, he is able to expose many of the comic flaws of his own character, including the diagnosis of his laughable chronic vanity. He recalls how as a youth he had been overly proud of his "soft handsome face, wasting [his] time in arrogant looks" (17), and even now, in his faded middle age, he admits to being "vain of his muscles, the breadth and strength of his hands, the smoothness of his skin" (12). But he can also cure himself of his infec-tious conceit with the most styptic humor of any of the Bellow heroes.

Gazing admiringly at his reflection in the mirror, he hyperbolically
compliments himself and then rationalizes away his self-love by
hazarding an overly ingenious explanation for man's narcissism: "Oh,
terrific—you look exquisite, Moses! Smashing! The primitive self-
attachment of the human creature, so deep, so old it may have a cellular origin" (159). Bellow as omniscient narrator pulls down Herzog's
vanity as well. In the courtroom scene he describes him as crossing his
legs "with a certain style" and then impishly adds that "his elegance
never deserted him even when he scratched himself" (225). But it is
Herzog's estimate of himself as an irresistible lady's man which is subject to the most devastating comic correction. Initially, he is confident
he can pass for a "grand-looking man" (159) and even in "fleeting
moments" fancies himself "the young and glossy stud" (154). But his
self-mockery promptly undermines his inflated claims of extraordinary
virility and disqualifies him from long-term participation in any kind
of sexual olympics. Even though he succeeds in satisfying Ramona, "a
true sack artist" (17), he still jeeringly dubs himself the "petit-bourgeois
Dionysian" (17) or a "prince of the erotic Renaissance" (186). And
although he still has the "strength to carry a heavy-buttocked woman
to the bed," he wryly concedes that "there were more faithful wor-
shipers of Eros than Moses Elkanah Herzog" (154).

Perhaps the best deflater of Herzog's affectation is the ever-present
obtrusiveness of his body. Although he is not plagued by the "enormities and deformities" of a Henderson, or burdened by the "indecently
big, spoiled" hulk of a Wilhelm, he is still embarrassed by the ravages
of age upon his once delectable corpus and is thus comically *"tantalized"* by irksome physical imperatives.[3] Herzog would, for example,
like to resemble the handsome, beatific rabbi his mother had wanted
him to become—but when he is dressed in bathing trunks and a straw
hat, he observes with rueful humor how "gruesomely unlike a rabbi"
he appears . . .

> his face charged with heavy sadness, foolish utter longing of which a
> religious life might have purged him. That mouth!—heavy with desire
> and irreconcilable anger, the straight nose sometimes grim, the dark
> eyes! And his figure!—the long veins winding in his arms and filling

3. Henri Bergson, "Laughter," in *Comedy*, ed. Wylie Sypher (New York: Doubleday
& Co., 1956), p. 93.

in the hanging hands, an ancient system, of greater antiquity than the Jews themselves (22).

Even though he is outfitted in the latest summer resort fashions, he cannot accept himself as the dapper *bon vivant,* because he cannot avoid identifying himself with those "paunchy old men" with their "pitiful puckered knees and varicose veins, pelican bodies and . . . haggard faces under sporty caps" (19). Most disappointing of all, Herzog cannot sustain the pose of the great humanitarian. Instead of improving the human condition, all he can do is take "a sleeping pill, to preserve himself" (107). By perpetually calling attention to the corporeal side of Herzog, or by having Herzog himself wryly deprecate his body, Bellow not only makes his hero the target of laughter, but also batters away at his comic presumption.

Even if no mention were made of Herzog's uncomplimentary physical features, he would still be funny as the confirmed bungler or, as he describes himself, "the stumbling, ingenuous, burlap Moses" (307). Like Tommy Wilhelm, he is another *schlemiel,*[4] that "agent of cultivated disability . . . [who] runs toward his goal over an obstacle course where he himself is responsible for strewing about most of the obstacles."[5] Wilhelm allows vampires and confidence men to bleed him of his funds; in like manner Herzog's "dignified blundering" (31) has financially exhausted him. He shamefacedly admits, "With me, money is not a medium. I am money's medium. It passes through me—taxes, insurance, mortgage, child support, rent, legal fees" (31). Herzog is also derelict in his religious obligations, obligations which he usually takes seriously. Unlike Updike's Bech, the Jew as spawned by the Protestant imagination, who is familiar with only the ethnic clichés and sociological parodies of Judaism, Herzog is an authentic Jew who is deeply committed to the Jewish heritage. When he becomes too intimate with beloved infidels and is in danger of neglecting his own creed, he is especially severe with himself. Making love to his Oriental mistress, Sono, on her unclean, disheveled bed, he hyperbolically reproaches himself for being a renegade from the faith. "Have all the

---

4. For an excellent discussion of Herzog as the "schlemiel as liberal humanist," see Ruth R. Wisse, *The Schlemiel as Modern Hero* (Chicago: University of Chicago Press, 1971), pp. 92–107.

5. Chester E. Eisinger, "Saul Bellow: Love and Identity," *Accent* 18 (Summer, 1958): 200.

traditions, passions, renunciations, virtues, gems, and masterpieces of Hebrew discipline . . . brought me to these untidy green sheets and this rippled mattress?" (170). In his courtship of Madeleine, when he commits the unpardonable sin of accompanying her to mass, he is appalled by the absurdity and sacrilege that he, a Jewish family man whose middle name, Elkanah, means "possessed by God," should be attending a service in the Catholic Church. Herzog amusingly but accurately characterizes his religious failings when he confesses to the God of the Old Testament, "Lord, I ran to fight in Thy holy cause, but kept tripping, never reached the scene of the struggle" (128). Herzog is also a poor judge of women, especially when it comes to selecting a marriage partner. Just as Wilhelm "had made up his mind not to marry his wife, but ran off and got married" (23), so Herzog knows what he "should avoid. Then, all of a sudden, [he's] in bed with that very thing, and making love to it" (334). Instead of choosing the submissive, thrifty Sono, he marries the domineering, extravagant Madeleine. Herzog is, moreover, an unwitting accomplice to his own cuckoldry. While he obligingly spends four afternoons on the psychiatrist's couch, Valentine Gersbach conveniently spends his time in Madeleine's bed. Herzog even permits Gersbach to take Madeleine's diaphragm to her in Boston, where she had gone to save their marriage. Like Isaac Bashevis Singer's Gimpel the fool,[6] who is repeatedly cuckolded yet continues to believe in his wife's innocence despite the most damning evidence of her adultery, Herzog believes Madeleine when she insists that Gersbach is not her lover but the "brother [she] never had" (193). Later, of course, Herzog realizes the cruel joke that has been played on him, for which he himself has provided the climactic, humorous twist. Or, as he mordantly describes the *ménage à trois,* "I sometimes see all three of us as a comedy team . . . with me playing straight man" (190). As a father, Herzog is also incompetent. Unlike the patriarchs of old who protected the entire tribe from injury and destruction, Herzog cannot even take his little daughter on an outing without almost killing her. Despite his fine intentions and his conscientious efforts, Herzog is still one of those "bungling child-men" (266), "an incorrigible character, doing always the same stunts, repeating the same disgraces" (182)—in other words, the *schlemiel.*

---

6. Isaac Bashevis Singer, "Gimpel the Fool," trans. Saul Bellow, *Partisan Review* 20 (May–June, 1953): 300–313.

As a *schlemiel,* Herzog is chiefly responsible for his own "humiliating comedy of heartache" (166). But like Wilhelm and Leventhal, Bellow's other obsessed abuse-seekers, he also relishes this heartache. As he says, "When a man's breast feels like a cage from which all the dark birds have flown—he is free, he is light. And he longs to have his vultures back again. He wants his customary struggles, his nameless, empty works, his anger, his afflictions and his sins" (169). Unlike his tormented fictional brethren, however, Herzog recognizes the perverse delight he derives from anguish and can see the humor in such masochism. When he subjects himself to his own brutal self-scrutiny and finds himself grossly inadequate as a husband, father, son, brother, citizen, friend, lover, and thinker, he claims to be "satisfied with his own severity, positively enjoying the hardness and factual rigor of his judgment" (5). Yet he undercuts the harshness of his self-criticism by wryly adding, "But how charming we remain, notwithstanding" (5). Without benefit of a Tamkin or a Dahfu to clear his vision, he realizes that his entire life has been one prolonged love affair with suffering, what with "writhing under [Madeleine's] sharp elegant heel" (76), lending "his attackers strength" (4), and inflaming himself with "failure, denunciation, distortion" (208). He is able to point up the inanity of such an existence by presenting a facetiously melodramatic account of its basic pattern. "I fall upon the thorns of life, I bleed. And what next? I get laid, I take a short holiday, but very soon after I fall upon those same thorns with gratification in pain, or suffering in joy—who knows what the mixture is" (207).

Similarly, Herzog can see the humor in his chronic lamentation. This is not to say that he is without any genuine sorrows. He is not an Alexander Portnoy, whose chief rage is directed against a nasty Mommy and whose complaint is but a puerile temper tantrum interspersed with prurient exhibitionism. Herzog has experienced severe personal indignities and deserves a certain measure of commiseration. Yet, as Bellow has pointed out, "*Herzog* makes comic use of complaint."[7] For example, when he considers telling Ramona his much rehearsed tale of victimization, he likens himself to "an addict struggling to kick the habit" (156). Or recalling how he "suffered in style"

[7.] Gordon L. Harper, "Saul Bellow—The Art of Fiction: An Interview," *Paris Review* 37 (Winter, 1963): 62.

(16), he admits to turning his " 'personal life' into a circus, into gladiatorial combat" (307). Fully recognizing his tendency toward hyperbolic confessions of woe, he, unlike the earlier Bellow protagonists, has the necessary detachment to call himself "that suffering joker" (11).

While Herzog is amusing because he is a "real, genuine old Jewish type that digs the emotions" (84) and compels others to "dig" his emotions, he is "to the point of death, 'comical'" (92) because of the all-absorbing project he has undertaken, a project which throws him "out of gear with the fundamental norms and orders of human existence."[8] Augie is obsessed with seeking a distinctive fate, and Henderson is driven to transcend human limitation; so Herzog has "tried to be a *marvelous* Herzog" (93). As a high school youth, brought to a boil by Emerson, he fervently believes that "the main enterprise of the world . . . is the upbuilding of a man" (160). As an adult he is still filled with "high cravings" (166) for the good and the true. It is, according to Bellow, Herzog's obsession with being an exceptional individual that makes him so humorous: "I don't think that I've represented any really good men. . . . I often represent men who desire such qualities but seem unable to achieve them on any significant scale. . . . Herzog wants very much to have effective virtues. But that's a source of comedy in the book."[9] Herzog does not wish to achieve merely personal excellence, to upbuild only himself. He is consumed with the far more lofty aim of making a significant intellectual contribution to society. He hopes to write a highly original, systematic study of the social ideas of the Romantics. It is his high-minded intention to come up with no less than a "new angle on the modern condition, showing how life could be lived by renewing universal connections; overturning the last of the Romantic errors about the uniqueness of the Self" (39). While such a noble endeavor is most laudatory, it turns out to be most ludicrous, since it is such an inconceivably large order for even the best-equipped supplier of information. Bellow himself has commented on the "comic impossibility of arriving at a synthesis that can satisfy modern demands."[10] In a *Chicago Tribune Books Today* interview he elaborates on this point with respect to *Herzog:*

8. Nathan A. Scott, Jr., "The Bias of Comedy and the Narrow Escape into Faith," *The Christian Scholar* 44 (Spring, 1961): 30.

9. Harper, "Saul Bellow—The Art of Fiction: An Interview," p. 67.

10. *Ibid.,* p. 69.

One of the sources of comedy in my book is the endless struggle of people to make sense of life and to sort out all the issues, and to get the proper historical perspective on oneself. . . . The whole world runs through your head like an oceanic tide and you have to, for the sake of your balance and even your sanity, sort everything out. My hero makes use of a phrase coined by President Wilson's Vice President, who was a man named Marshall, a Hoosier cracker barrel philosopher, and a great wit, who said, "What this country needs is a good 5 cent cigar." Herzog translates this for himself as "What this country needs is a good 5 cent synthesis." We live in these tides of information and fact which sway us back and forth. . . . The human mind seems to be not prepared for this kind of unprecedented modern crisis, and it is the humor of that kind of floundering that I try to get into Herzog. Even the qualified intellectual doesn't know what he's doing.[11]

Initially Herzog does not realize how absurd both he and his project are. He is supremely confident of his ability and feels that he can "wrap the subject up . . . pull the carpet from under all other scholars, show them what was what, stun them, expose their triviality once and for all" (119). Yet he assures himself that he is motivated not by the need for personal acclaim, but by a sense of genuine responsibility to his fellow man. Indeed, he regards himself as "the man on whom the world depended for certain intellectual work, to change history, to influence the development of civilization" (105). To accomplish such a momentous task, he deems it necessary to absent himself from society; only in splendid isolationism can he develop his splendid ideas. In a ramshackle hideaway he, like Thoreau, attempts to carry out "his plan for solitary self-sufficiency" (310–311). His plan, however, soon goes awry. Instead of writing a work which takes "into account the revolutions and mass convulsions of the twentieth century" (6), he becomes sidetracked by his own personal convulsions. Instead of elucidating Hegel's "ideas on consensus and civility" (6), he suffers the deterioration of his own civility. Instead of defining "the importance of the 'law of the heart' in Western traditions" (119), he is at a loss to define his own "throb-hearted" nature.

Unable to "legislate mentally"[12] for mankind, let alone govern him-

---

11. Robert Cromie, "Saul Bellow Tells (among Other Things) the Thinking behind *Herzog,*" *Chicago Tribune Books Today,* January 24, 1965, p. 9.

12. Tony Tanner, *Saul Bellow* (Edinburgh: Oliver & Boyd, 1965), p. 100.

self, Herzog heeds the promptings of his lawless id. Unable to cope
with the more complicated issues of life, he copes with women. Yet
Herzog is not consumed with achieving what Mailer in "The White
Negro" describes as the "orgasm more apocalyptic than the one which
preceded it."[13] Since his need for order is ultimately stronger than his
need for orgy, he can see the absurdity of his lust, revealing it to be
"the most wretched form of human struggle, the very essence of
slavery" (219). Yet he cannot entirely free himself from this form of
bondage. He ingeniously convinces himself that sexual gratification
is essential to his health and well-being. He further rationalizes his
personal need by generalizing it to a societal need. "The erotic," he
authoritatively claims, "must be admitted to its rightful place, at last,
in an emancipated society which understands the relation of sexual re-
pression to sickness, war, property, money, totalitarianism" (166). Bellow undoubtedly had such a remark in mind when he jocosely informed
a French reviewer: "En Amérique, la sexualité est moins plaisir
érotique qu'hygiène indispensable."[14] Herzog devastates his own rationalization by suggesting a similar *reductio ad absurdum* conclusion
that can be drawn from it: "Why, to get laid," he states with tongue
in cheek, "is actually socially constructive and useful, an act of citizen-
ship" (166). Despite his mockery of the worth of sexual therapy, he is
"powerless to reject the hedonistic joke of a mammoth industrial civilization" (166), and he eagerly puts himself in the hands of Ramona,
therapist *par excellence*. After a night-long treatment, he is still the
same idiosyncratic Herzog with "his problems as unsolved as ever" in
addition to "a lip made sore by biting and kissing" (207).

Along with being the erotic playboy of the western world, Herzog is
the erratic correspondent of the western world. Since his intellect is
temporarily in a state of disrepair and thus incapable of providing his
reading public with any sustained discussions of his views, he continually scribbles brief dispatches filled with his unfinished thoughts and
private associations. Although he addresses these messages to political
figures, psychiatrists, theologians, past and present philosophers, academic colleagues, living and dead relatives, and even to God, he never

---

[13.] Norman Mailer, "The White Negro," *Advertisements for Myself* (New York:
Berkeley Publishing Corporation, 1966), p. 321.
[14.] Pierre Dommergues, "Rencontre avec Saül Bellow," *Preuves* 17 (January, 1967):
41.

posts them. Joseph, unable to complete his essays on the Rationalists in an age of general irrationality, is driven to keep a journal to preserve his sanity; likewise Herzog, prevented from writing about the Romantics by his own tumultuous romances, must write his mental notes if he is to restore his balance—indeed, if he is to continue living. For, as he claims, he has always performed "elaborate abstract intellectual work . . . as if it were the struggle for survival," fully convinced that he "would die when thinking stopped" (265). This is not the only reason for his letter-writing. It also enables him to put "his troubles into high-minded categories" (58), allowing him to be dispassionate and even profound, meanwhile disguising the fact that he is settling his personal grievances. Through these letters he also plays the game of one-upmanship with the masterminds of all time. Since he has not been able to write a work which confounded and dazzled everyone, he is compelled to expose loopholes in the experts' thinking, furnish brilliant corrections, and overwhelm them with his own flawless theories. But Herzog soon realizes how inane it is for him to match wits with disembodied spirits, no matter how much his battered ego requires a victory. Even more disconcerting is his discovery that in these letters he has tried to impose his ideas on others. Therefore he, too, like the Reality Instructors he detests, is "a very special sort of lunatic [who] expects to inculcate his principles" (125). Yet this was not his conscious intention. What he had essentially wished to do through his "helter-skelter" correspondence "in all directions" (272) was to fathom the complexities of history and society in order to make sense of his own complexities. Also, by engaging in imaginary communication with people in the here and the hereafter, he had hoped to break out of his solitary confinement. But he ends up erecting verbal structures which only further distort the view of the world he is trying to understand and further separate him from the people he is trying to reach.

Love-making and letter-writing are not Herzog's only diversions when his "all-powerful human intellect . . . has no real occupation" (219). He also plays the role of the mad avenger. When he learns that his arch-rival, Valentine Gersbach, has locked his little daughter in a car at night to prevent her from hearing his argument with Madeleine, Herzog is outraged. He clamors for justice. He fantasies how he will annihilate the guilty pair. But for the time being he is not prompted to act out this fantasy. Only after he encounters the brutal-

ity of actual child-killers in a New York courtroom is he driven to
seek revenge upon Madeleine and Valentine.

Just as Henderson's confrontation with the malignant lion who
kills Dahfu forces him to recognize his own evasions of evil and
death, Herzog's hearing of the crimes of others leads him to acknowledge his own crimes. Initially, however, as he waits for his lawyer
in the hall of justice, he regards himself as the thoroughly upright
professor, the "Jesus" who has no "flies" (230) on him. But after
witnessing one case of human depravity after another, his composure
is visibly shaken. Unlike Leventhal, he does not attribute his uneasi-
ness to the presence of evil in an Allbee; unlike Joseph, he cannot be
entirely convinced that only the next man is "full of instinctive bloody
rages, licentious and unruly from his earliest days, an animal who
had to be tamed" (39). Rather, Herzog has the "floating suspicion"
(231) that he, too, has his own generous endowment of evil. He begins
to realize that his ridiculous obsession to become "a marvelous
Herzog" has not purged him of his wickedness, but has merely
forced it to go into hiding. On the surface, therefore, he appears to be
the tamed animal, the "pet goose" (231) who, like the outwardly submissive Tommy Wilhelm, makes the "psychic offer—meekness in
exchange for preferential treatment" (154). If any evil were to be
committed, he would never be the perpetrator of it. "Others were
appointed to do it to him, and then to be accused (by him) of wickedness" (245). But for the most part, striving for perfection and pursuing his humane studies in the "coop of his privacy" (9), he had been
shielded from the vile side of life. Even as a teenager he had tried to
escape the most unpleasant reality of all—death. Henderson fled to
Africa, "the real past" (46), to avoid death; so Herzog, "a bookish,
callow boy" (235), immersed himself in Spengler's Magian era to
ignore the fact that his mother was dying. He was incensed that as a
Jew he was considered a relic, but he did not seem particularly
distressed that his mother, already a walking skeleton, was soon to be
a corpse. When her eyes finally told him, "My son, this is death,"
Herzog reflects: "I chose not to read this text" (234). As the insulated
young intellectual, he would rather read *The Decline of the West,*
preferring to consider cultural decline than personal decline." [15] But in

15. John J. Clayton, *Saul Bellow: In Defense of Man* (Bloomington: Indiana University Press, 1968), p. 209.

the courtroom Herzog cannot fail to recognize personal decline, nor can his scholar's immunity to evil prevail. He can no longer be comforted by the naive view that "once cruelty has been described in books it is ended" (238). When he comes up against real cruelty—the abysmal neglect and then fiendish murder of an innocent child—he experiences in full force "the monstrousness of life" (240). Identifying his own daughter with the slain child, and Madeleine and Valentine with the villainous mother and her lover, he can no longer suppress his own internal evil—the "acrid fluid in his mouth that had to be swallowed" (239). Moses, the would-be law-giver, therefore flies to Chicago to violate the most sacred commandment, "Thou shalt not kill." But like Bellow's other outraged heroes, with the possible exception of Henderson, he only murders in his imagination. Far from being a Stephen Rojack, the college professor who in Mailer's *An American Dream* actually does kill his wife, Herzog only poses as the fierce vindicator, never firing his father's antique pistol. When he sees Madeleine and Valentine, he is able to dissociate them from the heinous criminals he had recently witnessed. And when he catches sight of his little daughter, not beaten to death but very much alive and thoroughly enjoying her bath, he does not have to commit a Valentine massacre. He immediately recognizes the absurdity of the revenge which has consumed him. As Bellow indicates, Herzog's "intended violence turned into *theater*, into something ludicrous. He was not ready to make such a complete fool of himself" (258).

Herzog's foolishness, however, is not at an end. When he finally gets to spend the afternoon with his daughter, he has an automobile accident. The accident is not his fault, but concealing his father's "clumsy horse pistol with [its] two cartridges" (284) is his fault and is considered a misdemeanor by the police. Too late, he realizes that he should have left the revolver in his friend's apartment and "stopped being quixotic" (286). Booked for carrying a loaded weapon, he and his daughter are taken to the police station. Although this is what he may have been seeking in his "earnest Herzog way"—to be "down in the ranks with other people, ordinary life"—he has to admit that this was an inane way of going about it. He had to smash a car, fracture his ribs, and terrify his little girl to "determine which reality is real" (287). As he sardonically remarks, "You burn the house to roast the pig. It was the way humankind always roasted pigs" (287). But

Herzog is now through burning houses. In his jail cell he vows to bring down the curtain on his "daily comedy" (159). "No more of this hectic, heart-rent, theatrical window-peering; no more collision, fainting, you-fight-'im-'e-cry encounters, confrontations" (303). When Herzog is freed from his brief imprisonment, he is also freed of most of his comic vices.

Returning to his Berkshire haven, Herzog is able to divest himself of his former affectation—in the words of Whitman, to escape "from the life that exhibits itself" (324). He can surrender his sorrows without feeling robbed of them; he can give up his sackcloth and ashes without feeling naked. Unlike Tommy Wilhelm, he is now able to go "with joy" and not think he is committing "adultery" (98). As he greets the radiance of the sun, he is filled with "true cheerfulness, not the seeming sanguinity of the Epicureans, nor the strategic buoyancy of the heartbroken" (319).

Herzog has also ceased being a "junkie—on thought." [16] He has given up what Bellow describes in *The Last Analysis* as "the mind's comical struggle for survival in an environment of Ideas." [17] When Herzog now encounters a myriad of facts, he is not compelled to explain their precise meaning or to organize them in any systematic way. When he finds a note card in his study reminding him "to do justice to Condorcet" (312), he does not have to exhaust himself championing any theorist who agrees with him or lash out at any other who opposes him. No longer placing such a high premium on intellectuality for its own sake, Herzog comes to understand that "habit, custom, tendency, temperament, inheritance and the power to recognize real and human facts have equal weight with ideas." [18] This does not mean that Herzog will never return to his intellectual endeavors, yet we are assured that he will not rely exclusively on solitary intellection and thereby lose his grasp on ordinary reality. He has already discovered what distortions and strange views such separatism produces. Recognizing that he can achieve meaning not in isolation, but in the midst of other men, Herzog vows, "I mean to share with other human beings as far as possible and not destroy my remaining years in the same way" (322).

[16.] Saul Bellow, *The Last Analysis* (New York: The Viking Press, 1965), p. 10.
[17.] *Ibid.*, p. vii.
[18.] Harper, "Saul Bellow—The Art of Fiction: An Interview," p. 71.

Above all, Herzog is no longer one of those intellectuals who love only "an imaginary human situation invented by their own genius" (304). Like Henderson after his lion shock therapy, he can accept reality for what it is without altering it to suit his fancy. As Herzog inspects his property, he can accept both the incomparable beauty of the land and the ugly ruins beyond repair, the contaminated well water and the overgrown garden—"hopeless—past regretting" (310). He can accept his tumbledown house, knowing full well that he will never have the strength to renovate it. He is no longer disgusted with the "ruins of his scholarly enterprise" (311), nor is he outraged or envious that his sanctuary has become the trysting place for village lovers. Although saddened by the skeletons of young birds trapped in the drained toilet bowl, he can even accept their untimely death. Perhaps more significant, he is able to accept the eventuality of his own death, not with rancor but with a "holy feeling" (340). With the same "spirit of comedy" (233) with which his mother had tried to prove to him that Adam was created out of dust, and with the same "wit you can have only when you consider death very plainly" (233), Herzog declares, "I look at myself and see chest, thighs, feet—a head. This strange organization, I know it will die" (340). Meanwhile, even though his face is "too blind," his "mind too limited," and his "instincts too narrow" (340), he opts to make do with his flawed being during his brief span of survival. Herzog ends up being "the comic man" whom Nathan Scott defines as the "contingent, imperfect, earth-bound creature" whose function it is "to awaken in us a lively recognition of what in fact our true status is."[19] Herzog, as comic man,

> asks us not to be afraid to acknowledge that we are only human and that our residence is not in the heavens. And he asks us to examine critically all the spurious stratagems that we employ to evade a frank acceptance of our finitude, whether they be those of bourgeois worldliness or of philosophical and religious mysticism. What the comic man cannot abide is the man who will not consent to be simply a man, who cannot tolerate the thought of himself as an incomplete and conditioned creature of a particular time and a particular space.[20]

19. Scott, "The Bias of Comedy," p. 19.
20. Ibid.

In addition to viewing himself as comic man, Herzog is endowed with "passionate satire" (129) which enables him to express what is worthy of laughter in the next fellow. Because he has been "swindled, conned [and] manipulated" (156) by chance acquaintances and supposed friends alike, his satire is, for the most part, of the harsh Juvenalian brand. Unlike Augie, whose resilient youth and larky good nature allow him to playfully mock and genially exonerate his exploiters, Herzog is initially too embittered to contain his vitriol or even to dilute it. All he can do is transform it into corrosive wit and wait for the opportunity to discharge it. But since Herzog has limited his contact with most people, they exist only as fleeting figures in his thoughts. He therefore cannot furnish any sustained caustic analysis of what makes them funny; he can merely fulminate about their most salient comic features. Aunt Zelda he scathingly dismisses as the vain and hypocritical suburban *hausfrau* who fancies herself a cut above the other ladies of the neighborhood, even though she, too, dyes her hair, wears "purplish lines on her lids" (37), and believes that every married girl is entitled to "nightly erotic gratification" (40) along with every conceivable luxury. Dr. Edvig, the Protestant Freudian, he lampoons as the unprofessional psychiatrist who prefers to treat Madeleine rather than Herzog, since she has a more intriguing body and a leaning toward Christianity. Shapiro, the intellectual historian, he denounces both as a ridiculously affected academician and as the gluttonous offspring of a rotten apple vendor. The lawyers Himmelstein and Simkin he ambivalently views as representative mass men foully "cutting everybody down to size" (86) and as a pair of old-fashioned Jews, oozing with "schmaltzy" affection.

It is only when Herzog recalls the droll characters who inhabited his childhood that he employs the milder Horatian kind of satire. Since his nostalgia rather than his wrath has been kindled, he is prompted to take a wistful inventory of all the odd dwellers of Napoleon Street. Although he detects their flaws and itemizes them with benign laughter, he still wants to retain these imperfect creatures as permanent fixtures in his memory. An unexpected meeting with Nachman, a former grade school friend, causes Herzog to begin his own ruefully humorous remembrance of things past. He calls to mind Nachman's father, the tyrannical, Mongolian-hued Hebrew teacher who immediately assumed that all of his pupils were not only bastards and thieves but, far worse, devourers of ham and bacon. Far less threatening was Nachman's uncle, Ravitch, the incurable tipster, who, having lost his wife and children in the Russian Revolution, boarded with the Herzogs. Nightly serenading the family with alternate snatches from Hebrew liturgy and popular tunes, this ineffectual Jewish drunkard, unable to become cheerful even when inebriated, evoked both laughter and tears. A greater disturber of the peace was Aunt Zipporah, who, like Augie March's Grandma Lausch, was "witty, grudging, at war with everyone" (141). A sharp-tongued critic of the Herzog pursuit of "dignities, honors" (141), she strove only for material objects. Father Herzog, just the opposite of his crass sister, was the refined though improvident gentleman. Although he "could calculate percentages mentally at high speed" (138), he was slow to realize any of the profits. Having repeatedly failed as a businessman, he still prided himself on being a fierce struggler. Herzog amusingly remembers that, as with himself, all of "Papa's violence went into the drama of his life, into family strife, and sentiment" (146).

There are characters whom Herzog wants to blot out of his memory —the two who have most sorely wronged him, Valentine and Madeleine. Yet his hatred of them keeps them uppermost in his mind. Unlike the Napoleon Street figures whose defects become less offensive and even endearing through his mental revival of them, the aberrations of the two "love actors" are magnified through Herzog's compulsive dwelling upon them. They alone incur his most searing and unrelenting invective.

Valentine, "a paper imitation of the real man of heart," [21] has many of the same comic vices as Herzog, only his vices are more extreme. Valentine also evokes more unsympathetic laughter than Herzog, since he does not have his redeeming virtue of self-mockery. Although Valentine has a more advanced case of ridiculous vanity than Herzog —jauntily wearing the flashy apparel which Herzog is ashamed to purchase and fancying himself the prize cock of the walk—never once does he wryly puncture his full-blown conceit.

Valentine considers himself the prize sufferer as well. Herzog's psychic scars are obviously insignificant compared to his devastating

21. David D. Galloway, "Moses-Bloom-Herzog: Bellow's Everyman," *Southern Review* 2 (Winter, 1966): 73.

physical wound—the amputation of his leg at the age of seven. Unlike Herzog, who makes fun of his own feeble bids for sympathy, Valentine without the slightest trace of levity demands as just compensation all the compassion the world can give him. "A frequent weeper of distinguished emotional power" (45), he generally obtains the desired response. But a good part of the time he ends up receiving the greatest share of compassion from himself. Valentine has a monopoly on other kinds of emotion also. As Herzog sardonically says of him, "He *was* a king, an emotional king, and the depth of his heart was his kingdom" (61). However, once any serious emotions become Valentine's possessions, they soon sound like foolish dimestore sentiments.

Valentine is also the caricature of the "real, genuine old Jewish type" (84). Vastly ignorant of the religious, ethical, and cultural traditions of Judaism, he thinks he can pass himself off as the choicest of the chosen people by writing heart-rending poems about his quaint old Jewish grandfather and delivering easily understood lectures on Martin Buber to Hadassah groups. Above all, he purposely loads his speech with vivid Yiddish expressions. Herzog jeeringly informs us that Valentine grossly misuses and mispronounces most of these; thus he is an *ersatz* Jew as well as an *ersatz* man of feeling.

Valentine is most ludicrous in his specious pose as the intellectual. Whereas Herzog experiences great difficulty in making sense out of very complex ideas, Valentine, the great "popularizer," has no trouble in simplifying such ideas so that they are readily understood by the average third-grade viewer of television. Whereas Herzog fails to produce a grand synthesis of all existing knowledge, Valentine is "a regular Goethe [who] finished all your sentences, rephrased all your thoughts, explained everything" (155). Whereas Herzog actively engages in honest battle with the great minds of past and present, Valentine, the television "ringmaster" (215), pits one contemporary thinker against another and passively looks on as they feign tearing into each other. Whereas Herzog desperately wishes to leave his ivory tower to share his talents with other human beings, Valentine, readily established in the world at large, effortlessly gives of himself and is able to be all things to all people. "With pinochle players he plays pinochle, with rabbis it's Martin Buber, with the Hyde Park Madrigal society he sings Madrigals" (217). Whereas Herzog gives thoughtful advice to his disturbed friend Lucas Asphalter, the "lectures Gersbach read [Herzog] . . . were . . . a parody of the intellectual's desire for higher meaning, depth, quality" (60). Valentine Gersbach is a superb example of the buffoon as thinker, "the kind of man who makes intellectuals wish they were dead when they hear him parroting their words." [22]

In George Meredith's opinion, the higher the comedy, the more prominent the part women play in it.[23] While this is not the case in most of Bellow's novels, where the female characters have no significant effect upon their menfolk, it is the case in *Herzog*, where Madeleine plays a leading role in the hero's "painful emotional comed[y]" (269). The Madeleine we see, however, is not a fully realized personality, but the grotesquely funny creature that emerges from Herzog's angry recollections and perverse fantasies. Lacking any fixed psychic identity, she is above all the quirky dilettante, much like Henderson's wives who, in the earlier versions of that novel, are by turns intensely interested in the Crimean War, Kierkegaard, Jung, and leprosy.[24] The only difference is that Madeleine's tastes are more diversified and that she pursues each of them with a vengeance, albeit a short-lived one. Like the predators of Bellow's other novels, the imposters Allbee and Tamkin, she exhibits manifestations of inauthenticity—a flare for theatrics and an obsession with role-playing. When Herzog first meets her, she is in fact caught up with acting the Catholic convert. Not only does she relish transforming herself into "a woman of forty—some white, hysterical, genuflecting hypochondriac of the church aisles" (112); she especially looks forward to confessing her sins to the eminent Monsignor Hilton, the proselyter of celebrities. But after she falls prey to the lascivious Jew, she feels too sullied to take communion and thus deprives herself of an invaluable association with one of the most famous Princes of the Church. Madeleine, then, leaves off being the "high-minded Christian

22. Irving Howe, "Odysseus, Flat on His Back," *New Republic* 151 (September 19, 1964): 21.

23. George Meredith, "An Essay on Comedy," in *Comedy*, ed. Wylie Sypher (New York: Doubleday & Co., 1956), p. 14.

24. Saul Bellow, *Henderson the Rain King* manuscripts, Harper Library, University of Chicago, Chicago, Illinois. Information about Henderson's wives' bizarre interests is found in typewritten draft, Ch. 7, p. 112; miscellaneous typewritten pages (B:8:9); and miscellaneous typewritten pages (B:8:33).

lady" (112) to become the "queen of the intellectuals" (76). She is amusingly unconvincing as a practicing Catholic; she is also unbelievable as a genuine bluestocking. This is not to suggest that she is without any intellectual passions. She has, to be sure, been consumed with Soloviev, Joseph de Maistre, "the French Revolution, Eleanor of Aquitaine, Schliemann's excavations at Troy, extrasensory perception . . . then Christian Science, before that, Mirabeau" (73). But Herzog informs us that her overriding interest is in reading murder mysteries and gossip columns. When she isn't straining her eyes over the printed word, she is out making costly purchases at the most elegant shops. Yet, absurdly enough, she has illusions of invading and taking possession of Herzog's intellectual stamping grounds, when in fact her constantly shifting enthusiasms would indicate that she is incapable of even self-possession.

Along with fancying herself the bluestocking *extraordinaire,* Madeleine considers herself the grand lady. With her affected British accent, "[her] patrician style" and "the crazy clear hauteur of [her] eyes" (298), she tries to conceal her unrefined bohemian background. But frequently her crude self humorously bursts out of hiding. That she never bothers to clean up the eggshells, chop bones [and] tin cans under the table, under the sofa" (59) is not in itself a sign of poor breeding, since noblewomen were never meant to be ignoble servants. But her tongue-lashing, fouler than any fishwife's, and her physical attacks, more vicious than any street fighter's, indicate that she is not the lofty individual she represents herself to be. Despite the fact that we are limited to Herzog's impression of Madeleine, we have to concede that his general assessment of her is not only clever but to some degree accurate: "Ah, this Madeleine is a strange person, to be so proud but not well wiped . . . —such a mixed mind of pure diamond and Woolworth glass" (299).

If Madeleine is the bizarrely comic *belle dame sans merci,* then Ramona Donselle is the comically pathetic woman with too much *merci.* Not only does she give Herzog "room . . . in her soul, and . . . the embrace of her body"; she also supplies him with "asylum, shrimp, wine, music, flowers, sympathy" (199). And if for some reason he could not sexually satisfy her, she would understand. "If anything, such humiliations would challenge or intrigue her, bring out her generosity" (208).

In addition to being the excessively understanding woman, Ramona strains to be the *femme fatale*. But since she is approaching the desperate age of thirty-eight, her performances as a "tough Spanish broad" or one of those tarts in a "girlie magazine" turn out to be more silly than seductive. Although Herzog ultimately succumbs to her contrived charms, he sees that beneath her masquerade she is the fatigued middle-aged woman who very much wants a husband. If she must perform elaborate rituals to secure one, she is willing to do so. Thus Ramona's "erotic monkey-shines" (17) prove more pathetic than amusing.

Ramona is totally amusing as theoretician of sex and sensibility. Trusting in the power of positive love-making, she urges Herzog to give full expression to his instincts and revel in her style of hedonism. It is her firm conviction that sexual release can eliminate man's "constitutional tension of whatever origin" (201), along with curing the world of most of its ills. Should one fail to satisfy the needs of the body, she is certain it would be a "surrender to malignancy, capitulating to the death instinct" (185). To lend support to her claim, Ramona not only quotes "Catullus and the great love poets of all times" (202), but also cites the unimpeachable conclusions of such neo-Freudians as Marcuse and N. O. Brown. Despite her "florid" lecturing and her exuberant practical demonstrations, she is unable to convince Herzog that "the body is a spiritual fact, the sinstrument of the soul" (208–209). Like the passive resister Augie March, Herzog finds such theorizing, even Ramona's ridiculous brand of it, a "dangerous temptation [which] can only lead to more high-minded mistakes" (209). By making Ramona out to be the caricatured sensualist, Bellow discredits the belief in that kind of indulgence which does not allow for any self-regulating principles.

While Herzog focuses his comic lens primarily on his own flaws and the flaws of those close to him, he occasionally directs it outward at mankind in general. Although he sometimes transforms his personal spite into public scorn, the incisiveness of his insights cannot be denied. They are not "sophomoric tag-lines,"[25] as Poirier claims, but expressions of a gifted intelligence which enlarge a tale of private folly into a wide-ranging ideological comedy. Unlike Joseph, whose social indictment is but an inchoate quarrel with the profiteering,

25. Richard Poirier, "Bellows to Herzog," *Partisan Review* 32 (Spring, 1965): 271.

war-mongering usurpers of his freedom, or Augie and Henderson, who never stop moving long enough to make any sustained inquiries as to what bothers them in the external world, Herzog is the painstaking examiner of many of the mid-twentieth century's inane practices and values. Yet his unsent letters, the vehicles for his criticism, are not, like Norman Mailer's *Presidential Letters,* exclusively of the editorial axe-grinding variety; nor do they reek of the author's sense of himself as intellectual saviour of mankind. They are instead expressions of a man who, because he occasionally emerges from Plato's cave and has unimpaired glimpses of reality, is in a position to expose the faulty vision of those who are still in the cave and can see only the shadow of things. He does not presume that his exposure will cause humanity to vacate entirely from the realm of appearances. He would be satisfied if his perception of the disparity between the actual and the fancied would every now and then shatter illusions and promote lucidity.

Chaotically and arbitrarily dispersed throughout the narrative, Herzog's letters vary in length and concerns. Their degree of seriousness depends upon the importance he ascribes to the subjects he is discussing. When, for example, he happens to think about the American style of bureaucracy, he complains of the Internal Revenue regulations which "turn us into a nation of bookkeepers" so that "the life of every citizen is becoming a business" (11). Since man's pursestrings rather than his heartstrings are most at issue, Herzog's pique is playfully expressed. But when he considers the country's insane nuclear policies which could endanger the lives of his own children and the entire population, he becomes one of those "bitter Voltairean types whose souls are filled with angry satire and who keep looking for the keenest, most poisonous word" (50). In a letter to the *New York Times* he directs his angry satire at Dr. Teller, whose remark about tight pants affecting the gonads more than fallout is grossly misleading, and at Dr. Strawforth, whose "Philosophy of Risk," the specious comparison of "human life to Risk Capital in business" (50), could trigger rather than deter a nuclear holocaust. Herzog mordantly observes that we prudent citizens are not innocent victims, for we willingly entrust our safety to such careless annihilation experts and persist in the belief that the "universe was made for our safe use" (50). Because Herzog has harbored a similar delusion in his private life, he is compelled to ridicule it by presenting a ludicrous example of such thinking. "Light travels at a quarter of a million miles per second so that we can see to comb our hair or to read in the paper that ham hocks are cheaper than yesterday" (50). Meanwhile, protected by such childish, erroneous notions, we remain at the mercy of those who have the power to obliterate us. And so Herzog ruefully concludes that de Tocqueville's impression of the American democratic society was incorrect, since its strongest impulse is not toward well-being, but toward self-destruction.

Herzog also takes the American democratic society to task for its lack of political acumen. Since he never does enter "politics in the Aristotelian sense" (94), he does the next best thing: he becomes the scathing assessor of national affairs. Although his assessment does not resemble the homely debunking of a Will Rogers and would never induce people to acknowledge what foolish political mortals they are, it does in its own urbane, sophisticated fashion reveal the fatuities of the Eisenhower era and sardonically censures the silent generation responsible for them. In a letter to Governor Stevenson, Herzog, the vocal majority of one, bitterly notes that instead of allowing intelligence to work for the public good, the people reject "mentality and its images, ideas, perhaps mistrusting them as foreign" (66). Instead of basing their choice of a president on sound judgment, they permit themselves to be swayed by degenerate sentimental affection, or what Herzog mockingly terms "low-grade universal potato love" (66). They bypass the intense humanist, Adlai, and pick as their standard-bearer the low-keyed military hero, Ike. They do not object to his appointing corporation lawyers and executives, those whom Herzog with tongue in cheek calls "Industrial Statesmen," to determine what America's aims should be. The people unquestioningly accept the Statesmen's "collection of loyal, helpful statements to inspire us in the struggle against the Communist enemy" (161–162) and devote their energies to manufacturing commodities in no way germane to their needs. Overly deferential to authority, the majority are content to be not Pascal's "thinking reeds," but "reed[s] bending before centrally generated winds" (162). Given such a state of affairs, Herzog can only mordantly conclude, "So things go on as before with those who think a great deal and effect nothing, and those who think nothing evidently doing it all" (66).

The Church, too, is subject to Herzog's wry scrutiny. His scrutiny, however, is colored by personal bias. Because Monsignor Hilton had been his rival for Madeleine's affections, and had been revered by her as the fount of all knowledge, Herzog transfers his animus for the man onto the institution he represents. Not only does he label the Church's claim of "universal understanding" to be a "harmful, Prussian delusion" (155), but he also punctures this delusion by stating, "Readiness to answer all questions is the infallible sign of stupidity" (155). Herzog's other objection to the Church has nothing to do with the waging of private vendettas. Angered by the maltreatment of others for a change, he chastens the clergy for its scant regard for the impoverished masses. While they purport to aid the indigent, they have done nothing constructive to eliminate the ugly poverty existing everywhere. If they genuinely tried to persuade the affluent to share their wealth, they would alienate their principal benefactors and be deprived of their own creaturely comforts. Out of self-interest, then, they minister only to the spiritual needs of their charges. And so the beggars still exist, whose wretchedness continues to make the rich men feel all the more superior because of their riches. As Herzog ironically observes, "Skid Row is the contrasting institution, therefore necessary. . . . Because of Lazarus, Dives gets an extra kick, a bonus, from his luxuries" (47). But Herzog's severest indictment is leveled at Dr. Edvig's Protestant Freudian version of Christianity for its depreciation of mankind. Like Augie March, who inveighs against the prevailing low estimate of man, Herzog cannot abide Calvin's "lousy, cringing, grudging conception of human nature" (58). Buttressed by the Jewish faith in the blessedness of creation and the sanctity of the temporal, Herzog ridicules that "Christian view of history" which sees "the present moment always as some crisis, some fall from classical greatness, some corruption of evil to be saved from" (54).

Even greater peddlars of doom are those pseudo-intellectual secular pessimists who have appropriated "visions of genius" (74) and in the process have perverted their meaning. In many of his essays and lectures Bellow has tried through wit and wily argument to upset their rotten pushcarts and run them out of business. In his earlier novels his heroes also made sporadic attempts to ferret them out and give them their eviction notices. But it is Herzog who most relentlessly pursues them, devastates them with his gall, and drives them into bankruptcy. He first exposes them as "pipsqueaks" ranting "about Inauthenticity and Forlornness" (75) and then denigrates the second-hand merchandise they are trying to foist on the public as "the canned sauerkraut of Spengler's 'Prussian Socialism,' the commonplaces of the Wasteland outlook, the cheap mental stimulants of Alienation" (74–75). Finally, to insure their never having a market for their wares, Herzog casts aspersions on the middle-class consumers of such damaged goods. One explanation Herzog offers for their gullibility is that their lives have grown so safe and tedious that they are quick to purchase any thrills, no matter how contrived or injurious they might be. Because they have not had many opportunities to witness firsthand "apocalypses, fires, drownings, stranglings, and the rest of it" (316), they attempt to satisfy their craving for the lurid by reading about the cataclysmic decline of the West, the ghastly void, and the fall into the terrifying quotidian. The other explanation Herzog suggests for the bourgeoisie's fascination with morbid ideas is similar to the one Diana Trilling furnishes: since the view of life as absurd has been highly endorsed by the best philosophical and literary circles, "to subscribe to this particular vision . . . is unmistakably to qualify for membership in a cultural elite."[26] Herzog evidently has this in mind when he wittily remarks, "Literate people appropriate all the best things they can find in books, and dress themselves in them just as certain crabs are supposed to beautify themselves with seaweed" (217). Frantically striving to be intellectually fashionable, to be at one with their cultural betters, they pretend to be crisis-ridden, alienated, and desperate. Indeed, Herzog underscores the inanity of having desperation as a prerequisite for belonging to the privileged class by hyperbolically commenting, "The day is fast approaching . . . when only proof that you are despairing will entitle you to the vote, instead of the means test, the pole tax, the literacy exam" (179).

Along with making sport of the overrated *Angst* of the spurious cognoscenti and those aspiring to join their ranks, Herzog ridicules the recent unwholesome preoccupation with death. The particular necrophiles he attacks are those German existentialists who lecture that "God is no more. But Death is" (271). If man would only lingeringly contemplate death, they claim, he would be rescued from distraction,

26. Diana Trilling, *Claremont Essays* (New York: Harcourt, Brace and World, 1964), p. 221.

gain freedom, and become "authentic." Herzog finds such a view nonsensical and dismisses it as another variation of "the old *memento mori,* the monk's skull on the table, brought up to date" (271). This is not to say that he objects to man's facing up to his mortality. Unlike Augie, who only fleetingly alludes to death in his euphoric disquisitions, or Henderson, who tries to avoid its imminence with acrobatic zeal, Herzog has reconciled himself to his eventual passing. Without such a reconciliation, he believes that the human spirit, "racing and conniving to evade death . . . holds its breath and hopes to be immortal because it does not live" (165). But Herzog cannot accept the "notion that a practiced and deliberate confrontation with death and despair will lead man to greater human depth." [27] The intentional courting of death, that is, purposely "disintegrating ourselves by our own wills in proof of our 'freedom' " (314), is, in his opinion, the worst kind of folly rather than the best kind of wisdom. The alternative he proposes is "acknowledging that we owe a human life to this waking spell of existence, regardless of the void" (314). Rather than practicing "over-kill" on ourselves, we would have time for the most meaningful task of all: "our employment by other human beings and their employment by us" (272).

Similarly, Herzog looks askance at the current adulation of suffering for its own sake. Unlike Malamud's heroes who define themselves through their experiences with sorrow and obtain a certain ecstacy through agony, it is a sign of Herzog's emotional recovery that he can relinquish the harrowing for the halcyon. As he sees it, the only kind of people who benefit from adversity are the truly religious, because they use it as an "opportunity to experience evil and change it into good" (317). But for the majority of people suffering is not in the least ennobling. If anything, it robs them of their dignity and blunts their sensitivity. To say that suffering is the necessary "antidote to illusion" (317) is to spout a vacuous cocktail party expression. Herzog realizes that man will inevitably experience his fair share of pain through the course of a lifetime, so it is utterly ridiculous to "expound suffering for anyone or call for Hell to make us serious and truthful" (317–318).

Closely related to Herzog's mockery of the recent obsession with

27. Donald Markos, "The Humanism of Saul Bellow" (Ph.D. diss., University of Illinois, 1966), p. 151.

despair, death, and suffering is his diatribe against modern cynicism. Like the prophet Amos, lamenting the fall of the "virgin Israel . . . with none to raise her up,"[28] he upbraids this generation for thinking "that nothing faithful, vulnerable, fragile can be durable or have any true power" (290). In the novel the principal advocates of this cynical view are Herzog's legal advisers, Simkin and Himmelstein, who, to use the words of Oscar Wilde, "know the price of everything and the value of nothing." For them as well as for Augie's "Machiavellians," the world is populated not with honest men, but with "whores" (85). Nobility, sincerity, and goodness do not exist. Only the "nasty" constitutes the real, or, as Herzog trenchantly reduces their perverted code to its most ludicrous extreme: "You must sacrifice your poor, squawking, niggardly individuality . . . to historical necessity. And to truth. And truth is true only as it brings down more disgrace and dreariness upon human beings, so that if it shows anything except evil it is illusion, and not truth" (93). Appointing themselves Herzog's "Reality instructors" (125), Simkin and Himmelstein continually blast away at him with their truth and insist that he accept their "brutal version of the . . . American way of life" (291). Herzog refuses to become their pupil, however. He still has faith that even in the twentieth century one can "live in an inspired condition" (165). Like Augie, he believes there can be "Man, with a capital *M*, with great stature" (434). Herzog disregards those "snarling realists" (291) and ends up viewing them merely as grotesque characters in the currently running "drama of disease, of self-revenge" in "an age of special comedy" (163).

These are just a few of the ideas which Herzog's nimble wit has played with. As Tony Tanner has indicated, "[All of] Herzog's thoughts and concerns are too various to summarize; indeed their profuse, unrelated multiplicity is an essential part of the meaning of the book."[29] But from the sampling that has been presented it is very apparent that, until Artur Sammler, Herzog is Bellow's most deft "vaudevillian of the mind"[30] who is able to amuse his audience with both obvious and subtle intellectual comedy.

As one of those humanists who have dedicated themselves to the

---

[28.] Amos 5:2, Revised Standard Version.

[29.] Tanner, *Saul Bellow*, p. 96.

[30.] Robert Shulman, "The Style of Bellow's Comedy," *PMLA* 83 (March, 1968): 116.

"struggle toward suitable words" (272), Herzog has a ready talent for verbal humor. He generally knows which words precisely convey his serious intentions and which ones humorously camouflage them. He can draft sentences of great profundity and great parody. He can employ phrases which flatter his ego and those which deflate it. Moreover, each time he tampers with language to trivialize his concerns and minimize his achievements, he not only amuses himself with his clever distortions, but he changes our perspective as well. His rhetorical twists upset our expectations and compel us to reassess him and his insights. In the process we laugh at his verbal deviations and perceive new shifts of meaning which we would not have had if Herzog had not taken any liberties with language. We see this technique best in Herzog's bastardization of quotations. A master of sleight-of-word, he produces ingenious adaptations of popular and erudite lines to mock and modify his behavior. For example, he both spoofs and stresses his masochistic tendencies by changing Emerson's "Hitch your wagon to a star" to his own "Hitch your agony to a star" (16). Guilt-ridden over his purchase of pagan clothing and his flight to hedonistic Martha's Vineyard, he both ridicules and underscores his frailty by parodying the Lord's Prayer: "O Lord! . . . forgive all these trespasses. Lead me not into Penn Station" (20). He also employs his antic coinages to reprove others. Upset by the disappearance of privacy in American life, he comes up with his own sardonic variation of Gresham's Law: "Bad money drives out good." Herzog's amended law, which is equally astute, reads, "Public life drives out private life" (162). He expresses his enmity for Valentine by playfully suggesting how such an intellectual faker might pervert Martin Buber's words. "Maybe [Valentine] wants to swap wives with a rabbi. He'll work his way round from 'I and Thou' to 'Me and You'—'You and Me, Kid!'" (260). Herzog gives vent to his hatred of Madeleine by splicing two commonplace adages, "A stitch in time saves nine," and "Familiarity breeds contempt," thereby originating his own satiric portmanteau maxim: "A bitch in time breeds contempt" (21). Herzog's mongrelized expressions amuse us with their unusual combination of hackneyed strains and increase our understanding of the principal concerns of the novel through their unexpected emphases.

In addition to fragmenting and reconstructing quotations for comic effect, Herzog takes well-known quotations out of context and introduces them in the context of his narration. While they give evidence of Herzog's amazingly fertile and retentive mind, they initially appear entirely inappropriate and irrelevant to the proceedings at hand. But upon reconsideration and by a wild stretch of the imagination, they are in some respects fitting and even contribute an added dimension to our interpretation of character and situation. As for the other respects in which they are incongruously out of place and hyperbolically ungermane to what is going on, they provide us with whimsical relief from the woeful. For example, Herzog, overwhelmed with a mass of intellectual and household chores, turns his plight into mock tragedy by melodramatically citing a Latin translation of a line from Euripides: *"Quos vult perdere dementat* [Whom God wills to destroy he first makes mad]" (121). He wryly exposes his penchant for luxuriating in sorrow by quoting the Johnsonian epigram, "Grief, Sir, is a species of idleness" (3). He makes his vindictiveness toward Madeleine and Valentine appear ridiculously excessive by uttering the same curse against them which the Hebrews reserved for their most vile enemies, the Amalekites:[31] *"Yemach sh'mo!* Let their names be blotted out!" (202–203). He points up the absurdity of his trying to become a genuine New Englander by quoting with tongue in cheek the sententious line from Robert Frost's Kennedy inaugural poem, "The Gift Outright": "The land was ours before we were the land's" (309). He causes us to laugh about the homosexual assault he received as a child. Shortly after describing it in awful detail, he recalls the passages from the New Testament which "the good Christian lady" (289) read to him in the hospital: "Suffer the little children to come unto me,"[32] and "Give and it shall be given unto you. Good measure . . . shall men give into your bosom"[33] (289). By exhuming such quotations long buried in Herzog's consciousness and having them interrupt his

---

31. Exodus 17:14 (Revised Standard Version) reads, ". . . I will utterly blot out the remembrance of Amalek from under heaven." Deuteronomy 25:19 (Revised Standard Version) reads, "Therefore when the Lord your God has given you rest from all your enemies round about, in the land which the Lord your God gives you for an inheritance to possess, you shall blot out the remembrance of Amalek from under heaven." In both instances the Hebrew word which has been translated as "remembrance" could also be translated as "name." However, Psalms 109:13 (Revised Standard Version) is the closest equivalent of Herzog's curse: "May his name be blotted out in the second generation!"

32. Luke 18:16 (King James Version).

33. Luke 6:38 (King James Version).

thoughts at the most unlikely yet apt times, Bellow undercuts Herzog's troubles by casting them within mirth-provoking frames of reference.

Herzog uses allusions in much the same way. Since he is adept at juggling a wide assortment of ideas, he is equally adept at tossing out a great variety of allusions. Unlike Augie March, his aim is not to show off the breadth of his knowledge. More certain of his intellectual endowments than his newly learned predecessor, he does not frenetically muster into active duty all the allusions at his command. He calls into play only those which could conceivably refer to his own life, yet at the same time are the most preposterously unlike his own life. He thereby enables us to see him in a newer light because of the chain of associations which his imaginative allusions have set in motion. He simultaneously makes himself more ludicrous because of the farfetched comparisons he does make. By dubbing himself a "patient Griselda" (64), the adoring wife in Chaucer's "Clerk's Tale" who remained faithful to her husband even though he took away her children and pretended to remarry, Herzog emphasizes how idiotic he was to endure Madeleine's cruel treatment of him for such a long time. By admitting that he intended to become the "Lovejoy" of his generation (191), Herzog makes fun of his intellectual presumptions. By referring to his "Faustian spirit of discontent" (68), he ridicules his sudden concern for "social questions . . . the external world" (68) when all along he had been hibernating in his private world of books. By calling his Berkshire retreat "Herzog's folly" (309), he humorously links his imprudent acquisition to Seward's shrewd purchase of Alaska. And when he surveys the ruins of his estate, he mock-heroically compares himself to Shelley's Ozymandias, the Egyptian pharaoh whose mighty kingdom decayed beyond recognition in the desert sands. To be sure, Herzog realizes that he falls short of the illustrious personages with whom he facetiously claims kinship. Yet these facetious claims allow him to escape momentarily from "the agony of consciousness and separate being" (93). By comically relating himself to universal figures, he can move beyond his own dilemma and see it with some detachment.

Herzog aims his most deprecating allusions at the chief traitors of the camp—Valentine and Madeleine. By pointing up their similarity to the least admirable and their dissimilarity to the most admirable men of the past, he gets his verbal revenge. By likening Valentine to

Cagliostro, the eighteenth-century Italian charlatan who pretended to be a noble and duped the credulous with his feats of alchemy and magic, Herzog comically accentuates Valentine's spuriousness. Conversely, by referring to Valentine as a *Shofat,* a judge in ancient Israel noted for being a supremely righteous man and a charismatic leader, Herzog points up Valentine's ludicrously deficient portrayal of the role. Madeleine is damned with the same kind of perverted praise. By suggesting that she expects to give birth to a Louis XIV since she purchases a five-hundred-dollar maternity outfit, Herzog ridicules her delusions of royalty and her habitual prodigality. By contrasting her with the Duke of Wellington, "the victor of Waterloo [who] drew apart to shed bitter tears" (76) for his slain enemies, Herzog mordantly stresses how uncompassionately Madeleine treats him, her vanquished foe.

Herzog directs his barbs at less offensive parties as well, although it is not his intention to injure them seriously. He simply enjoys amusing himself by mildly grazing their weak spots. By observing that the pedant Shapiro combs his hair "in the Rudolph Valentino" (68) style, he waggishly indicates the incongruity of such a "dumpy"-looking creature straining to appear the glamorous figure. By describing his brother Shura as a "true disciple of Thomas Hobbes," who asks "nothing better than to prosper in the belly of Leviathan" (78), Herzog makes light of Shura's opportunism. By referring to his Ludeyville neighbors as "Jukes and Kallikaks," the feebleminded and morally degenerate families studied by sociologists at the end of the nineteenth century, Herzog playfully exaggerates his neighbors' mental obtuseness and moral laxity. Even the benevolent Ramona does not escape Herzog's raillery. By ironically calling her "a priestess of Isis" (160), the Egyptian fertility goddess, he reveals her elaborate worship of Eros to be a highly developed form of nonsense.

Along with employing allusions to divert and distance himself from his anguish, Herzog is an expert at verbal retrieval. Since he is the most articulate of the Bellow heroes mentioned thus far and experiences the keenest sense of outrage, he originates the most ingenious "verbal phrases and kinetic metaphors with which suffering man escalates implacable defeats into comic impasses."[34] Herzog ruefully

34. Earl Rovit, *Saul Bellow,* University of Minnesota Pamphlets on American Writers, no. 65 (Minneapolis: University of Minnesota Press, 1967), pp. 40–41.

jests, for example, about the misery he endures as a result of Madeleine's encroaching intellectualism. "She's built a wall of Russian books around herself. Vladimir of Kiev, Tikhon Zadonsky. In my bed! It's not enough they persecuted my ancestors!" (59). He hyperbolically likens Madeleine's traits of paranoia, whose effects he has suffered, to the ten plagues visited upon the Egyptians. He laughs bitterly at the fact that he has been chosen to be the butt of Madeleine's wrath. "It would not be practical for her to hate herself. Luckily, God sends a substitute, a husband" (174). A frequent victim of female treachery in general, he expresses his misogyny in the caustic quip, "What do [women] want? They eat green salad and drink human blood" (41–42). Herzog "doggedly persists in twisting a smile . . . under the grip of . . . adversity,"[35] while his astringent wit permits him to take the sting out of that adversity.

In addition to his verbal retrievals, Herzog is a man of letters. The epistles of Moses, however, are not always gospel. Like Bummidge in *The Last Analysis,* he is "earnest when he is clowning and clowning when he means to be earnest."[36] Yet Herzog's portfolio includes not only soberly foolish and foolishly sober correspondence. He dashes off conciliatory and antagonistic, naive and sophisticated, petty and magnanimous letters. His other literary accomplishments include giving a "Great Books course" (162) to Nehru, Churchill, and Eisenhower, improvising whimsical children's stories, composing an "Insect Iliad," and reciting charming nursery rhymes. He is equally adept at drawing satiric vignettes of those he detests and idealized portraits of those he loves. He is able to rattle off rarefied abstractions and dignified biblical Hebrew, as well as colorful ghetto Yiddishisms and off-color gutter Americanisms. Herzog is a skilled wordsmith who forges many kinds of language which, when rubbed against each other, throw off the sparks of verbal comedy.

Herzog's utterances are drolly voluble as well as drolly versatile. Like Wilhelm and Henderson, Herzog "has a compulsion to tell all, to overtell, to explain all, to explain away."[37] Indeed, Ramona calls

35. Earl Rovit, "Bernard Malamud and the Jewish Literary Tradition," *Critique* 3 (Winter-Spring, 1960): 5.

36. Bellow, *The Last Analysis,* p. ix.

37. Stanley Edgar Hyman, "Saul Bellow's Glittering Eye," *The New Leader* 47 (September 28, 1964): 17.

attention to this particular compulsion: "What is funny is how completely you answer any question" (183). Herzog is also aware of how funny his "strict and literal truthfulness" (187) is; yet he cannot stop revealing the whole truth about himself, no matter how uncomplimentary it may be. We receive a detailed account of his poor grooming habits, his absentmindedness, his physical ailments, his social *faux pas,* his sexual victories and defeats. Herzog is even more garrulous when discussing intellectual matters. As he himself observes, "People legislate continually by means of talk" (191). He, too, is bursting with pronouncements and believes that the only way he can exert his authority is by inundating reality with his language. Hence he is compelled to be always in the "full flood of discourse":[38] "Quickly, quickly, more! . . . Herzog . . . felt his eager, flying spirit streaming out, speaking, piercing, making clear judgements, uttering final explanations, necessary words only" (68). But by the end of the novel Herzog feels that such judgments and explanations are no longer necessary. Having served his sentence of wracking cogitation, he no longer has "to control the world with words and ideas" and can "live unencumbered as another creature in the world that is."[39] And so we leave Herzog with his spell of intense consciousness at an end and his jocosely profuse words temporarily silenced.

Herzog does not possess the range of comedy that exists in *The Adventures of Augie March* and *Henderson the Rain King.* Although it does capture the rueful mirth of Herzog's corporeal imperfections obstructing his bids for spiritual perfection, it does not contain the humor of the body worsted in unusual physical action, nor does it reveal that body caught up in a rash of preposterous situations. It is primarily what was said of *Tristram Shandy,* that "history book . . . of what passes in a man's mind."[40] Throughout most of the novel we are in Herzog's mind, observing not his physical, but his mental pratfalls. This is not to say that Bellow wants to stifle our admiration for Herzog's extraordinary speculative powers; these powers catapult him into all spheres of the learned domain and are responsible for generating his all-inclusive ideological comedy. But what Bellow

38. Malcolm Bradbury, "Saul Bellow and the Naturalist Tradition," *Review of English Literature* 4 (October, 1963): 81.

39. Clayton, *Saul Bellow,* p. 224.

40. Quoted in David D. Galloway, "Moses-Bloom-Herzog: Bellow's Everyman," p. 76.

proves to be ridiculous is Herzog's presumption that he can intellectually resolve all of the complex issues of his age, or at least control
his environment solely through an intellectual awareness of it. Moreover, Bellow illustrates the folly of Herzog's grasping at lofty ideas to
avoid coping with his own problems, and his clinging to childish
views of reality which prevent a mature confrontation with it. Yet
despite Herzog's mental pratfalls, he does manage through hard-won
insight and gratuitous intuition to regain his equilibrium. Having employed his rapier wit for both self-dissection and salvation, he is able to
make the steadiest gesture of comic affirmation of Bellow's euphoric
heroes. Unlike Augie March, who can never be still enough to locate
his "axial lines," or Henderson, who can never stop "making such a
noise" in order to "hear something nice" (284), Herzog is no longer
compelled "to enact the peculiarities of life" (340), and can accept his
limited condition. Having "broken out of [his] own skull," he is
"ready to break into other skulls." [41] At the novel's end, however, we
find him in his Eden communing only with God and nature. His
privacy as yet uninvaded and his newfound tranquillity as yet undisturbed, he awaits the arrival of another human being. To observe the
Bellow hero interacting with society outside Eden, we must turn to
Artur Sammler and his disturbing planet.

[41.] Saul Bellow quoted in *Newsweek* 64 (September 21, 1964): 114.

This Droll Mortality

8

Mr. Sammler's Planet[1] appears at first glance to be the staking out of new fictional territory. Unlike the earlier heroes whose age and experience corresponded to Bellow's own age and experience at the time of their creation, his new protagonist, Artur Sammler, is some twenty years older. Far removed from the petulant underground man, the exuberant picaro or the enraged cuckold, he is a septuagenarian Tiresias figure who comments with the wisdom and the weariness of the aged on the recent American wasteland. Unlike the native-bred heroes who often lack the detachment to grasp all the complexities of their moral landscapes, Sammler, uprooted from Europe and relocated in this country at middle age, is equipped with the singular vantage point of the alien observer. Even with his one good eye, his perception of things is more insightful than the unimpaired vision of his fictional brothers. Nor does he feel embarrassed by his lengthy ruminations and thus compelled to parody his efforts or disrupt his flow of thought with irrelevant witticisms. Moreover, unlike the other central characters, he does not generally star in the "painful emotional comed[y]"[2] of his own making. A survivor of the holocaust, he has been more the victim of history's machinations than of his own masochism. Absent

1. Citations from this novel are to *Mr. Sammler's Planet* (New York: Viking Press, 1970).

2. Saul Bellow, *Herzog* (New York: Viking Press, 1964), p. 269.

for the most part is the customary Bellow humor involving the protagonist's outrageous self-executed follies, his hyperbolic reproaches for committing them, and his bungling attempts at redressing them. Unlike the other heroes, each with his readily discernible kind of daftness, Sammler has less overt aberrations which he gradually comes to acknowledge. Rather, the secondary characters are the turbulent ones who disrupt his calm and force him to become a "confidant of New York eccentrics; curate of wild men and . . . a registrar of madness" (118). Their more obvious idiosyncrasies and the mayhem they beget constitute the primary source of the novel's drollery.

Apart from these differences, *Mr. Sammler's Planet* has marked resemblances to Bellow's earlier work. There is the reproduction of the Augie March carnival world, peopled with all manner of sideshow grotesques. There is the teeming, barbaric Sodom and Gomorrah city which petrifies Leventhal and Wilhelm. There is the oppressive imminence of death from which Henderson flees. As a means of distraction from this imminence or as a way of coming to terms with it, there are comparable metaphysical flights alternating with earth-bound racy talk. There is the same strong yearning for affirmation which has characterized most of Bellow's anti-alienation writing. Mr. Sammler struggles to deny that "reality was a terrible thing, and that the final truth about mankind was overwhelming and crushing" (280). Although he has been exposed to more brutality than any other Bellow hero, as spent as his resources are, he still resists the temptation to reach such a negative conclusion. Likewise, he has his own quest to perform—not, to be sure, Henderson's grandiose mission of bringing succor to Africa and hygiene to America, or Herzog's lofty enterprise of synthesizing all knowledge and enlightening mankind. Sammler strives to realize what would appear to be a more modest aim but is, according to Bellow's values, the most difficult to achieve: first clarifying for himself and others what it means to be human, and then fulfilling the responsibility of being human. The novel recounts how successful a preacher and practitioner Mr. Sammler is.

Although *Mr. Sammler's Planet* has been in the literary orbit for a time, the critics, while initially awed by the marvels of its topography, have been slow to delve into its interior. Aside from being dazzled by its ideological sparks and glowing prose, they have not done justice to the complexity of Mr. Sammler's character. There has been a tendency to regard him merely as the undefiled, unchanging oracle, divulging unflattering truths about his frantic mortal petitioners. Seen in this light, he is represented not as a viable fictional creation, but as an artificial "perspective for viewing the lunacy of our age." [3] There has been the attempt to deny him any individual autonomy, to fuse his identity with that of his author. He is, according to this opinion, the crochety, exasperated old man in Bellow who emerges whenever the world becomes too much for him. But such impressions of Sammler are inaccurate. While his intelligence may be as ripe as Bellow's, his omniscience is still limited. Even though he has more self-knowledge than previous Bellow heroes, he does not have a complete understanding of himself or those around him. Through the course of his three-day earth exploration and the memories and musings it stirs up, he, like Herzog, comes to recognize that he is not "marvelous," that he is not a "Jesus" who has no "flies" (230) on him. Far from being the flawless superhuman collector, Mr. Sammler, Bellow tells us in no uncertain terms, shares the same imperfect fundamentals as his assemblage of deviants.

One would think that Artur Sammler, entering the eighth decade of his life, would be more concerned with impressing the other world than with impressing this one. To a large extent this is the case. Unlike Wilhelm, he is beyond the need to feign influence. Unlike Henderson, he does not have to prove his physical strength to satisfy the natives. Unlike Herzog, he is not driven to perfect his sexual charms to woo the ladies, or to match wits with every living and dead mental giant he encounters. Although Sammler is freed of such paltry desires, he still cannot fully emancipate himself from being the spoiled only son, "not easily pleased, haughty" (61), who read Trollope and Bagehot to transform himself from a coarse Pole into a refined Englishman. Even though he was a Polish Jew in the eyes of the Nazis who almost murdered him during a return visit to Cracow, and even though he has lived in the United States since 1947, he persists in exhibiting the airs of an English gentleman. Although he claims to have divested himself of all this Anglophile "nonsense" (6), Bellow, as omniscient author, frequently reminds us that Sammler has not done so. Bellow plays up the ruefully comic incongruity of having a half-blind Yeatsian "coat upon a stick,' who should be beyond van-

3. Beverly Gross, "Dark Side of the Moon," *Nation* 210 (February 9, 1970): 154.

ity, clinging to his outmoded affectations. Instead of carrying a white cane, Sammler sports a "furled umbrella, British-style" (5) and "developed expressions suited to an Oxford common room" (6). Especially when Sammler experiences an unusually sordid event or mingles with flagrantly crude people, he becomes all the more precious and arrogant. Just as Bellow mocks Herzog's contrived elegance before evil in the courtroom, he likewise mocks Sammler's forced primness before the black pickpocket and his Polish-Oxonian hauteur before the boorish student audience. In the context of the illicit and the vulgar, Mr. Sammler, the fastidious "polite Slim-Jim" (26), appears not only misplaced, but humorously conspicuous.

Even if Sammler didn't have his absurdly British mannerisms, his tall body and small face with its "overhanging hairs of the brow as in some breeds of dog" (4) would still make him appear humorously conspicuous. But Bellow, unlike his light-hearted treatment of his earlier physically marred heroes, refrains from making sport of Sammler's body. Because Sammler is "an old Jew whom they had hacked at, shot at, but missed killing somehow" (197), he is entitled to make a great issue of his ailments, to advertise what Henderson calls his "bargain basement of deformities" (83). Yet aside from minor complaints of tachycardia, "damaged . . . nerve-spaghetti" (5), and an itching anus, Sammler seems peculiarly unpreoccupied with somatic concerns. "So intellectualized is his way of being," claims Kenneth Atchity, "that Sammler is unmoved even by the physicality of his own body. It is not, as in the fiction of Nathaneal West, that he is *detached* from his corporeality and observes it as a spectator; no, Sammler is too far removed even to be interested in observing it." [4] While this may be true in part, another explanation for Sammler's disregard of his flesh and blood dimensions might be that a large part of him still feels dead, is still unresurrected from the mass grave he narrowly escaped. As he himself admits, it was not until twelve years after the war that he once more discovered he was human. Only then did "creatureliness" creep in again with "its low tricks, its doggish hindsniffing charm" (117). In any case the Sammler we observe through most of the novel is more of a hyperactive mind, rarely encumbered by an irksome body or diverted by a waggish one. When

4. Kenneth John Atchity, "Bellow's Mr. Sammler: 'The Last Man Given for Epitome,' " *Research Studies* 38 (March, 1970): 47.

he is dressing, his characteristic state is "trancelike. At several removes from the self in the glass, opposite" (144). Even when he is urinating in the washbasin, he is deep in "meditation on the inherent melancholy of animal nature, continually in travail, according to Aristotle" (15). While Leventhal, Wilhelm, Henderson, and Herzog evoke hearty laughter by being continually obstructed by and chronically fretting about their undelectable corpi, Sammler's frequent obliviousness of his own physicality is not without its own subdued kind of levity.

Although Sammler is relatively free from the tyranny of the body, he is not free from the tyranny of his mind. Like Herzog, he feels oppressed by the chaotic world about him with its hydra-multiplying facts and sensations, its crumbling certainties and renovated truths, its insoluble crises and facile reforms. Along with such external barrages, nightmares from his past—the barbarism of the Nazis, the liquidation efforts of the Poles, and the more recent specter of bloated corpses from the Israeli Six-Day War—consume his waking hours. His thoughts are therefore in perpetual motion, trying to make coherent sense of what has happened and what is happening. Yet he recognizes the futility and anguish of such "unrelenting analytical effort" (21). Like Herzog, he believes, "If the unexplained life is not worth living, the explained life is unbearable, too" (322). Sammler denigrates intellectual man both for his compulsion and for his presumption to make plain what is not immediately obvious or entirely known. Echoing the Hasidim, the more mystical sect of Judaism who believe that life, although essentially inscrutable, can in some ways be understood through nonrational means, Sammler claims that the soul has "its own natural knowledge" (3). Unfortunately, however, the soul, beset with distractions, does not always harken to its own knowledge and is thrown into confusion. It sits "unhappily," writes Bellow, "on superstructures of explanation, poor bird, not knowing which way to fly" (4–5). This is Sammler's position. Deep within, his spirit knows, without benefit of tortuous intellectual formulation, that its growth through interaction with humanity "is the real aim of existence" (236). Yet ponderous internal debates to arrive at "short views" about the depravity of others and the disorder of things deter him from acting upon such innate knowledge.

It is understandable that Sammler, whose life has already been so rudely interrupted and whose departure from earth is not too distant, wishes like Job to be let alone, not "to be visited every morning, to be called upon" (252). Beyond the need for the solace of other creatures, he claims to require only what his favorite author, Meister Eckhart, the medieval German mystic recommends—the consolation of God. But like Bellow's other solitaries, he is not permitted to be an uninvaded "meditative island on the island of Manhattan" (75). By accident he catches sight of an elegantly dressed black pickpocket, skillfully fleecing the passengers on the bus he takes home from the library. The thief, discovering that Sammler has witnessed his operations, follows him into the lobby of his apartment building. He corners the terrified old man, exposes himself, and silently threatens him with his formidable penis. The symbolic intent of the confrontation is obvious: in this day and age reason and decency are subject to intimidation by brute, lawless, primitive forces. But reason and decency are also inspired by equally strong appeals for benevolence. Sammler's nephew, Elya Gruner, who has rescued him from a displaced persons camp after the war and has comfortably supported him in this country, is suffering from a fatal aneurysm and now seeks a kind of rescue and support from Sammler. Sammler, in turn, extremely fond of and indebted to Gruner, is moved to perform any kind of service he can for him. But Sammler's benevolence has its limits. While he is willing to leave off his self-communings to comfort the virtuous and stable individual, he is not eager to be of comfort to the "wretched, itching, bleeding, needing, idiot[s]" (74) who wish to confide in him. Unlike Augie March, who often has nothing better to do with his time than consort with antic characters and listen to their preposterous accounts of themselves, Sammler, mentally preparing his valedictory summaries about the current *Zeitgeist* and on his way to express some meaningful valedictory word to Gruner, resents the intrusion of his quirky visitors. Whereas Augie is charmed by his idiosyncratic companions, Sammler has no patience with them and is sometimes repelled by them. This can be partially attributed to the kinds of comic characters Bellow creates to trespass upon Sammler's privacy. More like allegorical figures of vice in medieval morality plays or like vile Jonsonian humors, rather than multidimensional human beings, they remain on the scene only long enough to exhibit their prominent deviations from the norm. Bellow also makes it apparent that Sammler cannot readily make allowances for their deviations. Unlike Augie, he usually does not make the effort to discover their redeeming virtues or view their vices in terms of the person as a whole. Scathed by experience and always expecting the worst, Sammler dwells only upon their most glaring flaws which represent for him the entire character as well as the debased aspects of the age.

Even when he knows, for example, that one of his callers, the hopelessly perverted Walter Bruch, has experienced many of the same indignities that he has during the war, he still focuses on what is saliently freakish about him. Never having recovered from near extermination by the Nazis, Bruch is compelled to reenact his death, but always in the most mocking and histrionic fashion—playing the corpse and chanting Latin sepulchral music. Seeking a release from being the victim, he is also given to impersonating his persecutors— "ranting like Hitler" (58) and improvising the sound effects from Nazi mass meetings. As a finale to his morbid humor, he ends up with his maudlin, over-elaborated Buchenwald reminiscences. For Sammler, Bruch exemplifies the survivor, not ennobled through suffering but crazed and ultimately made clownish by it. In addition to having been a prisoner of the concentration camps, the sixty-year-old Bruch is a prisoner of sexual fetishism—deriving erotic thrills from ogling the fleshy arms of young Puerto Rican women. Equally thrilling is his belief that he alone is afflicted with such a terrible vice. He provides Sammler not only with a lurid account of all the sensual particulars of his adventures, but, like Wilhelm before his father, he engages in an orgy of self-recrimination. Sammler, like Dr. Adler, devoid of any compassion, flippantly assures Bruch that he is not singular and diagnoses his fixation as "an old nineteenth-century Krafft-Ebing trouble" (60). The only interest Sammler has in Bruch is clinical and theoretical. Along with attributing Bruch's sexual anomaly to the "repressions of another time" (60), Sammler relates Bruch's pride in the uniqueness of his anomaly to Kierkegaard's comical account of the majority of people who want to be gaped at, to be the "birds of rare plumage, the queerly deformed fishes, the ridiculous breeds of men" (62–63). Bruch's worth for Sammler lies not in his intrinsic being, but as a psychological curiosity and as a catalyst for reflection on more universal themes.

Sammler views the young as even greater curiosities and is even more intolerant of what he construes as their shortcomings. The students who are paid to read to him he finds "hairy, dirty, without style, levelers, ignorant" (36). While Sammler can theoretically account for their grossness—a form of ineffectual protest against the false, unfeeling society—he cannot contain his hostile reactions. His meticulous self takes offense at their rank smells and his sense of propriety takes umbrage at their lack of self-respect. Strangely enough, Sammler is charmed in spite of himself by a student confidence man, Lionel Feffer, who battens off the system rather than being beaten by it. Perhaps a type sprung from Leslie Fiedler, he is a prime example of what Bellow has described elsewhere as one of those "media managing intellectuals," those "college-educated swinging, bearded, costumed, bohemianized intellectuals [who] are writing the ads, manufacturing the gimmicks, directing the shows, exploiting the Woodstocks."[5] Like them, Feffer is so caught up with chasing the phantom of the dollar, manipulating aimless friends to do his shady bidding, and seducing their wives on the side that he is on the verge of mental and physical collapse. Feffer is also a junior version of Dr. Tamkin in his compulsion to invent and exaggerate former business successes and to fantasy grandiosely about future ones. Possessing the same kind of specious brilliance and partial knowledge about a wide variety of topics, he glibly analyzes the complicated ways of the world. He pries into other people's affairs and forces his advice upon them. Although Sammler realizes that Feffer is a devious operator who capitalizes on his dealings with others, he cannot resist his magnetic powers. While he refuses Feffer's request to be a television entertainer of the decadent masses, he does agree to share his civilized reminiscences with a presumably academic audience. Yet even when the intellectual thinks he is negotiating on his own terms and has not prostituted his standards, Bellow implies that he is invariably duped by the self-seeking promoter; or perhaps the belief in the importance of what he is saying blinds the intellectual to the corruption of the in-

5. In addition to censuring "media managing intellectuals" in general, Bellow in his essay, "Culture Now: Some Animadversions, Some Laughs," his first published piece since *Mr. Sammler's Planet,* specifically attacks Leslie Fiedler for attempting to "close the gap between high culture and low" by assuming the pose of "The Desperado, the Primitive, the Redskin, the Sense-Deranged Poet, the Child, and then the Bard chanting to the tribe. . . ." See *Modern Occasions* 1 (Winter, 1971): 172–174.

stant wisdom hucksters with whom he willingly associates. Feffer, the bogus entrepreneur, has conned Sammler, the enlightened old liberal, into discussing the rational scientific attitude in pre–World War II England before an audience of unenlightened youth, expecting a talk about "Sorel and Modern Violence" (109). When Sammler quotes Orwell's facetious claim that the British radicals were protected by the Royal Navy, an obtuse youth takes the remark seriously. He lashes out at Sammler with a crude form of the *juvenis-senex ad hominem* argument: "Why do you listen to this effete old shit? What has he got to tell you? His balls are dry. He's dead. He can't come" (42). Although there is no doubt that Bellow intends this student to represent "sex-excrement-militancy" (43) carried to its most deplorable and ludicrous extremes, he does not intend him to be the spokesman for all youth. It is Sammler, insulted and outaged, who draws this conclusion and proceeds to vilify all those under thirty.

Sammler's opinions of the young are not based only on brief encounters with the impudent and unwashed. He draws his conclusions from more prolonged exposures to his incurably prodigal and erratic grand-nephew Wallace Gruner. Wallace is clearly Bellow's caricature of the young man trying to find himself, trying to assert his financial and emotional independence, yet floundering miserably. Whereas Augie March is more original in his floundering, Wallace imitates what every overindulged feckless though high-minded member of his generation has done—studying the backward peoples of Europe, yet being bilked by them; volunteering for the domestic peace corps, yet fainting at a movie about childbirth; scorning his father's wealth, yet using and ruining the family limousine. Amply endowed with unearned largess and the intellectual potential to become whatever he wishes, he avoids realizing any of his ambitions. Postponing his entry into the adult world, he remains forever the *enfant terrible*. Whereas Augie has Bellow's respect for his resistance to define himself in terms of any one function, Wallace's abortive careers and endless becomings incur Bellow's mockery. He is jocosely described as "nearly" a physicist, "nearly . . . a mathematician, nearly a lawyer . . . nearly an engineer, nearly a Ph.D. in behavioral science. . . . nearly an alcoholic, nearly a homosexual" (88).

Since Bellow has made Wallace out to be such "a high-IQ moron" (177), there is justification for Sammler not to look kindly upon him. It is especially difficult for him to listen to Wallace's unruly thoughts without silently condemning them or regarding them as symptomatic of the lunacy of the young. Although they are filled with non sequiturs and fraught with prejudices and confusions, some of them strangely echo Sammler's own thoughts. Wallace's appeals to abstruse intellectual authority to make sense of ordinary events resemble the "special pedantic awkwardness" which Sammler brings to "commonplace situations" (7). His involved explanations for the rise of homosexuality in America are like some of Sammler's own labyrinthine speculations about the origins of kindred socio-psychological phenomena. His denunciations of women as the raunchier and the more destructive of the species sound like Sammler at his most misogynistic. His terror of and fascination with black phalluses are the same kind of feelings Sammler has but suppresses. Thus, in censuring Wallace for his waywardness, Sammler may be unwittingly censuring himself as well. Such reproach may prevent him from sharing the sympathetic view which Emil, the family chauffeur, has of Wallace: an already troubled youth who has become even more crazed by the prospect of his father's death and who desperately seizes upon any harebrained scheme to distract himself from such an awful reality. But Sammler can only aloofly regard Wallace as the incorrigibly anarchistic son who rebels without dignity against the dignified old order.

Sammler is even more contemptuous of Angela Gruner, Wallace's pampered and dissolute sister. Even though she is Bellow's caricature of the modern emancipated woman who is more enslaved than liberated by the free expression of her sexuality, Sammler upbraids her for being a vile temptress of the flesh. Like the prophet Isaiah, castigating the "daughters of Zion" for their "stretched forth necks . . . wanton eyes" and provocative adornments,[6] Sammler censures Angela for her stretched forth bust, whorish eyes, and "microskirts."

Herzog has all kinds of reasons for his vitriolic character assassinations of Madeleine, who for such a long time ground her heel into his groin. But Sammler, who is presumably Bellow's "post-coital" man, has never been personally wronged by Angela; hence his revilings seem extreme and unearned. He is disconcerted by Angela's undisguised sensuality in the same way that his white man's sensibilities

6. Isaiah 3:17, King James Version.

have been riled by the imperious sexuality of the black criminal. Although he merely listens to her disjointed tales of unbridled eroticism, his imagination, despite his superego's restraints, supplies any lurid omissions. His penchant for generalization, however, quickly takes over and makes Angela's petty sexual license representative of the large-scale revival of Roman paganism sweeping the country. But Bellow makes it apparent that Angela is not only an unregenerate libertine; often she is the pseudo-humanitarian sending defense funds to free black rapists, the insufferable psychotherapy patient compulsively reciting her problems, or merely the petulant child demanding instant satisfaction of her whims and total forgiveness for her naughty ways. While Sammler recognizes these other sides of Angela, he chooses to view her primarily as an infernal sex machine or a mocking imitation of one, a woman who tempers her "powerful message of gender . . . with comedy" (70). Like Herzog, who is struck by the inauthentic and authentic in Madeleine, her "mixed mind of pure diamond and Woolworth glass" (299), Sammler notes in Angela both "low comic and high serious . . . Goddess and majorette" (164). But because she refuses to ask her dying father's pardon for the vexation she has caused him, Sammler is only disgusted, not amused by her. In this instance Sammler's disgust is warranted, for Bellow does not permit Angela to have a miraculous Mary Magdalene conversion. Infuriated with Sammler for urging her to be reconciled with her father, she, like the brash Columbia radical, insultingly claims that Sammler doesn't know what life is like because he is old, unaware and, above all, sexually impotent.

Sammler's lack of charity toward the other women in the novel is not warranted. He harbors many of the same prejudices which his namesake, Arthur Schopenhauer, expressed in his essay, "Of Women." His disparagement of his niece Margotte's ability to discuss ideas and her penchant to champion the cause of all unfortunates echoes Schopenhauer's claim that the mental faculty of women is "very niggard in its dimensions" so that they "show more sympathy for the unfortunate than men do." [7] His criticism of her girlish preoccupation with inconsequentials is reminiscent of Schopenhauer's condescending view that "women remain children their whole life long; never

---

[7.] Arthur Schopenhauer, "Of Women," *The Works of Schopenhauer,* ed. Will Durant (New York: Frederick Ungar Publishing Co., 1928), pp. 447–448.

seeing anything but what is quite close to them, cleaving to the present moment, taking appearances for reality, and preferring trifles to matters of the first importance." [8] Even Sammler's unflattering description of Margotte's physical characteristics is not far removed from Schopenhauer's deprecating picture of women as that "under-sized, narrow-shouldered, broad-hipped, and short-legged race." [9] Despite Margotte's well-meaning efforts to make Sammler comfortable and her compliance with his every wish, he considers her a bothersome, inept creature who makes "cruel inroads" (21) into his time with her earnest "German wrongheadedness" (17).

Sammler is even less compassionate toward his own daughter, Shula, even though she has more than her share of quirky liabilities. In her person she manifests most of the ridiculous aspects found in Bellow's previous fictional women. Like Sono, Herzog's Oriental mistress, she garners the wretched refuge of America's teeming shores and stashes it all in her tiny apartment. Like Madeleine, she is a scavenger of ideas which she never bothers to examine, but haphazardly deposits in her already cluttered mind. Like her, she is a religious quick-change artist, switching from Judaism to Catholicism, depending upon whether the current holiday's ritual appeals to her. Like Mildred, Einhorn's orthopedic-shoed handmaiden, she tries to be sexually desirable, even though she clumps about in her space shoes and wears ethnic costumes inappropriate to her age and figure. And like Lily Henderson, she resorts to the most farfetched dissimulation to achieve her aims. But she is most laughable because of her "single-minded, persistent, prosecuting, horrible-comical obsession" (51) to have her father write the memoirs of H. G. Wells. A fanatic in her devotion to Daddy and the dissemination of knowledge, she steals scientist Govinda Lal's printed moon lectures, which she assumes will yield fascinating comparisons with Wells's lunar science fiction. Such conduct, while devious, is not for all time damnable. But Sammler, filled with righteous indignation, associates his mischievous though well-intentioned daughter with the malevolent Negro pickpocket and magnifies her minor theft into the heinous criminality of the age. Above all, he resents her implicating him, the impeccably upright man, in such unlawful behavior. Although he eventually forgives her, he is still exasperated by her loony

8. *Ibid.*, p. 447.
9. *Ibid.*, p. 451.

meddling and not in the least grateful for the lengths she has gone to in order to be of service to him. Still filled with regret that he and his wife "had not blended better" (116), he is ashamed of the "unhinged, wavering-witted" (198) creature she has turned out to be. Near the end of the novel, however, as Sammler increasingly compares himself to the dying Elya Gruner, a man of genuine family feeling, and finds himself sorely lacking in this area, he comes to realize his own failings as a parent. Arriving at the same discovery that Bellow's other "junkie[s]-on-thought"[10] inevitably reach, Sammler admits to being "too delicate for earthly life, too absorbed in unshared universals" (198). So consumed with spawning ideas, he has neglected the daughter he begot. By excluding her from his rarefied preoccupations, he has not only alienated himself from someone who craves his presence, but his inaccessibility, Bellow implies, may also have driven Shula to behave more outlandishly than usual to gain his attention. It is one of the novel's subtle ironies that Sammler, a man who prides himself on his moderation and rationality, should in any way be responsible for his daughter's "extravagance . . . animal histrionics," madcap larceny, "goofy business with shopping bags, trash-basket neuroses" (198). But Sammler, much as he would like to deny it, is of this world and inextricably bound up with its imperfections. There is still a final wry twist concerning his relationship with Shula. All along he has credited her with no self-awareness and thus no capacity to alter her daft ways. In a last exchange with her he is astonished to learn that she deliberately masquerades as an eccentric, since it has been her only way of securing male admirers. Were she permitted to keep some of Elya Gruner's hidden money, she claims she could afford to be more conventionally stylish and so attract a worthwhile mate. Thus not even Sammler, who excels at distinguishing (a higher form of mental activity than mere explaining), can discern the complexity of his presumably simple-minded daughter. So engrossed with fathoming the strange phenomena of the times, he has not bothered to acquaint himself with his own troubled offspring and in any significant way minister to her needs. It has been far less taxing on him merely to dismiss her as his incurably defective contribution to posterity. Now that he recognizes that she is not an all too predictable demented type, but an intriguing, protean human being, he is fascinated

10. Saul Bellow, *The Last Analysis* (New York: Viking Press, 1965), p. 10.

by her and fully appreciates her. His parting words to her are appropriately, "You're a good daughter. The best of any. No better daughter" (311).

In addition to suffering from a disorder common to many of Bellow's intellectual heroes—an underdeveloped heart caused by an overworked mind—Sammler tries to deny the existence of the evil impulse within him, or that he has ever acted upon it. Bellow created an Allbee to expose Leventhal's victimizing tendencies; likewise he creates a black pickpocket to reveal Sammler's own power of blackness. When Sammler first watches the thief plying his trade, he is impressed with his majestic bearing and surgeon-like dexterity. Instead of avoiding the scene of the crime, Sammler continues to ride the same bus, secretly desiring a reenactment of the thief's masterful exploitation of the "slackness, the cowardice of the world" (47). Even when he exhibits himself before Sammler, flaunting his symbol of indisputable potency and malice, Sammler is filled with voyeuristic curiosity. While it is Bellow's intention to have the black thief, who makes public his privates, epitomize twentieth-century depravity, it is also his intention to show the "ironic appeal" [11] of such depravity to the supposedly righteous. Sammler, the man of highly developed moral restraints, is attracted to the embodiment of criminal and sexual abandon. Although he claims he has no "use for the romance of the outlaw" (11), he has to concede that the gruesome actions of the outlaw lend verve and intensity to the most tedious commonplace events. In his past he had experienced first-hand the vivifying effects of murdering his fellow man. A near-corpse, hiding out from the Nazis, he felt a surge of reanimation from shooting a German straggler in the head. This violation of the most serious commandment Sammler had all along tried to blot out, to pretend that it had never occurred. But seeing the black pickpocket perform his nefarious feats not only illuminates Sammler's external world so that it is "wickedly lighted up" (12); it also illuminates the dark spots in his own interior. But Sammler chooses not to dwell on these—it is far less painful to damn the black thief for his "galloping impulses" (162). To avoid confronting his own iniquity, Sammler even succumbs to becoming a bawdy teller of tales by allowing the opportunist Feffer to wheedle information

11. Charles Thomas Samuels, "Bellow on Modernism," New Republic 62 (February 7, 1970): 28.

from him about the black man's baring of his crotch. Thus he is responsible for putting Feffer, the sensation- and money-hungry bloodhound, on the trail of the black criminal, and he is obliquely to blame for the clash that follows. En route to visit the dying Gruner for a final time, Sammler is waylaid by a traffic-stopping fight between Feffer and the black thief. Having photographed the pickpocket in action for lucrative magazine coverage, Feffer refuses to give up his camera, no matter how violently the black man throttles him. Sammler's reaction is to sympathize with the outmatched "prying . . . idiotic" (287) white boy and to view his black assailant as a lethal, overpowering animal whose glaring sexuality makes him even more repugnant: "Considering the Negro's strength—his crouching, squeezing, intense animal pressing-power, the terrific swelling of the neck and the tightness of the buttocks as he rose on his toes. In straining alligator shoes! In fawn-colored trousers! With a belt that matched his necktie—a crimson belt! How consciousness was lashed by such a fact!" (288). Too old and weak to reckon with such a force and free Feffer, Sammler has to appeal to his crazed son-in-law Eisen to intervene. The irony of what ensues is all too familiar. Crises necessitate the forming of strange alliances. Sammler, the professed humanist, has to depend on Eisen, the dehumanized man of iron, to put an end to the fracas. Powerless in his own right, he turns to any power, no matter how specious it might be. But when Eisen, the victim of the holocaust turned victimizer and mercenary artist to boot, uses his bizarre iron sculpture to strike the black man and almost crushes his skull with it, Sammler is appalled. He claims he never instructed Eisen to injure the fellow, only to loosen his grip on Feffer. Yet Bellow implies that Sammler is not so naive as to believe a cessation of hostilities can occur without the perpetration of counter hostilities. From his partisan warfare days he essentially knows that Eisen's actions, while unduly vicious, are still defensible: "You can't hit a man like this just once. When you hit him you must really hit him. Otherwise he'll kill you" (291). But in the midst of the bloodletting he has indirectly ordered, Sammler has a change of heart. Although he never assumes the full burden of guilt for the damages already committed, he musters his waning strength to deter Eisen from administering the final death stroke. Sammler's attitude toward the Negro pickpocket is marked by the same "ludicrous inconsistency" (291). When he watches him choke the defenseless Feffer, he considers him a loathsome "black beast," but when he views him felled by Eisen's devastating blows, he detects a "certain princeliness" (294) in him. Thus Sammler no longer plays an enfeebled old Jew who must rely on his Jewish Defense League henchman to settle a conflict through violence; he combats his own murderous leanings and through a last-minute resurgence of right conduct preserves a human life. From being the prey and predator of the ignoble savage, he becomes the protector of the noble savage.

Sammler minimizes the significance of his attempted destruction and the subsequent about-face rescue of his black Fury. He views the occasion not as one which has allowed him "to affirm the human bond" (273), but as a sordid embroilment which delays him from engaging in purposeful communication with Elya Gruner. Only to Elya he believes "there was something to say. Here there was nothing to say" (292). Similarly, at this moment of intense frustration he looks back with disgust at all of the previous entanglements which have prevented him from reaching Elya. Rather than viewing the agitators as distraught individuals whom he might have helped, he caustically dismisses them as desperate showmen "in the great fun fair [who] do this droll mortality with one another. . . . entertainers of your near and dear" (294). Never having any use for their vapid acts, he has tried to elude their company, but could never avoid becoming their captive audience. Ironically, Sammler is not permitted to remain very long in the company of Elya, the man he most esteems, because when he extricates himself from this most recent mess and finally arrives at the hospital, Elya is dying. Sammler never gets the opportunity to exchange any parting words with him. All he manages to do is extol Elya's virtues to his daughter and deliver a silent eulogy before Elya's corpse. The eulogy, while it expresses Sammler's respect for Elya, contains more an implied recrimination of himself. In a short story, "Mosby's Memoirs," [12] written just before *Mr. Sammler's Planet,* Bellow describes a similar response. Willis Mosby, an erudite, controlled, supercilious Wasp, "having disposed of all things human" (184), reminisces about Hymen Lustgarten, a comic fumbling Jew. By recalling incidents which reveal Lustgarten's unshakable trust in his fellow man, his warm, guileless manner, and his "passionate father-

---

12. Saul Bellow, "Mosby's Memoirs," *Mosby's Memoirs and Other Stories* (New York: Viking Press, 1968).

hood," Mosby vaguely realizes the limitations of his own personality
and the aridity of his own life. Sammler, an older and more complex
version of Mosby, is no Wasp, but a nouveau "Britisher" who finds
himself deficient when he assesses the worth of Elya Gruner, the same
kind of demonstrative *Ostjude* [Eastern Jew] as Lustgarten. Sammler
praises Elya for performing his assignment, for being a man of "feeling, outgoingness, expressiveness, kindness, heart" (303). By contrast,
Sammler knows he has been remiss in doing what is required of him.
Describing himself as a relatively useless "Anglophile intellectual"
(303), he admits to slighting his obligations to family and friends.
Rather than accepting people unconditionally the way Elya did, he
admits to being obsessed with denouncing them for their sham
"dramatic individuality" (230). Sammler does not claim that Elya
has been a flawless creature, however. He mentions his pride, vanity,
and irritability. Nor does he conceal the fact that Elya performed
illegal abortions and had furtive connections with the Mafia. He even
suggests that Elya may have had his own "lustful tendencies" (161)
and derived vicarious satisfaction from Angela's perverse sexuality.
Sammler himself has been guilty of many of the same offenses but
has acted as if they were nonexistent. Usually representing himself as
a pillar of society, he has attributed any visible imperfections to the
influence of adverse external forces rather than to any internal erosion.
Yet even with his lapses, Elya is not disqualified from being named an
earthly saint. As Bellow maintains earlier in the novel, "It is the
strength to do one's duty daily and promptly that makes saints and
heroes" (93). And Elya, Sammler admiringly relates, daily practiced
surgery which he loathed, promptly catered to the extravagant wishes
of his children, obediently conformed to his strait-laced wife's concep-
tions of the model husband, and habitually "took thought for others"
(85). Eager to be of service when alive and even obliging in answering death's summons, Elya has, in Sammler's estimation, met the
"terms of his contract" (313). Through steady and often painful effort,
he acquired and demonstrated what Bellow throughout most of his
novels has considered the greatest ability: "Not being more than human or less than human, but exactly human." [13]

Sammler is aware of what it means to be human and what the
terms of the contract are. Unlike Henderson, however, he is not

[13.] Saul Bellow, *The Victim* (New York: Vanguard, 1947), p. 133.

bathed in high feeling at his discovery, or, like Wilhelm, overcome with tears at the "consummation of his heart's ultimate need" (118), or, like Herzog, filled with religious awe before his newfound revelation. His final words in the novel, "We know, we know" (313), are more those of self-reproach for his perpetual breaches of contract. Unlike many of the hopeful endings of the other novels, where there is a strong indication that the protagonists will act upon their new insights and effect a positive change in their lives, there is no easy triumph intimated in *Mr. Sammler's Planet*. When he concludes his soul-searching death vigil and returns to the ever-recurring vexations of the earth, Artur Sammler at age 70-plus will remain pretty much the same: the high-minded sage, "thumping the rest of his species on the head" (75), with himself not exempt from the thumping.

The fact that Sammler's own conduct does not end up being exemplary does not detract from the incisiveness of his pronouncements on the conduct of the age. But the question which arises is, how skillfully have these pronouncements been woven into the narrative? Hemingway would answer, "Prose is architecture, not interior decoration, and the Baroque is over. For a writer to put his intellectual musings, which he might sell for a low price as essays, into the mouth of artificially constructed characters which are more remunerative when issued as people in a novel is good economics, perhaps, but does not make literature.[14] In *Mr. Sammler's Planet*, however, where the acrobatic turns of mind of a finely delineated gentleman of higher learning take the place of daredevil heroics of non-introspective adventurers, "intellectual musings" are an integral part of the novel, not tasteless ornamentation. They constitute a large part of the dynamic action and are not the tedious and often irrelevant commentary on the action.

Herzog's mental rehashings are a form of therapy leading to psychic recovery, but Sammler's voluminous thoughts do not resolve any of his quandaries; they are indispensable guides to the perplexities of the times. Not his own personal breakdown, but the imminent collapse of the world as he knows it, with the earth as the only habitation of man, gives him occasion to make final appraisals of that world. These appraisals are not drenched with the self-mockery which usually occurs whenever the Bellow hero sounds like a prophet or a didact. Nor is

14. Hemingway quoted in Forest Read, *"Herzog:* A Review," *Epoch* 14 (Fall, 1964): 95.

their severity diminished by the inclusion of any palliative humorous asides. In *Mr. Sammler's Planet* Bellow's criticisms of society differ in their mode of expression. In former books it has been his strategy, claims Irving Howe, "to protect his flanks through smoke screens of elaborate comic rhetoric. He has maintained two narrative voices signifying two world outlooks, the first sentterious and the second sardonic, yet with the declamations of the sentterious voice never quite undone, and sometimes even slyly reinforced, by the thrusts of the sardonic voice."[15] In *Mr. Sammler's Planet* Bellow has more or less abandoned the sardonic for the sentterious. If any driblets of the sardonic remain, they add a piquant flavor to the sentterious, but never overpower it. And the sentterious, unlike in *Herzog* or *Henderson the Rain King,* is self-assured and sustained until it conclusively makes its intended point. Gone are the bits and snippets of conspicuous erudition which the author straining to be thinker intersperses at random to impress rather than edify his readers. Bellow has confessed as much in a recent interview: "[*Mr. Sammler's Planet*] is my thoroughly non-apologetic venture into ideas. In *Herzog* . . . and *Henderson the Rain King* I was kidding my way to Jesus, but here I'm baring myself nakedly."[16]

What Bellow bares himself nakedly about in *Mr. Sammler's Planet* is the future of the earth now that the Apollo venture into space has given rise to a brave new lunar world. Unlike Norman Mailer's *Of a Fire on the Moon,* his focus is not on the self-seeking political Daedaluses who campaigned for the expedition, the maze of technological data connected with the flight, or the feats of the foolproof Icaruses, soaring in the empyrean and exploring the *terra incognita.* Rather, Bellow is concerned with the metaphysical ramifications of the Apollo moon landing. Should man continue his herculean struggle to make the morally and physically contaminated earth habitable, or should he vacate it to settle a new, presumably chaste planet? Bellow entertains each alternative long and hard. He marshals all the arguments he can conceive of, those in accord with his own thinking and those inimical to it, and gives them all an equal hearing. This careful weighing of the writer's own beliefs as well as those heretical to them

15. Irving Howe, Review of *Mr. Sammler's Planet* by Saul Bellow, *Harper's* 240 (February, 1970): 106.
16. Jane Howard, "Mr. Bellow Considers His Planet," *Life* 68 (April 3, 1970): 59.

is what makes *Mr. Sammler's Planet* such a distinguished novel of ideas. Bellow himself has said that the novel of ideas becomes art only when "the views most opposite to the author's own are allowed to exist in full strength. Without this a novel of ideas is mere self-indulgence. . . . The opposites must be free to range themselves against each other, and they must be passionately expressed on both sides." [17] In *Mr. Sammler's Planet* there are two clearly differentiated intellectual spokesmen, each with his opposing persuasion which he vigorously champions. Unlike Henderson, who seldom challenges the mantic wisdom of African King Dahfu, Sammler takes issue with the earth-moon views of the Indian scientist Govinda Lal. Paradoxically, Lal the Oriental is more occidental in his values than Sammler the Westerner. Demonstrating no inclination for the passive contemplative life, he is more a self-styled pioneer and pragmatist, committed to opening new frontiers and finding the best way to live in them. He is also more Wellsian in his outlook than is Sammler, a former intimate of Wells. Not only does his book, *The Future of the Moon,* have a Wellsian title, but Lal, like Wells, is also an apostle of inevitable scientific progress. He differs from Wells, however, in that he does not think the scientific elite will be able to build a technologically organized world society on this earth. Painfully aware from his own background of the Asiatic hordes desperately sparring for existence, he finds the beginnings of the same congestion and dissatisfaction in all areas. Knowing the extremism and fanaticism of the majority for whom there are no options, and anticipating the destructive powers of such a hopelessly trapped society, he is ready to declare this planet doomed beyond amelioration. He therefore advocates an exodus to the moon, not as an imagination-expanding experience, but as a means of salvation from an unfit place to live. Although he doesn't foresee the establishment of an instant lunar utopia, he believes there will at least be sufficient territory to ensure the preservation of the race. Under the inspired leadership of noble and resourceful space technicians and as a result of the austerities of the voyage and relocation, Lal predicts that an improved order of man will eventually evolve. But if man in his present imperfect state refuses to leave his terrestrial prison, the repressed savage in him will erupt and he will turn against his fellow

---

17. Saul Bellow, "Where Do We Go from Here: The Future of Fiction," in *To the Young Writer,* ed. A. L. Bader (Ann Arbor: University of Michigan Press, 1965), p. 146.

inmates. Equating human beings with biological specimens in whom there is no "sovereign obligation to one's breed" (220) and in whom the desire to die follows the act of reproduction, Lal forecasts the imminent extinction of the species through self-consumption. He thus entreats man to turn his sights moonward and muster all of his energies to get there, instead of awaiting sure oblivion on native ground.

Sammler disagrees. While he is impressed with the scientific ingenuity which has made travel possible in a "dayless, nightless universe" (222) and has brought about visitation to an unexplored satellite, he does not believe it will contribute to the survival of man. While he considers it a luxury to contemplate ultimates in remote lunar privacy, he knows that is not what is most conducive to the growth of man's spirit. Finding no metaphysical advantages for a moon voyage, Sammler can be said to share the view Robert Frost expresses in "Birches": "Earth's the right place for love: I don't know where it is likely to go better." This does not mean that Sammler has no misgivings about earth and that he gives his unqualified endorsement to earthlings. In his colloquies with himself and others, favorable and unfavorable opinions of man vie with each other. He is, on one hand, an exponent of Schopenhauerian pessimism. From the time he was sixteen, when, Bellow tells us, Sammler's mother had him read *The World as Will and Idea,* he became aware of Schopenhauer's claim that the Will holds sway over the intellect, that it is an endless striving, a blind urge which can never be satiated or obtain a measure of tranquility. In human life, which manifests the nature of the Will, there is accordingly the same kind of striving and absence of lasting fulfillment. If there is a cessation of desire, the state we call happiness, it is only temporary. It soon changes to boredom, and the yearning for satisfaction again comes to the fore. Moreover, when man is not overcome with boredom or yearning, he, like the lower orders of creation, is bent on asserting himself at the expense of his fellows so that the world is a perpetual battleground. With a superabundance of empirical evidence from the present age staring him in the face, Sammler reaches the same dim conclusions as Schopenhauer. He observes the Will's defeat of reason in Nazi Germany. Shattering Hannah Arendt's "banality of evil" thesis, he shows how "banality is the adopted disguise of a very powerful will to abolish conscience" (18). He detects another form of the Will's tyranny in this country. Concurring with Schopenhauer's view that the organs of sex are the instrument of the Will, he decries the libidinal revolution taking hold of America, with the black man elevated to the position of erotic leadership and the white man trying to emulate him. Yet even though everyone is permitted to indulge in the grossest creaturely acts, he is still not satisfied. Sammler, echoing Schopenhauer, claims that each individual, believing that happiness is what others have, constantly strives for instantaneous gratification of all his demands and refuses to be evicted from the earth until he gets his money's worth. But because he knows his eviction will surely come to pass and because he dreads the prospect of "futurelessness" (75), he frenetically avails himself of life's every possibility, no matter how bizarre it might be. He even resorts to criminality as a means of self-actualization or as a way of attaining equality with the most glamorous villains of all time. If criminality is not to his liking and if his sense of inconsequence is extreme, he succumbs to madness and acts out his "fantasies of vaulting into higher states" (93). But what usually occurs, according to Sammler, is that man turns toward histrionics to lend interest to his banal life and to avoid thinking about death. In *The Adventures of Augie March* Bellow praises man for his ability to "catch up with legends" (333), and in *Henderson the Rain King* Bellow has Dahfu extol the redeeming powers of the imagination. In *Mr. Sammler's Planet* Bellow reverses his position. He has Sammler condemn man for mythologizing himself and giving free rein to his imagination in an attempt to emancipate himself from the bondage of the commonplace. Instead of acquiring any authenticity, becoming "the thing itself," man's search for personal distinction, Sammler contends, leads him to imitate inferior models. Especially after the Industrial Revolution, when the privilege of individuality was bestowed on all, did man abuse that privilege. Overly impressed with his newly gained sovereignty of self and having the liberty and leisure to experiment with its powers, he becomes obsessed with cultivating the most scintillating personality imaginable. Sammler's description of this scintillating personality is like D. H. Lawrence's description, which Bellow quotes in his essay, "Where Do We Go from Here: The Future of Fiction." Lawrence compares "the civilized conception of character to a millstone—a painted millstone about our necks."[18] Sammler

18. *Ibid.,* p. 137.

employs the same metaphor: "The Self may think it wears a gay new ornament, delightfully painted, but from outside we see that it is a millstone" (234). In *Seize the Day* Bellow called this millstone self the "pretender soul" and dramatized how it parasitically fed off and depleted the strength of Tommy Wilhelm's real soul. It is only at the end of the novella that his real soul subdues its predator and assumes control. No such victory is recorded in *Mr. Sammler's Planet*. According to Sammler's bleak point of view, the counterfeit, meretricious self continuously weighs man down and prevents his desirable self from emerging. When the novelty of his exhibitionism wears off and he is left stranded with his worthless, cumbersome trappings, he finds his existence unbearable. From the extreme of over-prizing his individuality, he goes to the opposite extreme of wanting to disown it entirely. He longs for nonbeing. Only this nonbeing takes the form of "round trips through evil, monstrosity, and orgy, with even God approached through obscenities" (229).

So much for Sammler's Schopenhauer-inspired negative estimate of man. Opposing it, but not as vehemently and frequently expressed, is his Jewish-inspired positive estimate of man. Bellow informs us in the novel that Schopenhauer called the Jews "vulgar optimists" (209), and Sammler, much as he would like to think of himself as an emancipated, secular intellectual, cannot free himself of this designation. He, like Bellow, has a "Jewish feeling"[19] within him which resists the despair and cynicism of twentieth-century apocalyptic romanticism. Although he does not possess the full measure of the *shtetl* Jew's *bitochon,* what Maurice Samuel defines as "certainty, assurance, trust . . . instinctive faith in every form of life,"[20] Sammler is still enough of a yea-sayer to denounce those who "stressed too hard the disintegrated assurances . . . [and] bitterly circled in black irony" (9) all vestiges of idealism. Unlike many of the survivors of the holocaust for whom God died in the concentration camps, Sammler, after a long period of apostasy and viewing himself as the supreme judge of his actions, gradually regains his belief in God. This confidence in the higher authority of God makes possible whatever confidence Sammler has in the potential of man. Sammler's backward leap of faith from

19. Nina A. Steers, "'Successor' to Faulkner?" *Show* 4 (September, 1964): 38.
20. Maurice Samuel, *The World of Sholom Aleichem* (New York: Schocken Books, 1943), p. 43.

God to man thus qualifies as an expression of Jewish optimism which holds that man is "able to realize in himself the good which first finds its reality in God." [21] Because Sammler has not abandoned hope that there is "a splash of God's own spirit" (189) in every being, he can, although not as zealously as Herzog, defend man against his wasteland discreditors. Even though he is sorely affected by the nasty, brutish nature of the present, Sammler can still commend our weak and crazy species for fighting against its fear and criminality. He can, above all, argue against Lal's scientific reduction of man to a death-craving, purposeless creature, driven only by biological necessity. Drawing on the affirmative Jewish doctrine which advocates the choice of life over death and the consecration of that life through meaningful action, Sammler observes that once man is born, he elects to go on living. Although he encounters many obstacles, he respects "the powers of creation"; he obeys "the will of God" (220). Because he has been given an invaluable gift which he wants to preserve, he is not eager, as Lal assumes, to leap into "Kingdom Come" (220). Nor do his insufferable tasks prompt him to leave this world. Thus man's clinging to life, despite all its confusions and uncertainties, and his arduous performance of duties are what Sammler deems most laudable. As for other, more spectacular evidence of man's magnanimity, he is hard pressed to discover it. While Sammler does grant that there were times when love seemed to be the ruling force in man's life and noble actions unexpectedly emerged from his error-strewn ways, he still finds humankind "doing the same stunts over and over. The old comical-tearful stuff" (174). No matter how strongly Sammler yearns to do so, he cannot, like Bellow's other defiers of gloom, uncover only the "radiance" of life. For him there are too many shadows which darken its light. Sammler's optimism, while discernible, is not finally strong and abiding enough to counteract his pessimism. Unlike Camus in *The Plague,* he cannot conclude there are "more things to admire in man than to despise."

The earnest airing of views on matters of great import has always been a prominent feature of Bellow's novels. But in *Augie March* and *Henderson the Rain King* he introduced jarring comic situations which often derailed his train of thought. He was not at all concerned

21. Leo Baek, "The Optimism of Judaism," in *Contemporary Jewish Thought,* ed. Simon Noveck (B'nai B'rith Department of Adult Jewish Education, 1963), p. 182.

that his ideas would lose their continuity or be forgotten in the com-
motion; he relished the ingenious pratfalls he devised as much as the
intellectual proceedings they interrupted. This is not so with *Mr.
Sammler's Planet*. Rather than valuing comic situations for their own
droll sake, Bellow seems to include them so as not to disappoint
fans who have come to expect a certain combination of mayhem and
meditation in his novels. The initial impression one gets is that he per-
functorily interspersed the minimum number of antic interludes
needed to fulfill expectations. He surely did not consider Sammler's
reflections so weighty and interminable as to require incidents of diversionary action. For him there was excitement enough in Sammler's
"ferris wheel" revolvings of mind without the introduction of lesser
forms of amusement. But Bellow still could not give up communicat-
ing with those readers who might not be intellectual heavyweights.
He thus felt compelled to maintain their interest by offering them
comic relief from the novel's sustained mental inquiry. Moreover,
having assumed the role of morality instructor in *Mr. Sammler's
Planet,* Bellow realized that the best way of reaching all his readers,
keen-witted and dullards alike, was to use his comic situations as lively
exempla of his preachings. As Irving Howe has noted, "Bellow has
the rare gift of transforming dialectic into drama, casuistry into
comedy, so that one is steadily aware of the close relationship between
his discursive passages and his central narrative." [22] Early in the novel,
for example, Sammler states that "humankind, knotted and tangled,
supplied more oddities than you could keep up with" (37). Bellow
then proceeds to create odd and incongruous situations which corroborate this observation. To be sure, not all of them are funny in
the conventional sense. A near-blind old man being spooked by a
black bogeyman and his penis resembles Leventhal's freakish persecution by a Gentile he never knew he wronged. In both encounters the
sinister overwhelms the ridiculous. The same is true for the scene in
which the bogeyman is apprehended. What started out to be a harmless prank on the part of Lionel Feffer ends up being a brutal black
and white clash in which Feffer is almost choked to death by the
thief and the thief is almost clubbed to death by the bellicose Eisen,
engaged by the pacifist Sammler. The wry aspects of the situation are
at once overshadowed by the pervasive violence.

[22.] Howe, Review of *Mr. Sammler's Planet*, p. 108.

Not all of the situations in *Mr. Sammler's Planet* are so grisly, with horror almost totally effacing the humor. Although many of them arise out of desperation, there is considerable levity in them. Sammler provides the explanation for the origins of such situations. "Unanimously all tasted, and each in his own way, the flavor of the end of things-as-known. And by way of summary, perhaps, each accented more strongly his own subjective style and the practices by which he was known" (278). Bellow, in turn, creates episodes in which the more frantic characters give full expression to their subjective style and unrestrainedly enact their eccentric practices. Shula, fearing that death might soon prevent her father from writing his projected memoirs of H. G. Wells, graduates from looting trash bins to pilfering Govinda Lal's *The Future of the Moon*. Thrilled with the same kind of "game fever" (193) she had exhibited as a five-year-old when playing hide and seek with her father in London, she spends most of the novel impishly concealing the manuscript from Lal and Sammler. In addition to gleefully repeating the cunning subterfuge of her girlhood, she unwittingly presents a giddy burlesque of the *femme fatale*'s wiles, for she attempts to seduce Lal in her own maladroit fashion. All too aware of her advancing middle age and the decline of her chances for matrimony, she overtaxes her feeble imagination to be as provocative as possible. Wearing a misbound sari and an orange Hindu circle on her forehead, she not only fails to win Lal, but cannot even distract him from talking to Sammler. Shula's abortive wooing is very much like Mtalba's unsuccessful courtship of Henderson. In both instances the humor originates in the contrast between the women's impassioned pursuit of the men and the men's total obliviousness to them. The difference is that Bellow in *Mr. Sammler's Planet* does not develop the episode, allowing the reader to immerse himself in its spirited fun. Since he has proved his point—demonstrating how Shula's thievery and seduction are excesses of the subjective style—he is eager to move on to other points, especially those which emerge from Sammler's dialogue with Lal.

Bellow regards their philosophical exchange as the ideological center of the novel, so he allows it to go on uninterrupted for some thirty pages. However, to prevent their flood of discourse from inundating the novel, Bellow feels compelled to stop it by having Wallace Gruner, the other leading instigator of comic situations, produce a literal flood.

Dreading the loss of his father and his financial sponsorship, Wallace is driven to ransack the family estate for illegal abortion money which he believes Dr. Gruner received from the Mafia and ingeniously concealed. Wrongheadedly searching for the buried loot in the attic's pipes, he bursts them so that water, not dollar bills, gushes forth and drenches the house and its inhabitants. Wallace's plumbing fiasco resembles Henderson's misguided destruction of the Arnewi cistern. Although the damage in each case is considerable and the result of calculated bungling, Bellow's treatment of each situation varies. He more fully elaborates the risible particulars of the havoc Henderson creates. He shows him before the deluge, perfecting his home-made bomb and preening as the great white technological savior; in the midst of the deluge, frenziedly trying to halt the rush of water as he is assaulted with dead frogs and the abuse of the Arnewi; and after the deluge, excessively castigating himself for his stupidity. Bellow makes no such comic extravaganza out of Wallace's waterworks display. He does not show Wallace plotting his mischief, executing it, or afterwards overcome with undue remorse for having caused it. He concentrates only on the immediate, humorously incongruous effects of it—water cascading through a densely furnished house with an inefficient bucket brigade of Wallace and Sammler to drain the flow, and the arrival of firemen with their water-filled hoses to save the day. Aside from being a temporary whimsical distraction, Wallace's aqueous antics serve primarily as a spur to Sammler's moralizing. Even in the midst of his emergency flood control duty, Sammler cannot refrain from associating Wallace with "symbols of turbulence" (242) and classifying him with infamous destroyers of their fathers' " 'valueless' success" (240). Wallace's botched treasure hunt, punctuated by Sammler's ongoing condemnation of it, fails to elicit its full share of hearty laughs. The same kind of diminished response is occasioned by Wallace's final madcap adventure on the day of his father's death—recklessly piloting a small plane and then crash-landing it while attempting to photograph the shrubbery of country estates. This time Bellow does not allow us much of an eyewitness view of Wallace's daredevil frolics. He provides us instead with Angela's and Shula's secondhand report of it. While their report conveys some of the absurdity of Wallace's aerial escapade, it is no substitute for the kind of highly embellished, on-the-scene account which Bellow presents of Augie March's eagle-training and iguana-hunting expedition. Bellow never dampens Augie's rollicking situation by interjecting sober analyses of its implications, but this is precisely what he does in *Mr. Sammler's Planet*. Even in the midst of a report of a comic situation, let alone the comic situation itself, Bellow has Sammler offer his didactic interpretations of it. Even though he only assumes that Wallace is buzzing overhead in his little Cessna, Sammler refers to him as a "roaring center" (267) unto himself, the kind of madman he earlier described as having "fantasies of vaulting into higher states" (93). Once again the ulterior purpose of the novel's comic situations becomes apparent. While they may entertain us with their surface mirth, they are expressly designed to teach us how not to behave. By revealing examples of ludicrous conduct, Bellow hopes to dissuade us from becoming so inclined.

The novel's comedy of language is also enlisted in the higher service of academic sermonizing. Unlike Augie, Henderson, and even the tormented Herzog, who often trifle with words for the mere sport of it, Sammler is so intent upon composing and delivering his peroration that he does not indulge much in meaningless verbal diversion. Consumed with "thinking [his] way to the ultimate reason of things"[23] and summing up his findings, he carefully chooses that language which best implements his needs. If his needs require the use of antic discourse to express his opinions most effectively, he does not hesitate to employ it. Especially when his ire is provoked, he becomes unusually witty. But, unlike Herzog, who often waxes risible when indignant, Sammler does not rely on his wit to dispel his own melancholy or to dazzle others with his cleverness. He values his wit primarily for its worth in furthering his editorializing aims. To convey, for example, the plight of twentieth-century man overwhelmed with ever-mounting distractions, Sammler, drawing upon Freud's comparison of the establishment of the ego's sovereignty to a "work of reclamation, like the draining of the Zuider Zee,"[24] uses a similar metaphor of "a Dutch drudgery . . . pumping and pumping to keep a few acres of dry ground," yet unable to halt the "invading sea . . . of facts and sensations" (4). To register his contempt for those writers-turned-activists who clamor for instant revolution, he invents the commonplace but

23. Alfred Kazin, Review of *Mr. Sammler's Planet* by Saul Bellow, *New York Review of Books* 15 (December 3, 1970): 3.
24. I am grateful to Bette Howland for suggesting the source of this metaphor.

incisive metaphor of foolhardy malcontents proclaiming a "general egg-breaking to make a great historical omelet" (214). But the greatest source of vexation for Sammler, and thus the one which evokes his most derisive figurative outbursts, is "theatricality in people" (230). He accordingly inveighs against this unwholesome penchant for histrionics by describing offenders in the most unflattering commercial and theatrical images. Like Herzog damning Madeleine for her spurious facade, he refers to those tawdrily masqueraded personalities as Woolworth store products, "cheap tin or plastic from the five-and-dime of souls" (234). He likens their frantic bids for attention to the desperate and shrill playing of musical instruments. Especially irritated by their emotional exhibitionism, he hyperbolically pictures them as "swimming and boating in that cloudy, contaminated, confusing, surging medium of human feelings, taking the passion-waters, exclaiming over their fate" (234). It goes without saying that Sammler's anger-induced rhetorical leaps of imagination amuse us with their novelty. But they also command our interest and prompt us to examine Sammler's complaints more carefully. While we may not end up agreeing with him, we would not have paused to consider his position had he not enticed us with his droll figures of speech.

When exasperated, Sammler also distorts the language of popular quotations to express his unpopular views. Disgusted with today's clergy for their lasciviousness, he finds them not fulfilling Isaiah's prophecy of "beating swords into plowshares" (106), but practicing a bastardized version of it, "converting dog collars into G strings" (106). Equally annoyed with the gross congregants and their inferior spiritual leaders, Sammler trenchantly amends Matthew's "pearls before swine" phrase to his own: "Artificial pearls before real swine were cast by these jet-set preachers" (115). Sammler, however, does not provide us with many such tongue-in-cheek revisions of well-known sayings. Unlike Herzog, who feels uneasy in his role of moral spokesman and thus resorts to more circuitous ways of expressing his convictions, Sammler, confident as a seer, is straightforward in speaking his mind. Nor does Sammler usually adopt Herzog's practice of interjecting into the context of his thoughts seemingly incongruous quotations which end up amusing us with their unexpected appropriateness. One notable exception is Sammler's inclusion of the Latin phrase, *Quod erat demonstrandum* [That which has been demonstrated], right after the thief has displayed his penis. While the unlikely juxtaposition of the crude act and the formal quotation initially disconcerts us, it comes to make more sense than nonsense and thus possesses a jocular relevance. Just as the Latin phrase in its abbreviated form, Q.E.D., is used at the end of an argument in logic to signify it has been conclusively proved, Sammler assumes that the thief regards his demonstrated organ as conclusive proof of his superiority. But as a rule Sammler does not bother with those quotations which are germane only through comic indirection. Because he has so many important matters to consider, and because he realizes his time for doing so is limited, he incorporates only the most immediately apt and compelling quotations to lend breadth and depth to his speculations. For example, to emphasize his disapproval of the billions spent on highways rather than on public welfare, he recalls T. S. Eliot's remark that "statesmen [are] the foremost of the Gadarene swine" (277). Mulling over the topic of sex and old age, he calls to mind the elderly Sophocles' temperate views as recorded in Cicero's *De Senectute,* the more wanton views of the septuagenarian Wells, and Hamlet's grim estimate of man in his declining years. Because Sammler has been able to offer us a number of pertinent observations on the subject, he holds our interest. There is no need for him to introduce humorously inappropriate quotations as a way of camouflaging a lack of thorough coverage or as a way of providing entertaining digressions.

Nor does Sammler employ the rash of improbable allusions which Augie, Henderson, and Herzog freely develop. This is not to say that he entirely refrains from drawing unlikely parallels between his venal companions and venerable figures of history and literature. While he seldom undercuts himself through preposterous associations, he does by way of outlandish comparisons comically reduce those who violate his standards of decorum. The severity of his mockery depends upon the severity of the violation. Since Margotte's offense is the rather harmless one of unwittingly misrepresenting her late husband's political theories, Sammler with mild levity allies her with Plato and the twelve Apostles, who unintentionally distorted the ideas of Socrates and Jesus. Since Walter Bruch's practice of courting a refined lady while simultaneously indulging in the most perverse fetishisms is a more loathsome vice, Sammler jeeringly likens his conduct to the specious fidelity of the young rake in Ernest Dowson's 1891 poem, *"Non Sum Qualis*

Eram Bonae Sub Regno Cynarae" [I Am Not What Once I Was in Kind Cynara's Day], who, in the midst of his libertinism, professes his undying affection to an absent lover. But since Wallace commits what is to Sammler one of the most unpardonable sins of all—the desecration of another man's property—Sammler in a fit of caustic hyperbole links Wallace's accidental house-flooding with the terrorist campaign waged by Bakunin, the Russian nineteenth-century anarchist. Generally Sammler, who is more concerned with elucidating than with entertaining, calls into duty more probable allusions. A citizen of the world, with the world's learning still at his command, he can summon the most precise and graphic references to substantiate and vivify his reading of reality, particularly his impressions of the lunar age. Although he does not have Lal's knowledge of the biophysical properties of the moon, he is able to recall those moon allusions in mythology, folklore, poetry, and science fiction which shed particular light upon our own planet and present a temporary escape from it. When, for example, Sammler gets excessively disgusted with Angela's prurience and the prurience of the entire Western world, he becomes "pleasantly haunted by moon-visions, Artemis—lunar chastity" (67). But he also sees the moon the way it is viewed in popular folklore as somehow affecting sanity. He thus notes the collective madness of the American people, who are so obsessed with journeying into outer space and colonizing the moon that they squander billions of dollars desperately needed to help remedy grave social ills on this earth. As for those individuals who are already unhinged—the Shulas, Wallaces, and Eisens—he finds them more crazed than ever by the prospect of the end of their earth-centered world; therefore "lunatic" is his most frequent description of them. To suggest how much we are under the moon's sway, Bellow has Sammler recall a line from Milton's Comus: "Now to the Moon in wavering Morrice move" (97). Milton was referring to the fishes and seas "performing the dance" (97), but Bellow is implying that in this age we, the higher orders of creation, are equally influenced by the moon and do our equivalent aerospace dances. To Sammler such cosmic gyrations also resemble the bizarre feats depicted in science fiction. Our astronautical engineers, bent on catapulting themselves from the confining earth and heading moonward in "their flying arthropod hardware" (174), could be straight out of Wells's The First Men in the Moon, a work Sammler mentions. Similarly, Sammler's conception of the austere, highly disciplined life on the moon where only the technicians rule is very much like the Selenite anti-utopia which Wells's scientists discover when exploring the moon.

Despite Sammler's reliance on the most expeditious allusions and quotations to convey his meaning, his harangues are usually most prolonged affairs. Departing from the "traditional contractedness of Jewish thought,"[25] the sages of which nearly always preferred the shortest form of discourse, Sammler more closely resembles the individual who is "nervously loquacious on the edge of an abyss."[26] Instead of offering short views as he continually promises to do, he sputters on and on, making it virtually impossible for anyone to get a word in edgewise. Present at both the near-disintegration of his familiar world and the christening of an unfamiliar one, he feels compelled to give a detailed account of what is happening. Except for rare moments of pithiness, his eschatological bent causes him to dwell to the point of humorous prolixity on all the portents of doom. Instead of condensations, he offers catalogues, mostly of decadent human types. While these catalogues are improbably funny in their length, they do not possess the droll specificity that is found in Augie March's catalogues. Instead of being fond enumerations of quaint misfits, they are scathing inventories of the hopelessly warped, rattled off at the height of contempt. Sammler's analyses of sociological and metaphysical issues are also unabridged. Rather than submitting précis of his findings, he includes involuted and protracted reports of all phases of his investigations. Instead of "eliminating the superfluous" (278), as he professes to do, he is comically unable to sift out the unnecessary.

While the language of *Mr. Sammler's Planet* is verbose, it is not varied. Unlike many of Bellow's other novels, there are not stretches of distinctive levels and kinds of discourse which jocosely commingle with each other. Sammler's vocalized and unvocalized monologues dominate the book. Other voices are heard, but briefly and at sporadic intervals. There are only snatches of the policeman's overly familiar yet stolid replies, Walter Bruch's maudlin *mea culpas,* Lionel Feffer's pushy entrepreneur lingo, the student's Neanderthal crudities, Eisen's blunt refugee English, and Angela's psychiatric and *True Romance*

25. Kazin, Review of *Mr. Sammler's Planet,* p. 4.
26. Kenneth Burke quoted in Kenneth John Atchity, "Bellow's Mr. Sammler: 'The Last Man Given for Epitome,' " p. 53.

confidences. Conspicuously missing is the sound of the black man's accent and idiom in counterpoint with the Jewish white man's accent and idiom. Unlike Malamud, who records the verbal clashes between a Jewish and a black writer in *The Tenants,* Bellow keeps his black mute and allows his penis to speak for him. Sammler, as usual, takes over as chief articulator. Yet it would be a mistake to conclude that Sammler's language is all of a kind. While he is not a hyperactive verbal stunt man like Henderson, he is still agile enough to perform a fair number of rhetorical shifts. Should the occasion warrant it, he can move with ease from sober dialectics to skittish colloquialisms. He can interrupt his mandarin Oxonian talk with earthy Yiddish expressions and stilted Oriental forms of address. He can switch from the most biting tirades to the most banal jokes. He can alternate from eulogizing man in the sublimest terms to excoriating him with the most disparaging animal imagery. Although Sammler may be inflexible in many of his views, he cannot be accused of being inflexible in his use of language.

Since Sammler describes his state as one of "nonintimidation by doom" (134), he is not prompted to employ the desperate humor of verbal retrieval which Bellow's intimidated heroes resort to in periods of stress. Having lived through the worst times and become inured to subsequent adversity, he does not have to amuse himself with mirthful confessions of personal woes. Nor does he have to rely on wry self-deprecation as the only means of warding off despair. If necessary, he can call upon his spiritual reserves to buoy his sinking spirits. Should these reserves be temporarily depleted, he can summon into play his Old World irony as a way of distancing himself from the New World's madness. Although he ultimately fails to distance himself and finds that he is "a million times exceeded in strangeness by the phenomena themselves" (110), he manages to bear his confinement to the strangeness without forced grins, with his urbanity intact.

Mr. Sammler's Planet, while a product of great intellectual maturity and advanced writing craft, has much of the same testy humor that is found in Bellow's first novel, *Dangling Man.* The reason for its existence is, however, vastly different. Joseph rails against humanity for initiating a senseless war whose evils he has nightmares about but has never experienced; Sammler, having borne the full brunt of the same war's savagery, rails against humanity not so much for his former sufferings, but for the repetition of an identical savagery some twenty years later. Joseph's and Sammler's reactions are, nevertheless, alike. Powerless to arrest the accelerating chaos, Joseph retreats to record his venomous journal entries, while Sammler separates himself from the rest of his species to give his acerbic recitals. Exchanges with people outside his "six-sided box" only intensify Joseph's hostility; contacts with the fellow tenants of his planet only exacerbate Sammler's bitterness. But there the similarity ends. In contrast to the youthful Joseph's abbreviated and often oversimplified analyses of society's deficiencies, Sammler, the mature one-eyed prophet, exhaustively and intricately spells out what is wrong with the "country of the blind." He relies not merely on his own native intelligence and nimble wit to do so; he also unobtrusively taps the wisdom of the ages to aid in his forecasting. He most resembles Herzog in this respect, though he is more skillful at integrating his own insights with those gained from secondary sources. Because Sammler is more intellectually dexterous, he does not have to introduce levity to mask any clumsy handling of erudition, nor does he feel compelled to temper his austere judgments by couching them in whimsical language. Unlike Bellow's other faultfinding heroes, whose need to ingratiate proves stronger than their need to chastise, Sammler uses comic rhetoric only if it reinforces his views, no matter how pejorative they may be. Indeed, Beverly Gross argues that the "private drama of *Mr. Sammler's Planet* exists only as a vehicle for sounding public proclamations and moral mandates, for getting things off Bellow's chest."[27] While it is true that Sammler lacks the corporeal reality of a Wilhelm or a Henderson and that the scrapes he experiences serve merely to ignite his combustible mind, he has enough of what James terms the "solidity of specification" to engage our interest in him as a character in his own right. Although he appears most often as a withdrawn, cogitating figure observing the "gallery of fools" in his midst and mentally drafting what Benjamin DeMott calls his neo-Enlightenment "dunciad,"[28] he is not without his own ridiculous hypocrisies and obsessions. As long as he inhabits this planet, he is also implicated in its "confusion and degraded clowning" (313). There is no millenarian utopia, Jewish funeral home, mythic Africa, or rural promised land to which he can escape. The

27. Gross, "Dark Side of the Moon," p. 155.

28. Benjamin DeMott, "Saul Bellow and the Dogmas of Possibility," *Saturday Review of Literature* 53 (February 7, 1970): 28.

oldest yet the most adaptable of Bellow's heroes, he is the only one who has not fled from the world's horrors by theorizing about them or dreaming them out of existence. He has trained himself to live with "crazy streets, filthy nightmares, monstrosities come to life" (74). With such "cruel dissolution" (74) facing Sammler daily, he understandably does not deliver any euphoric praises of man or offer any charitably humorous excuses for man's lapses. Nevertheless, the impingement of brutal reality stifles but does not silence what remains of Sammler's comic response to life.

Conclusion

9

Saul Bellow has not written a divine comedy depicting the miraculous resurrection or redemption of man in some remote paradise. Rather, he has created a series of secular comedies revealing man in this sullied world, vacillating between recidivism and reform of his detestable practices. They are comedies in which the protagonists are not resolute pilgrims making their steady progress to the "celestial city," but faltering penitents, never quite able to extricate themselves from the snares of their terrestrial cities. Nor do they ever escape from their own private entanglements. Since the "human stuff" out of which they are made does not possess absolute purity, they cannot free themselves of their tainted nature. If they aspire to be "pure intellect . . . pure will" or pure eros, the grossness of their creatureliness impedes the realization of their perfectionistic strivings.[1] Since eternal life is not guaranteed them, they are compelled to settle for the contingency and finitude of their existence. If they try to hide from death, their fragility steals

---

1. Nathan Scott claims that the difference between tragic man and comic man lies in the way in which each regards his mortal limitations. The tragic man "would be pure intellect or pure will or pure something-or-other, and nothing wounds him more deeply than to be reminded that his life is a conditioned thing and that there is nothing absolute at all in the human stuff out of which he is made. But the comic man is unembarrassed by even the grossest expressions of his creatureliness." See "The Bias of Comedy and the Narrow Escape into Faith," *The Christian Scholar* 44 (Spring, 1961): 19–20.

over them unawares and reminds them of their impermanence. Bellow, however, does not lugubriously or vitriolically dwell upon man's limitations or magnify them beyond credibility. His is not the infernal vision of the contemporary black humorists who view this world as a hell where man's beginning is dust and his end stench. While Bellow does acknowledge that we are incorrigible creatures, "doing always the same stunts, repeating the same disgraces" (*H:* 182), he does not succumb to the black humorists' facile and sensational devaluation of human worth. Still believing in mankind's possibilities, he declares, "I cannot agree with recent writers who have told us that we are Nothing. We are indeed not what the Golden Ages boasted us to be. But we are Something." [2] In his secular comedies he elaborates on what this "Something" is. He shows his characters struggling to be men of feeling in a world devoid of feeling. He recounts the hard-won triumphs of their compassion over their self-pity. He causes us to marvel at their strenuous efforts to battle their iniquity and dread. He reveals them in rare intervals of magnanimity, eschewing meanness and acting charitably. Although they are burdened with social pressures and personal traumas, they resist surrendering to despair. Preserving their appreciation for beauty and their capacity for love, they are able to go on living in "this bondage of strangeness" (*AM:* 523). Yearning for affirmation, they are, nevertheless, too skeptical to be dogmatic proponents of it.

Though Bellow's concerns do not markedly vary from one secular comedy to the next, there has been a progressively sophisticated and versatile use of the comic mode in each of his novels. Its development has approximately paralleled the advancing maturity of Bellow's heroes and the increasing novelty of his fictional forms. In *Dangling Man* the humor is often as dilettantish and crabbed as the twenty-eight-year-old Joseph, the scholar *manqué* who, suspended between civilian and military life, can only impotently jeer at himself and the world. Because he is totally consumed with settling his grievance with the unjust deniers of his freedom, he is transformed from a humane rationalist into a spiteful "irrationalist." In such a distraught state he, who is but an apprentice in the art of learned wit, cannot draft a very sustained or devastating ideological comedy. With his ever-mounting

2. Saul Bellow, "A Word from Writer Directly to Reader," *Fiction of the Fifties,* ed. Herbert Gold (New York: Doubleday & Co., 1959), p. 20.

rage and dwindling intellectual resources, he can make only fitful and often aimless satiric thrusts at the pervasive regimentation and absurdity of the times. Far more satisfying, though equally ineffectual, are the bitterly ironic expostulations and replies carried on between himself and his alter ego. These take the place of any barbed debates which Joseph might have with his brothers. The journal form which Bellow employs to convey Joseph's experience also restricts his communication with anyone other than himself and thus diminishes the scope and vitality of the novel's comedy. Instead of capturing the immediacy of any prolonged encounters with the droll, unenlightened public, he has Joseph immediately remove himself from them to transcribe his purportedly enlightened reactions about them. His jaundiced, hurried impressions of the people outside his room pass for comedy of character. His frenetic sorties into society and his clumsy retreats from it to take up his scribbling suffice for comic action. Admittedly, such claustral scribblings in no way measure up to the lively scrimmages with humanity portrayed in Bellow's later novels. But if *Dangling Man* is to be judged solely as a "record of . . . inward transactions" (9), then it is a deft account of the besieged consciousness tending to its deadly serious and mordantly funny business.

In Bellow's next novel, *The Victim,* the transactions are filled with the same crotchety humor, but they are now carried on between two middle-aged aggrieved parties: Asa Leventhal, the self-righteous Jewish trade journalist, and Kirby Allbee, the outraged anti-Semitic dybbuk who seeks to possess Leventhal's soul. Although the heated wrangles between two quirky disputants yield more comic possibilities than do Joseph's listless quarrels with himself, they are not without their own tedium. Allbee's hysterical demands for occupancy clashing with Leventhal's equally hysterical declarations of no trespassing tend to monopolize their wry exchanges. Their verbal sparring is all too predictable and not sufficiently varied in content. The same might be said of their actions. While their alternations between playing the victim and the victimizer offer more cause for diabolical mirth than do Joseph's solitary writhings, they are repeated so often that they lose most of their shock value. What should have been Allbee's insidious infiltration is reduced to insipid pestering, and what should have been Leventhal's somber exorcism deteriorates into a series of facetious evictions. But then, who is to say that such a *reductio ad absurdum* strategy may not have been Bellow's intention all along? It may have been his aim to show not only the balefulness of evil, but the buffoonery of evil as well. If so, then he has generally succeeded within the limits he has set for himself. These limits have been further prescribed by the tightly structured, "well-made" novel form which he chose for telling his tale. Calling *The Victim* his "Ph.D. thesis,"[3] he adhered to all the rules and conventions of Flaubertian realism. With self-conscious artistry he methodically fashioned his "parallel plots and characters"[4] and introduced the requisite ironies. He was careful to remain consistently detached from his characters and exerted a Spartan control over his literary style. Most of the comedy is therefore constrained. Especially the thoughtful laughter which Allbee evokes when discussing the undeserved suffering of the innocent and the ruthless competitiveness of life is stiltedly academic. While Allbee is believable as a dybbuk, he is not convincing as a dialectician. Conversely, Leventhal, who never presumes to be a thinker, in his own stumbling fashion makes the more original observations about life's humorous anomalies. Although the sinister and ludicrous situations in which Bellow places Leventhal are contrived, his characterization is natural. It is his antic personality —his embarrassment by his body, his ursine abrasiveness, his shadow-boxing with anti-Semitic bogeymen, and his compulsion to keep "[his] spirit under lock and key" (146)—which makes Leventhal the forerunner of Bellow's fully fleshed comic neurotics and, more than anything else, prevents the novel from being merely a nightmare of accusation and guilt.

Bellow expressed a dislike for his first two novels because he found them "plaintive, sometimes querulous." Tired of their "solemnity of complaint,"[5] he wrote his rollicking denial of wretchedness, *The Adventures of Augie March*. Tired also of shackling himself to the

---

3. Saul Bellow quoted in George Garrett, "To Do Right in a Bad World: Saul Bellow's *Herzog*," *The Hollins Critic* 2 (April, 1965): 6.

4. For an elaboration of the ways in which *The Victim* fits into the "James-Flaubert tradition of conscious artistry" and for a discussion of the ways in which *The Victim* is an improvement in narrative form over *Dangling Man*, see Keith M. Opdahl, *The Novels of Saul Bellow: An Introduction* (University Park: Pennsylvania State University Press, 1967), pp. 50–52.

5. Gordon L. Harper, "Saul Bellow—The Art of Fiction: An Interview," *Paris Review* 87 (Winter, 1965): 62.

Flaubertian standard of meticulous craftsmanship, he "kicked over the traces" and wrote a "catch-as-catch-can picaresque," a form which allowed him to include "a great mass of sand and gravel," "a diversity of scene," and a "large number of characters." [6] With a gigantic leap of the imagination he went from the cramped, saturnine humor of *Dangling Man* and *The Victim* to the expansive, saturnalian humor of *Augie March*. There is no doubt that such a humor, which celebrates more than it censures so vast a troupe of motley figures, offers a broader and more generous perspective on life. In its tendency for affirmation even while focusing on the gaudy and the grotesque, it manifests the potential for "high" comedy which, according to Wylie Sypher, "chastens men without despair, without rancor, as if human blunders were seen from a godlike distance, and also from within the blundering self." [7] Saturnalian humor, however, is not without its limitations. Often intoxicated with its own mirth, it can become so obstreperous that it usurps the center of attention and drowns out the more subtle nuances of meaning. This unrestrained boisterousness is occasionally present in the comic language of the youthful Augie. His rambunctious desire to "touch all sides" makes for the frenzied inclusiveness of his observations. The legions of facts he musters up are so vast that he often loses control of them. While they superbly attest to the plenitude of American life and amply reveal the surface wonders of Chicago, they are not the most conducive for finely probing the hidden mysteries of the "sphinx-like" city. The same is true for the "free style" which Augie prides himself on originating. While the liberties he takes with language—syntax tampering, unholy alliances of disparate discourse, grammatical violations and neologisms—are piquantly truant, they are often so wildly clever that they steal the show from the more sedate thoughts they are meant to convey. Especially when Augie wants to avoid unpleasant realities, he employs excessively startling metaphors and farfetched allusions to conceal what threatens to undermine his optimism. Strained wit thus prevails, when the more natural response would be one of world-weariness. This forced verbal effervescence mars

6. Harvey Breit, "Saul Bellow," *The Writer Observed* (New York: World Publishing Co., 1956), p. 273.

7. Wylie Sypher, "Our New Sense of the Comic," in *Comedy*, ed. Wylie Sypher (New York: Doubleday & Co., 1956), p. 212.

the excellence of the novel's comic language and contributes to Augie's lack of substance as a fictional character.[8] He most often appears as a mouthpiece for euphoric sentiments and the good-humored defender of the aberrant Machiavellians, rather than as the complex tragicomic pursuer of "a good enough fate." And when he is not eulogizing his "version" of things, he is so caught up in and alternately rescued from a whirlwind of slapstick situations that he seems more like an unbreakable toy than a fragile human being. On the rare occasions when he is not engaging in "clownery, hiding tragedy" (454), he can curtail his evasive movement long enough to delve in his own way to the vital core of an issue. With the truths derived from his innocent and not so innocent knocks, he is able to draft his own speculative comedy and arrive at such disconcerting insights as: man's actions are determined by instincts rather than by reason; society judges an individual's worth by what he *does,* not by what he *is;* and the majority need to coerce others to accept their interpretation of reality. While such reflections seem to be "super-added to [Augie's] adventures, rather than an outcome of them,"[9] it cannot be denied that his urchin intellectual way of expressing them is one of the reasons why Augie's picaro's progress is so distinctive.

The Adventures of Augie March is Bellow's festive comedy, with lovable eccentrics and revels galore. Ruled by an energetic master of ceremonies and neophyte defier of fate, it is informed with the principle that man is "only ostensibly born to remain in specified limits" (240). In the following novella, *Seize the Day,* the festivities are over and replaced by the grueling labor of economic and emotional survival. Tommy Wilhelm is the enervated slave of ceremonies and seasoned acquiescer to fate; the prevailing principle in his quasi-naturalistic comedy is, "There's really very little that a man can change at will.

8. Other critics have commented on Augie's lack of fictional density. Robert Penn Warren attributes his thinness of character to his lack of "commitments," a trait with which Bellow has endowed him. See his review of the novel in *New Republic* 129 (November 2, 1953): 22–23. John Aldridge, on the other hand, blames Augie's given society for his lack of "dramatic centrality," since there exists within it "no price of spiritual opposition which might endow him with tragic or pathetic value." See "The Society of Three Novels," *In Search of Heresy* (New York: McGraw-Hill & Co., 1956), p. 135.

9. Tony Tanner, *Saul Bellow* (Edinburgh: Oliver & Boyd, 1965), p. 55.

He can't change his lungs or nerves, or constitution or temperament. They're not under his control" (24). While Bellow relies on the puckish Augie to put a "girdle around the earth in forty minutes," cursorily inspect things, and conclude what "fools these mortals be," in *Seize the Day* he acts as his own inspector and offers a more careful scrutiny of chiefly one foolish mortal. The resultant humor is certainly not as ebullient and wide-ranging as that of his "favorite fantasy," [10] *Augie March*. But neither does it confine itself to surfaces, resting primarily on a brimming inventory of risible externals. More concentrated in its energies and delicately attuned to register more subtle variations, it is able to penetrate Wilhelm's interior and convey a sense of the depths and hostilities unknown even to him. This is not to suggest that Bellow overlooks Wilhelm's exterior. With satiric disparagement tempered by amused sympathy, he comments on Wilhelm's corpulent body, his animal resemblances, and his disheveled attire. More than in any previous novel, he captures the pathos and folly of a flawed creature's inept coping with very real betrayers, both devious supporters and forthright renouncers. While Leventhal has only spectral confrontations with his shadowy double and Augie flees before any of the Machiavellians can pounce upon him, Wilhelm remains to be exploited by a very much alive quack analyst-investor and endures the repeated curses of his niggardly father. Still Wilhelm has the capacity to make light of his misfortune. Even though he faces destitution and feels about to drown in "the waters of the earth" (77), he can underscore the absurdity of his clinging to such a defective lifesaver as Dr. Tamkin. And Dr. Tamkin, all the while he is pulling Wilhelm under, is paradoxically able to offer advice which will later buoy him up. More patently a mountebank than Allbee, he is nevertheless the more coherent and persuasive comedian of ideas. Although he uses the bastardized clichés of an illegitimate psychology, he is able to impress upon Wilhelm the necessity to live in the here and now, divorce himself from suffering, and renegotiate with his true self. The fact that Wilhelm subsequently does make contact with this true self, even though it ironically takes place in the presence of an unknown corpse and sham mourners, makes *Seize the Day,* despite its prevailing

10. Bernard Kalb, "Biographical Sketch," *Saturday Review of Literature* 36 (September 19, 1953): 13.

atmosphere of "sad-sack" desperation, one of Bellow's more hopefully resolved comedies.[11] This resolution is not altogether believable, since it comes to pass after only one day and involves a character with so many defeats in his background that it scarcely seems possible he would discover who he is in such a short duration. But, in light of the qualified optimism about man's potential expressed in various parts of the novel, we are asked to accept this quasi-naturalistic story with its somewhat gratuitous romantic ending and believe that for the time being Wilhelm has achieved the "consummation of his heart's ultimate need" (118).

Wilhelm's petit bourgeois reversals of fortune in the all too common marketplace do not, by and large, require a vigorous suspension of disbelief. *Henderson the Rain King,* Bellow's full-scale exotic romance with its prodigious questor and comic improbabilities, taxes our wildest fancies. Yet Henderson, the fifty-five-year-old Tarzanesque *Übermensch* who uproariously bulldozes his way through all obstacles, is a refreshing change from Leventhal and Wilhelm, those Chaplinesque homunculi who are hemmed in by society's and their own self-erected barriers. Although Henderson shares many of the same laughable physical encumbrances which vex Leventhal and Wilhelm (and howls even more vociferously about these encumbrances), he is not permanently abashed by his Brobdingnag body. Unlike Leventhal and Wilhelm, whose corpulence makes them shy away from what they construe as disapproving glances from hostile bystanders, Henderson does not allow his ungainly body to prevent him from wrestling with the fiercest African prince, kissing the flabbiest African queen, and lifting the heaviest African idol. Nor does he possess Leventhal's aversion to the beasts in the jungle. Often acting as if he were P. T. Barnum's special attraction, Henderson is not loath to fraternize with all the animals on hand and in the process to absorb their brute wisdom. Because he wholeheartedly embraces so many disparate creatures, he is Bellow's most avid "adorer of life" and the hero who, at the end of his African education, is best able to realize the high aim of comedy: the unconditional acceptance and appreciation of the

---

11. Such a view is by no means unanimous, since there are a number of critics who consider *Seize the Day* one of Bellow's least hopefully resolved novels. Wilhelm's final submergence in tears is, in their opinion, evidence of his chronic self-pity and infantile rage.

other, no matter how peculiar that other may be. Because the literary romance in which Henderson is cast allows him to venture far out and discover fabulous kingdoms and rulers, he also enjoys greater opportunities for miraculous self-rejuvenation than do his fictional brethren who exist in the more closed forms of realism and naturalism. But this fact is also responsible for the major defect of the novel. In place of the dreary black and white world of Chicago's South Side and New York's Upper West Side, where puny Jonahs struggle to prevent the leviathan society from swallowing them up, Bellow creates a dazzling technicolor African playground where an oversized Daniel sports with more friendly than ferocious lions. Because too much of the world as we know it has been reconstructed to serve as a backdrop for antic frolic and human character has been transmogrified into caricature, the seriousness of *Henderson the Rain King* as a "pursuit of meaning" novel is not always credible. Although Henderson is eager to strike up the dance of ideas with any willing partner, he is generally unable to improvise his own steps. He dizzily follows the fancy footwork of King Dahfu, who, in his own drolly cryptic fashion, circles about such subjects as the transcending powers of the human mind, the vast difference between being and becoming, and the way to encounter death. The language used to express these ideas is often just as vertiginous as the discussants' way of approaching and developing them. Henderson's cumbersome bombast, seesawing with his glib vernacular, and Dahfu's elliptical native speech, alternating with his verbose Reichian theorizing, function like most comic language to defile what is presumably to be desecrated.[12] The damage occurs when this defilement runs rampant, leaving nothing to be consecrated so that the novel appears to be merely an extended spoof. When Henderson stops being the clown, compulsively entertaining everyone with his riotous pratfalls and cascade of wisecracks, and becomes the sainted fool, struggling to affirm that the "eternal is bonded onto us" (318) and that nobility will have its day, his consecration outweighs his defilement.[13] During such intervals the novel ceases to be the giddy burlesque of the ugly American seeking spiritual beauty

12. Wylie Sypher claims that "comedy desecrates what it seeks to sanctify" ("The Ancient Rites of Comedy," in *Comedy*, p. 224).

13. I am indebted to Tony Tanner (*Saul Bellow*, pp. 85–86) for suggestions leading to this conclusion.

to become the serious parable of the "fighting Lazarus" (217) aspiring to rise from the living dead. This rare combination of burlesque and parable makes *Henderson the Rain King* Bellow's most original comedy.

Herzog, the therapeutic confessional of a distraught, cuckolded intellectual, is undeniably Bellow's most sophisticated comedy. In place of the cartoonish physical action of *The Adventures of Augie March* and *Henderson the Rain King,* it has its equally frenetic though more intricate mental action. Its epistolary cum personal reminiscence narrative form makes possible the universalizing of personal concerns and the personalizing of universal concerns. The inappropriateness of these conversions and the sudden non sequitur shifts from one to the other account for some of the wry humor produced. The remaining humor is initiated by Herzog himself, Bellow's wisest fool, who, with the jumbled learning of the Western world throbbing in his overworked brain, assesses his own ridiculous values and those of society at large. Endowed with the comic vision and powers of perception which Bellow usually reserved for himself in his earlier novels, Herzog mercilessly and mirthfully indicts himself for his own deviant behavior, his narcissism, masochism, and anachronism. While he hopelessly mismanages his affairs to arrive at a "good five-cent synthesis" (207) of the complex issues of life, he, more than any of the other bungling Bellow protagonists, provides exhaustive, mocking commentary on his mismanagement. He is also a protagonist whose intelligence matches Bellow's own so that, as Albert Guerard observes, Bellow's authorial consciousness can "without strain" identify with him, thereby releasing his most authentic and versatile narrative voice.[14] What Bellow has noted about Montaigne can be readily applied to Herzog; he, too, "is able to pass with ease from kitchen matters to metaphysics."[15] More specifically, Herzog can recite nursery rhymes at the same time he is recapitulating difficult ideas. He can exchange saccharine endearments with his Jewish cronies and bitterly lampoon them immediately afterward. He can recall poignant snatches of Old World Yiddish as well as imitate the abrasive idiom

[14.] Albert Guerard, "Saul Bellow and the Activists: On *The Adventures of Augie March,*" *Southern Review* 3 (July, 1967): 595–596.

[15.] Saul Bellow, "Literature," in *The Great Ideas Today,* ed. Mortimer Adler and Robert M. Hutchins (Chicago: Encyclopedia Britannica, 1963), p. 135.

of urban America. Of all the Bellow protagonists, Herzog contains the most colorful, kaleidoscopic mind, sparkling with a comic array of diverse verbal fragments. Occasionally, however, these fragments are too scintillating and, like Augie March's "barbaric yawp" and *bon mots,* they call attention to themselves and do not always best convey the subtleties of the topics discussed. An observation of Karl Miller's about *Herzog*'s characterization could also apply to its language: "[It] seems less a way of saying something than of avoiding some of the responsibility for what is said."[16] Herzog intends to go "after reality with language" (272), but often he buries it with an avalanche of his clever retorts and cultural name-droppings. At such times he is not convincing as the intellectual, since he is so unsure of himself in this capacity and would rather amuse everyone than risk being taken seriously by them. When he is expatiating on his own aches and pains, we are delighted that the jester overtakes the sage in him. But when he is expatiating on the ills of the world, his jesting is not always in order and actually hinders rather than enhances our understanding of his analyses. This unfitting levity is not, however, an abiding characteristic of Herzog's comic perspective. When he stops being the self-conscious thinking man and becomes the more natural "Man Thinking," accepting his humble beginnings and end, he possesses a truly sublime sense of humor. This kind of humor does not occasion the affirmative trumpetings of Augie March and Eugene Henderson, but leads to a muted expression of joy issuing from the still, small voice within Herzog.

"Comedy tends to present a glass in which we glimpse ourselves (albeit distorted for humorous effect), whereas satire, as Swift wryly put it, presents a glass in which we tend to see others' failings, but seldom, willingly, our own."[17] *Mr. Sammler's Planet,* Saul Bellow's latest novel to date, is, in the above sense, more satiric than it is comic. Artur Sammler, a variant of the Plautine *senex iratus,* dwells on the failings of rascally youth, arrogant blacks, and willful females, but is loath to acknowledge his own failings. A sworn upholder of Apollonian values, he stridently lashes out at the Dionysian excesses of the times—"the right to be uninhibted, spontaneous, urinating, defe-

---

16. Karl Miller, "Leventhal," *New Statesman* 70 (September 10, 1965): 360.

17. John M. Stedmond, *The Comic Art of Laurence Sterne* (Toronto: University of Toronto Press, 1967), p. 89.

cating, belching, coupling in all positions, tripling, quadrupling, poly-morphous . . ." (33). Herzog, too, is contemptuous of the erotic revels of the hedonistic age, but because he occasionally succumbs to being one of the revelers, he is more sportive than spiteful in his indictment of them. Sammler, aged and holocaust-ravaged, suffers from a hardening of his jocular arteries and cannot be amused by any of the giddy creatures who revolve around him. Those who interrupt his "internal consultations" he harshly dismisses as idiotic supplicants and wayward distracters. Absent from *Mr. Sammler's Planet* is the genial, forgiving comedy of character which has graced Bellow's more euphoric novels. Absent, too, is the spontaneous, frolicsome comedy of situation whose merriment is its own excuse for being, found particularly in *The Adventures of Augie March* and *Henderson the Rain King*. The comic situations that do occur are contrived and hackneyed versions of their inventive forerunners. Yet they do perform an important function; not only do they serve as prime movers for the novel's static, almost nonexistent plot, but, more importantly, they and the daft individuals who figure in them serve as springboards for Sammler's ruminations. These ruminations are responsible for the novel's chief distinction. While many elements of Bellow's golden age of humor have in *Mr. Sammler's Planet* appreciably diminished in luster and have in certain areas become downright rusty, the novel's ideological comedy is the most luminous of all of Bellow's works. A superb example of what Northrop Frye designates as "second-phase satire," or literature assuming the responsibility of social analysis, it succeeds in "breaking up the lumber of stereotypes, fossilized beliefs, superstitious terrors, crank theories, pedantic dogmatisms, oppressive fashions, and all other things that impede the free movement . . . of society." [18] All of this upheaval is brought about by the verbal torrents of a frail old man who himself is not rid of the same evils against which he is fulminating. Although many of these verbal torrents have been precipitated by insufficient warning and provocation and have gone on interminably so as to impede the novel's narrative flow, they, in their caustic irony, most often strike their mark. Yet many of the readers who made *Herzog* a best seller have not fancied Sammler's dour scoldings and would have preferred more witticisms than *Weltschmerz*. But to require more jests and fewer jeremiads is to

[18.] Northrop Frye, *Anatomy of Criticism* (New York: Atheneum, 1965), p. 233.

misunderstand Bellow's overall intent, for *Mr. Sammler's Planet* is his book of lamentations about the difficulties of being a humanist in this world. To write a larky account of it would be dishonest.

Saul Bellow is not dishonest in his novels. If anything, he is compelled to tell the "Whole Truth," the Truth which the art of comedy is dedicated to telling.[19] From *Dangling Man* to *Mr. Sammler's Planet,* he has through his wit and wisdom instructed us to "accept the mixture as we find it—the impurity of it, the tragedy of it, the hope of it." [20] Yet he does not presume to have grasped the "Whole Truth." As he has stated in his address on "Recent American Fiction," "Modern writers sin when they suppose that they *know,* as they conceive that physics *knows* or that history *knows.* The subject of the novelist is not knowable in any such way. The mystery increases, it does not grow less as types of literature wear out. It is, however, Symbolism, or Realism or Sensibility wearing out, and not the mystery of mankind." [21] While Bellow's comedy has routed "superfluity and solemn nonsense" and has brought us "relief from the long-prevalent mood of pessimism, discouragement, and low-seriousness," [22] it has not unraveled the mystery. What his comedy has done is sharpen our perception of it, and increase our awe of it.

19. In his essay "Tragedy and the Whole Truth," Aldous Huxley argues that Homer in the twelfth book of the *Odyssey* refuses to treat the plight of Odysseus and his men tragically, since he has them eating heartily and resting peacefully after their harrowing day. Nathan Scott draws upon Huxley's essay when he amends the Aristotelian definition of comedy to say, "The art of comedy is not an art that is dedicated to the ludicrous, but is rather an art that is dedicated to the telling of the Whole Truth" ("The Bias of Comedy and the Narrow Escape into Faith," p. 21).

20. Saul Bellow, "Introduction," *Great Jewish Short Stories,* ed. Saul Bellow (New York: Dell Publishing Co., 1963), p. 16.

21. Saul Bellow, "Recent American Fiction," Lecture delivered under the auspices of the Gertrude Clarke Whittal Poetry and Literature Fund (Washington: Library of Congress, 1963). Reprinted in *Encounter* 21 (November, 1963): 29.

22. Bellow, "Literature," p. 164.

Sources Cited

BY SAUL BELLOW

I. Longer Works

The Adventures of Augie March. New York: Viking Press, 1953.
Dangling Man. New York: Vanguard, 1944.
Henderson the Rain King. New York: Viking Press, 1959.
Herzog. New York: Viking Press, 1964.
The Last Analysis [play]. New York: Viking Press, 1965.
Mr. Sammler's Planet. New York: Viking Press, 1970.
Mosby's Memoirs and Other Stories. New York: Viking Press, 1968.
Seize the Day. New York: Viking Press, 1956.
The Victim. New York: Vanguard, 1947.

II. Short Fiction, Articles, Reviews, and Lectures

"Address by Gooley MacDowell to the Hasbeens Club of Chicago." *Hudson Review* 4 (Summer, 1951): 222–227.
"Arias." *Noble Savage* 4 (New York: Meridian Books, 1961), pp. 4–5.
"Culture Now: Some Animadversions, Some Laughs." *Modern Occasions* 1 (Winter, 1971): 162–178.
"Deep Readers of the World, Beware!" *New York Times Book Review* 4 (February 15, 1959): 1.
"From the Life of Augie March." *Partisan Review* 16 (November, 1949): 1077–1089.

Translation of Isaac Bashevis Singer's "Gimpel the Fool." *Partisan Review* 20 (May–June, 1953): 300–313.

"Introduction." *Great Jewish Short Stories,* ed. Saul Bellow, pp. 9–16. New York: Dell Publishing Co., 1963.

"The Jewish Writer and the English Literary Tradition." *Commentary* 8 (October, 1949): 366–367.

Keynote Address before the Inaugural Session of the XXXIV International Congress of Poets, Playwrights, Essayists, Editors, and Novelists, June 13, 1966, New York University.

"Laughter in the Ghetto." *Saturday Review of Literature* 36 (May 30, 1953): 15.

"Literature." *The Great Ideas Today,* ed. Mortimer Adler and Robert M. Hutchins, pp. 135–179. Chicago: Encyclopedia Britannica, 1963.

"Saul Bellow on the Modern Novel." Radio lecture, July, 1961.

"A Sermon by Dr. Pep." *Fiction of the Fifties,* ed. Herbert Gold, pp. 66–73. New York: Doubleday & Co., 1959.

"Some Notes on Recent American Fiction." *Encounter* 21 (November, 1963): 22–29.

"A Word from Writer Directly to Reader." *Fiction of the Fifties,* ed. Herbert Gold, p. 20. New York: Doubleday & Co., 1959.

III. Interviews

Cromie, Robert. "Saul Bellow Tells (among Other Things) the Thinking behind *Herzog.*" *Chicago Tribune Books Today,* January 24, 1965, pp. 8–9.

Dommergues, Pierre. "Rencontre avec Saul Bellow." *Preuves* 17 (January, 1967): 38–47.

Galloway, David D. "An Interview with Saul Bellow." *Audit* 3 (Spring, 1963): 19–23.

Harper, Gordon L. "Saul Bellow—The Art of Fiction: An Interview." *Paris Review* 37 (Winter, 1965): 48–73.

Howard, Jane. "Mr. Bellow Considers His Planet." *Life* 68 (April 3, 1970): 57–60.

Steers, Nina A. "Successor to Faulkner?" *Show* 4 (September, 1964): 36–38.

ABOUT SAUL BELLOW

I. Biographical Material

Breit, Harvey. "Saul Bellow." *The Writer Observed,* pp. 271–274. New York: World Publishing Co., 1956.

Kalb, Bernard. "Biographical Sketch." *Saturday Review of Literature* 36 (September 19, 1953): 13.

II. Criticism

Aldridge, John W. "The Society of Three Novels." *In Search of Heresy,* pp. 126–148. New York: McGraw-Hill Book Co., 1956.

Allen, Mary Lee. "The Flower and the Chalk: The Comic Sense of Saul Bellow." Ph.D. dissertation, Stanford University, 1968.

Alter, Robert. "Heirs of the Tradition." *Rogues' Progress: Studies in the Picaresque Novel,* pp. 106–132. Cambridge: Harvard University Press, 1964.

———. "The Stature of Saul Bellow." *Midstream* 10 (December, 1964): 3–15.

Atchity, John Kenneth. "Bellow's Mr. Sammler: 'The Last Man Given for Epitome.'" *Research Studies* 38 (March, 1970): 46–54.

Baumbach, Jonathan. "The Double Vision: *The Victim* by Saul Bellow." *The Landscape of Nightmare,* pp. 35–54. New York: New York University Press, 1965.

Bradbury, Malcolm. "Saul Bellow and the Naturalist Tradition." *Review of English Literature* 4 (October, 1963): 80–92.

Chase, Richard. "The Adventures of Saul Bellow: Progress of a Novelist," *Commentary* 27 (April, 1959): 323–330.

Clayton, John J. *Saul Bellow: In Defense of Man.* Bloomington: Indiana University Press, 1968.

Davis, Robert Gorham. "The American Individualist Tradition: Bellow and Styron," *The Creative Present,* ed. Nona Balakian and Charles Simmons, pp. 111–141. New York: Doubleday & Co., 1963.

DeMott, Benjamin. "Saul Bellow and the Dogmas of Possibility." *Saturday Review of Literature* 53 (February 7, 1970): 25–28, 37.

"Dun Quixote–Henderson the Rain King," *Time* 73 (February 23, 1959): 102.

Eisinger, Chester E. *Fiction of the Forties,* pp. 341–362. Chicago: University of Chicago Press, 1963.

———. "Saul Bellow: Love and Identity." *Accent* 18 (Summer, 1958): 179–203.

Fiedler, Leslie A. "Saul Bellow." *Prairie Schooner* 31 (Summer, 1957): 103–110.

Galloway, David D. "The Absurd Man as Picaro: The Novels of Saul Bellow." *Texas Studies in Literature and Language* 6 (Summer, 1964): 226–254.

———. "Moses-Bloom-Herzog: Bellow's Everyman." *Southern Review* 2 (Winter, 1966): 61–76.

Garrett, George. "To Do Right in a Bad World: Saul Bellow's *Herzog.*" *The Hollins Critic* 2 (April, 1965): 2–12.

Gross, Beverly. "Dark Side of the Moon." *Nation* 210 (February 9, 1970): 153–155.

Guerard, Albert. "Saul Bellow and the Activists: On *The Adventures of Augie March.*" *Southern Review* 3 (July, 1967): 582–596.

Guttman, Allen. "Bellow's *Henderson.*" *Critique* 7 (Spring, 1965): 33–42.

Harper, Howard M., Jr. *Desperate Faith*, pp. 7–64. Chapel Hill: University of North Carolina Press, 1967.

Hartman, Hugh. "Character, Theme and Tradition in the Novels of Saul Bellow." Ph.D. dissertation, University of Washington, 1968.

Harwell, Meade. "Picaro from Chicago." *Southwest Review* 39 (Summer, 1954): 273–276.

Hassan, Ihab H. *Radical Innocence: Studies in the Contemporary American Novel*, pp. 290–324. Princeton: Princeton University Press, 1961.

Herzog, Review of. *Newsweek* 64 (September 21, 1964): 114.

Howe, Irving. "Introduction to *Seize the Day.*" *Classics of Modern Fiction*, ed. Irving Howe, pp. 457–466. New York: Harcourt Brace & World, 1968.

———. "Odysseus, Flat on His Back." *New Republic* 151 (September 19, 1964): 21–26.

———. Review of *Mr. Sammler's Planet* by Saul Bellow. *Harpers* 240 (February, 1970): 106–114.

Hyman, Stanley Edgar. "Saul Bellow's Glittering Eye." *The New Leader* 47 (September 28, 1964): 16–17.

Kazin, Alfred. Review of *Mr. Sammler's Planet* by Saul Bellow. *New York Review of Books* 15 (December 3, 1970): 3–4.

———. "The World of Saul Bellow." *Contemporaries*, pp. 217–223. Boston: Little, Brown and Co., 1962.

Klein, Marcus. *After Alienation*, pp. 33–70. Cleveland: World Publishing Co., 1962.

Kristol, Irving. Review of *The Adventures of Augie March* by Saul Bellow. *Encounter* 13 (July, 1954): 74–75.

Markos, Donald. "The Humanism of Saul Bellow." Ph.D. dissertation, University of Illinois, 1966.

Match, Richard. Review of *The Victim* by Saul Bellow. *New York Herald Tribune Weekly Book Review* 4 (November 23, 1947): 10.

Miller, Karl. "Leventhal." *New Statesman* 70 (September 10, 1965): 360–361.

Mudrick, Marvin. "Who Killed Herzog? Or, Three American Novelists." *University of Denver Quarterly* 1 (Spring, 1966): 61–97.

Opdahl, Keith M. "The Crab and the Butterfly." Ph.D. dissertation, University of Illinois, 1961.

———. *The Novels of Saul Bellow: An Introduction.* University Park: Pennsylvania State University Press, 1967.

Podhoretz, Norman. "The New Nihilism and the Novel." *Partisan Review* 25 (Fall, 1958): 576–590.

Poirier, Richard. "Bellows to Herzog." *Partisan Review* 32 (Spring, 1965): 264–271.

Popkin, Henry. "American Comedy." *Kenyon Review* 16 (Spring, 1954): 329–334.

Read, Forest. *"Herzog:* A Review." *Epoch* 14 (Fall, 1964): 81–96.

Rovit, Earl. *Saul Bellow.* University of Minnesota Pamphlets on American Writers, no. 65. Minneapolis: University of Minnesota Press, 1967.

Samuels, Charles Thomas. "Bellow on Modernism." *New Republic* 162 (February 7, 1970): 27–30.

Shulman, Robert. "The Style of Bellow's Comedy." *PMLA* 83 (March, 1968): 109–117.

Stern, Richard G. "Henderson's Bellow." *Kenyon Review* 21 (Autumn, 1959): 655–661.

Stock, Irwin. "The Novels of Saul Bellow." *Southern Review* 3 (Winter, 1967): 13–42.

Tanner, Tony. *Saul Bellow.* Edinburgh: Oliver & Boyd, 1965.

Warren, Robert Penn. Review of *The Adventures of Augie March* by Saul Bellow. *New Republic* 129 (November 2, 1953): 22–23.

Weiss, Daniel. "Caliban on Prospero: A Psychoanalytic Study of the Novel *Seize the Day* by Saul Bellow." *Psychoanalysis and American Fiction,* ed. Irving Malin, pp. 279–307. New York: E. P. Dutton & Co., 1965.

Wisse, Ruth R. "The Schlemiel as Liberal Humanist." *The Schlemiel as Modern Hero,* pp. 92–107. Chicago: University of Chicago Press, 1971.

MISCELLANEOUS

Alter, Robert. *Rogues' Progress: Studies in the Picaresque Novel.* Cambridge: Harvard University Press, 1964.

Ausubel, Nathan. "Introduction: Cabalists, Mystics and Wonder-Workers." *A Treasury of Jewish Folklore,* pp. 175–178. New York: Crown Publishers, 1948.

———. "Introduction: The Human Comedy." *A Treasury of Jewish Folklore,* pp. 264–266. New York: Crown Publishers, 1948.

——. "Introduction: *Schlemiels* and *Schlimazls.*" *A Treasury of Jewish Folklore,* pp. 343–345. New York: Crown Publishers, 1948.

——. "Introduction: *Schnorrers* and Beggars." *A Treasury of Jewish Folklore,* pp. 267–268. New York: Crown Publishers, 1948.

Baek, Leo. "The Optimism of Judaism." *Contemporary Jewish Thought,* ed. Simon Noveck, pp. 181–183. B'nai B'rith Department of Adult Jewish Education, 1963.

Bergson, Henri. "Laughter." *Comedy,* ed. Wylie Sypher, pp. 61–190. New York: Doubleday & Co., 1956.

Buber, Martin. *Hasidism.* New York: Philosophical Library, 1948.

Chase, Richard. *Walt Whitman Reconsidered.* New York: William Sloane Associates, 1965.

Collignon, Jean. "Kafka's Humor." *Yale French Studies* 16 (Winter, 1955–56): 53–62.

Dostoevsky, Fyodor. *The Brothers Karamazov.* Trans. Constance Garnett. New York: Random House, 1950.

——. *The Double* in *Three Short Novels of Dostoevsky.* Trans. Constance Garnett, rev. and ed. by Abraham Yarmolinsky. New York: Doubleday & Co., 1960.

——. *Notes from Underground.* Trans. Ralph E. Matlaw. New York: E. P. Dutton & Co., 1960.

Dresner, Samuel H. *The Zaddik.* New York: Abelard-Schuman, 1960.

Emberson, Frances G. "Mark Twain's Vocabulary." *University of Missouri Studies* 10 (July 1, 1935): 1–53.

Frye, Northrop. *Anatomy of Criticism.* New York: Atheneum, 1965.

Goldman, Albert. "Boy-man, schlemiel: The Jewish Element in American Humour." *Explorations,* ed. Murray Mindlin and Chaim Bermant, pp. 3–17. London, 1967.

Howe, Irving. "Introduction." *A Treasury of Yiddish Stories,* ed. Irving Howe and Eliezar Greenberg, pp. 1–71. New York: Viking Press, 1953.

——. "The Stranger and the Victim." *Commentary* 8 (August, 1949): 147–156.

Kafka, Franz. *The Trial.* Trans. Willa and Edwin Muir. New York: Alfred A. Knopf, 1964.

Koestler, Arthur. *Insight and Outlook.* New York: Macmillan, 1949.

Kristol, Irving. "Is Jewish Humor Dead?" *Mid-Century,* ed. Harold U. Ribalow, pp. 428–437. New York: Beechhurst Press, 1955.

Langer, Susanne K. *Feeling and Form.* New York: Charles Scribner's Sons, 1953.

Leacock, Stephen. *Humour and Humanity.* New York: Henry Holt & Co., 1938.

Lelchuk, Alan. "On Satirizing Presidents: An Interview with Philip Roth." *Atlantic* 228 (December, 1971): 81–88.

Mailer, Norman. "The White Negro." *Advertisements for Myself,* pp. 311–332. New York: Berkeley Publishing Company, 1966.

Melville, Herman. *Moby-Dick.* New York: Bobbs-Merrill Company, 1964.

Meredith, George. "An Essay on Comedy," *Comedy,* ed. Wylie Sypher, pp. 3–57. New York: Doubleday & Co., 1956.

Monro, D. H. *Argument of Laughter.* Notre Dame: University of Notre Dame Press, 1963.

Perls, Frederick; Hefferline, Ralph; and Goodman, Paul. *Gestalt Therapy.* New York: Dell Publishing Co., 1951.

Reich, Wilhelm. *Character-Analysis.* Trans. Theodore P. Wolfe. New York: Orgone Institute Press, 1949.

Rovit, Earl. "Bernard Malamud and the Jewish Literary Tradition." *Critique,* III (Winter-Spring, 1960): 3–10.

———. "Jewish Humor and American Life." *The American Scholar* 36 (Spring, 1967): 237–245.

———. "The Novel as Parody: John Barth." *Critique* 4 (Fall, 1963): 77–85.

Samuel, Maurice. *The World of Sholom Aleichem.* New York: Schocken Books, 1943.

Sartre, Jean-Paul. *Anti-Semite and Jew.* Trans. George J. Becker. New York: Schocken Books, 1965.

Schilling, Bernard N. *The Comic Spirit.* Detroit: Wayne State University Press, 1965.

Schopenhauer, Arthur. "Of Women." *The Works of Schopenhauer,* ed. Will Durant, pp. 446–459. New York: Frederick Ungar Publishing Co., 1928.

Scott, Nathan A., Jr. "The Bias of Comedy and the Narrow Escape into Faith." *The Christian Scholar* 44 (Spring, 1961): 9–39.

Stedmond, John M. *The Comic Art of Laurence Sterne.* Toronto: University of Toronto Press, 1967.

Sypher, Wylie. "The Ancient Rites of Comedy." *Comedy,* ed. Wylie Sypher, pp. 214–226. New York: Doubleday & Co., 1956.

———. "Our New Sense of the Comic." *Comedy,* ed. Wylie Sypher, pp. 193–214. New York: Doubleday & Co., 1956.

Trilling, Diana. *Claremont Essays.* New York: Harcourt, Brace and World, 1964.

Wallant, Edward. *The Children at the Gate.* New York: Popular Library, 1964.

Index

Abt, Morris (*Dangling Man*), 28, 29
Adler, Dr. (*Seize the Day*), 92, 96,
  108, 109, 111, 182
The Adventures of Augie March, 64-
  89, 92, 109, 115, 125, 128, 134, 174,
  197, 199, 214-216, 222; function of
  comedy in, 4; and language, 18, 19;
  secondary characters in, 66-73; and
  comic rigidity, 69; and comedy of
  situation, 77-79, 89, 199-200, 216; and
  comedy of ideas, 79-81, 216; comic
  style, 84-85; function of comic
  language in, 84-85; encyclopedic wit
  in, 85; allusions in, 85-86; humor of
  verbal retrieval in, 88; and joy, 113-
  114; high comedy in, 215; saturnalian humor of, 215; comedy of
  character in, 216. *See also* March,
  Augie
*The Adventures of Mottel the Cantor's
  Son* (Sholom Aleichem), 18
Aesop, 10
Affectation, 6-7; and Wilhelm, 91-95;
  and Joseph, 27; and Grandma
  Lausch, 68; and Henderson, 116-117;
  and the Bellow hero, 116-117; inverse and Henderson, 117; and
  Herzog, 145, 155; and Sammler, 178-
  179

Affirmation: in *Seize the Day*, 113-
  114; and *Henderson*, 142, 219; and
  Herzog, 143; in *Herzog*, 175; in
  Mr. Sammler's Planet, 177; and
  Bellow hero, 212
Agnus Dei (Mozart), 137
Albert, Charley (*Henderson*), 118
Aldridge, John, 216n
Aleichem, Sholom, 18, 20, 110
Alienation: and Joseph, 36
Allbee, Kirby (*The Victim*), 43, 213,
  217; and comedy of character, 48-
  52; as aristocrat *manqué*, 50; as
  bigot, 50-52; as philosopher, 52-53
Allen, Mary Lee, 54n, 88n
Allusions: in *Augie March*, 85-86; in
  Seize the Day, 109; and *Henderson*,
  137; and Herzog, 171-172; and
  Sammler, 205-206
Almstadt, Mrs. (*Dangling Man*), 27,
  37
Alter, Robert, 140
Amadis de Gaul (*Don Quixote*, Cer-
  vantes), 119
An American Dream (Norman
  Mailer), 154
Amorality: of Augie March, 76
Amos (*Dangling Man*), 28, 70
Amos (prophet), 16, 168

231